The Mammoth Book of
TATTOOS

Edited by Lal Hardy

RUNNING PRESS
PHILADELPHIA · LONDON

Constable & Robinson Ltd
3 The Lanchesters
162 Fulham Palace Road
London W6 9ER
www.constablerobinson.com

First published in the UK by Robinson,
an imprint of Constable & Robinson Ltd, 2009

A copy of the British Library Cataloguing in Publication
Data is available from the British Library

UK ISBN 978-1-84529-740-4

5 7 9 10 8 6

First published in the United States in 2009 by Running Press Book Publishers

9 8 7 6 5
Digit on the right indicates the number of this printing

US ISBN 9780762436316

Running Press Book Publishers
2300 Chestnut Street
Philadelphia, PA 19103-4371

Visit us on the web!
www.running press.com

Designed by Mitchell Associates
www.mitch.uk.com

Printed and bound in China.

Cover tattoos by Kahlil Rintye (front), Thomas Hooper (spine), and Jo Harrison (back)

Contents

Introduction

When I first took a decidedly serious interest in the colourful world of tattooing and body adornment in the early 1970s it was almost impossible to find any printed information on this ancient and fascinating art form. A little bit of research revealed that two books had been published in Britain, both of them way back in the 1950s – George Burchett and Peter Leighton's *Memoirs of a Tattoo Artist* and Hanns Ebensten's *Pierced Hearts and True Love*. However, trying to locate them proved a futile task – according to the chief librarian at my local library, both titles had been stolen some time ago!

Dai Cann

Then, one day in 1974, I asked again at a large bookshop if they had any books on tattooing, fully expecting to be told that they did not. Instead the assistant walked over to one of the lower shelves and presented me with a copy of a newly published book entitled *Skin Deep – The Mystery of Tattooing* by Ronald Scutt and Christopher Gotch. I handed over the princely sum of £8.50 (I was earning £23 a week in those days) and headed home to devour the contents. Reading it, I was transported to the Orient, the South Seas, Borneo, and other exotic locations described by the authors in an informative text illustrated by hundreds of photos of tattoos. In retrospect, the photos in the book don't show the best quality tattooing

Aaron Hewitt

work compared with what is being created today, but the book served as an introduction to the world of tattooing and it remains a reference volume that I treasure.

The Teddy boy revival and punk movements of the 1970s revived interest in tattooing and by the 1980s the tattoo ball was well and truly rolling. Although most tattoo studios were off the beaten track and the trade was pretty much a secret society, a few more publications were coming off the presses. In 1982, Don Ed Hardy – now a familiar name in the world of fashion due to his designs used on clothes worn by the rich and famous – hosted a tattoo convention, The Queen Mary Tattoo Expo, held on The Queen Mary liner in Long Beach, California. It attracted some of the most innovative artists from around the world, including Bob Roberts, Greg Irons, Bill Salmon, The Dutchman, Leo Zulueta, Mike Malone, Kandi Everett, Dennis Cockell, and George Bone, to name just a few. All the artists exhibited clients with their artwork etched into their flesh; it was a turning point in the world of tattooing. As the tattooists returned to their own towns and countries, their heads filled with inspiration and eager to put onto skin their newfound knowledge, the renaissance of tattooing had already begun. Soon, conventions were being held in more and more countries across the globe.

Biker magazines saw a market and began to print one-off "tattoo" editions, featuring biker tattoos. These in turn became more regular journals, eventually resulting in monthly colour tattoo magazines available in mainstream outlets, featuring a broad spectrum of tattooed folk.

Tattooists like Lyle Tuttle in San Francisco, Hanky Panky in

Theresa Gordon Wade

Holland, and Lionel Titchener in Britain all gathered together tattoo artefacts and collections and opened museums. Photographer Chris Wroblewski travelled the world producing numerous tattoo books documenting not just Western-style tattooing, but also Japanese, Thai, Burmese, Bornean, New Zealand, and so on.

The tattoo world was growing, and growing fast; inspiration was coming from all directions – from different art forms, from global tattoo styles, from the artwork of different subcultures, from punk . . . psychobilly . . . rock music. The fall of the Iron Curtain also resulted in an upsurge of tattoo artists in countries where tattooing had been banned. Places where tattoo had been falling into decline suddenly witnessed the art form rise like a phoenix from the ashes.

The United States had been the inspiration for much of the tattoo boom of the 1980s, but Europe now started to spawn incredible artists like Bernie Luther, Filip Leu, Klaus Faurhman, Tin Tin, Luke Atkinson, and Mick of Zurich. In the United Kingdom established artists like George Bone, Phil Bond, Saz Saunders, and Brent and Dennis Cockell began to push British tattooing ever upward, and with new artists such as Ian of Reading and Micky Sharpz pioneering new styles, demand for tattooing reached unprecedented heights.

More recently, satellite TV has opened new doors for tattooing. Tattoo reality shows like Miami Ink, Inked, LA Ink, and London Ink have brought tattooing into the home. The influence of such programmes cannot be overestimated; they have influenced a whole new generation of tattoo clients, who often seek to have a design they have seen on a TV show replicated. The Discovery and National Geographic TV channels have broadcast documentaries on tattooing among tribes and other groups

of people all over the world, further educating television audiences in the wealth and diversity of tattoo art.

For both tattoo artists and collectors of tattoos, the Internet has been perhaps the greatest innovation for a generation – web sites full of tattoos all over the world provide reference material while tattoo design sites, fan sites, and information are all there at the touch of a button – instantaneously.

The number of celebrities, rock stars, actors, and sports stars wearing hearts and other designs on their arms and other parts of their bodies has further brought the art of tattoo into the public eye and influenced people. I'd be prepared to bet that when David Beckham received his "Guardian Angel" tattoo on his back from Louis Molloy in Manchester neither of them thought that the image would become perhaps the single most famous tattoo image in the world today – and that it would be tattooed in various forms onto the hides of literally thousands of people worldwide.

The striking visuals of tattoo are now used in numerous adverts selling everything from ice cream to automobiles. Tattoo imagery, like that of 1970s' anti-establishment punk, has been groomed and taken into the mainstream of public life.

For those readers unfamiliar with tattoo techniques and styles, there are two ways to do tattoos. The first, by hand, is how tattooing originated and how it has been practised by various

Jondix

John Treharne

cultures since man first learnt that he could mark his body by puncturing the skin and introducing a pigment into it. The second is by using some kind of electric machine. Many people ask which method hurts the most; I would say, having experienced both methods, that they all hurt to some degree!

Part of the tattoo renaissance has been a resurgence of traditional hand tattooing in many places, such as New Zealand, Japan, Hawaii, Borneo, Thailand, Tahiti, and Samoa, to name just a few. Artists are creating traditional tattoos using traditional methods and various hand tools particular to their area, drawing on traditional imagery such as the beautiful moko, in the case of the Maoris of New Zealand, or the P'ea of Samoa. In many places where the Church and the State sought in the past to eradicate tattooing, it is now being recognized as an important part of the islanders' cultural heritage.

In traditional tattoo machines an electric motor drives the needles back and forth, but new technology has led to the development of air-powered machines. The first electric machine, patented in New York in 1891 by the American Samuel O'Reilly, made tattooing both faster and more precise. Today, most artists all over the world use a machine of some kind to create tattoos.

As technology advances, so, too, do many of the tools and materials of the tattoo trade. There is better sterilization today; an immense variety of brighter – and safer – colours; and better quality machines. But the quality of the art still depends on the skill of the practitioner.

Some artists specialize in just one of the myriad styles which exist while others are "jacks of all trades". Contemporary tattooists are required to turn their hand to just about any idea a client requests and turn it into

Yan Spencer

a piece of living art (as can be seen in the photographs which illustrate this introduction): a portrait of a loved one, or a favourite pet; a traditional Japanese image; a modern twist on an old classic design; a mystical or spiritual piece; one of the numerous tribal styles; a fantasy image; a realistic design; Old School; New Skool; or Americana.

This book features the work of nearly 80 tattooists from around the globe. It is a visual reference illustrating some of the many different styles of tattooing popular around the world today. Some of the artists featured, such as Phil Bond and George Bone, have been pioneering tattooing for over forty years, while Hannah Aitchison, Corey Miller, Chris Garver, and Kim Saigh have become household names through their beautiful art being shown on TV. Others, like Valerie Vargas, are new to the game, but already cutting a swathe. All of those featured, though, are accomplished and committed artists with a love and passion for the wonderful art of tattoo.

Lal Hardy

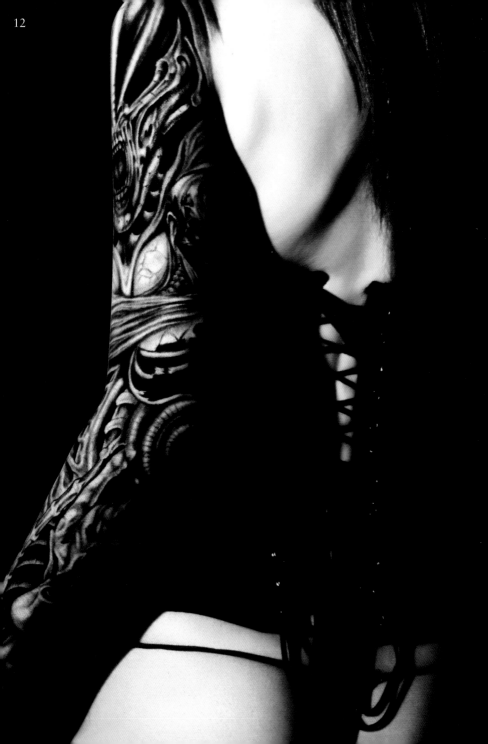

ADAM DA PUNK

Adam da Punk's tattoo adventure
started in the dark depths of
Deptford in south-east London in
1992. He now works at New Wave
Studio in north London, following
16 years of madness buried up to
his elbows in ink and tattoo fun
all around the world. He doesn't
specialize in styles and says that
anyone who comes through his
studio door can get tattooed
by him as long as they're not
"dragging an attitude". "If you are
cool," he says, "your tattoo will be
cool. So sit down, tell me your life
story and DON'T MOVE!"

Adam da Punk photographs
© Paul Mann Photography.

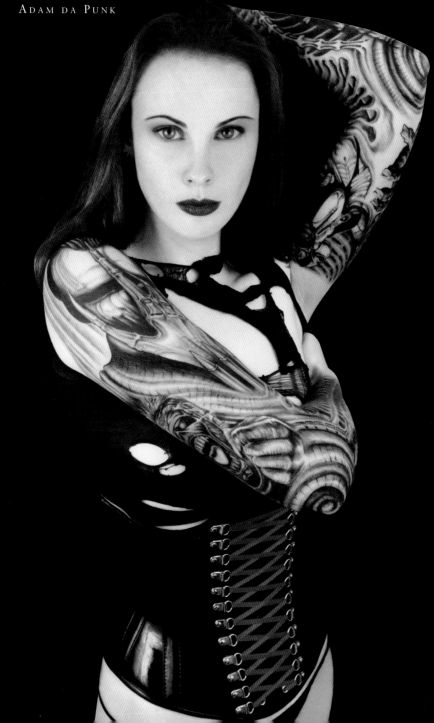

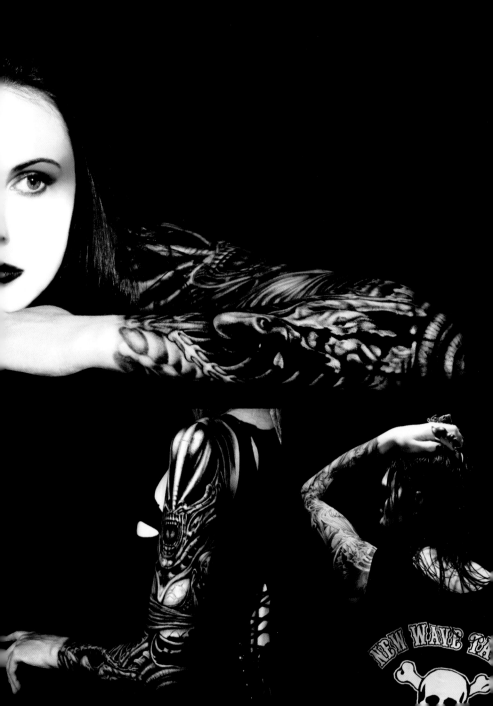

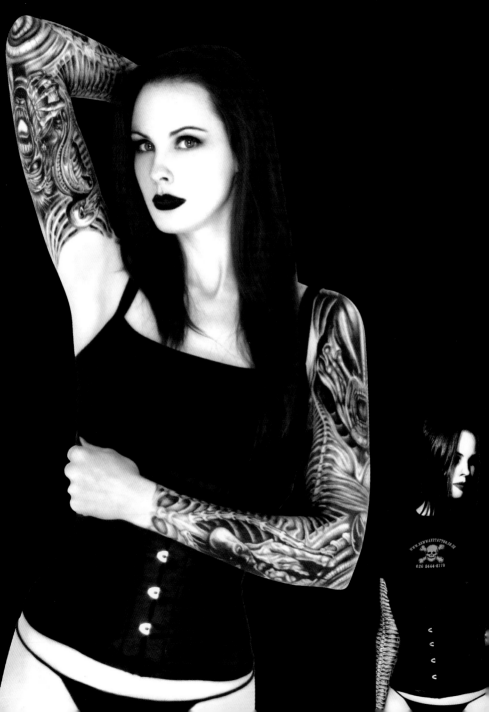

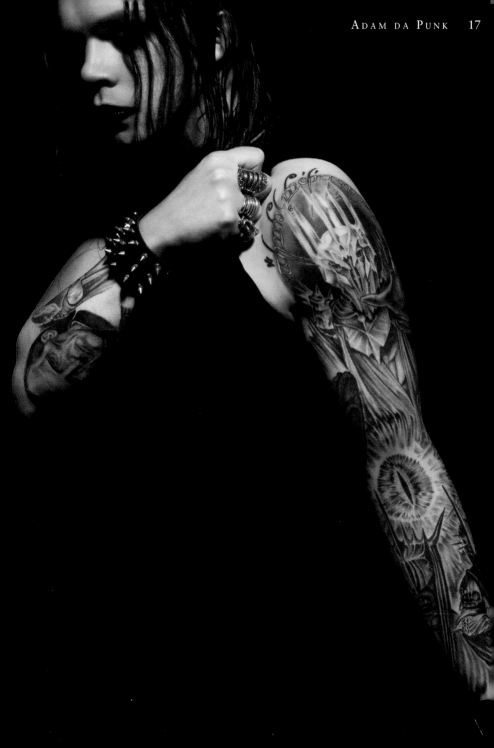

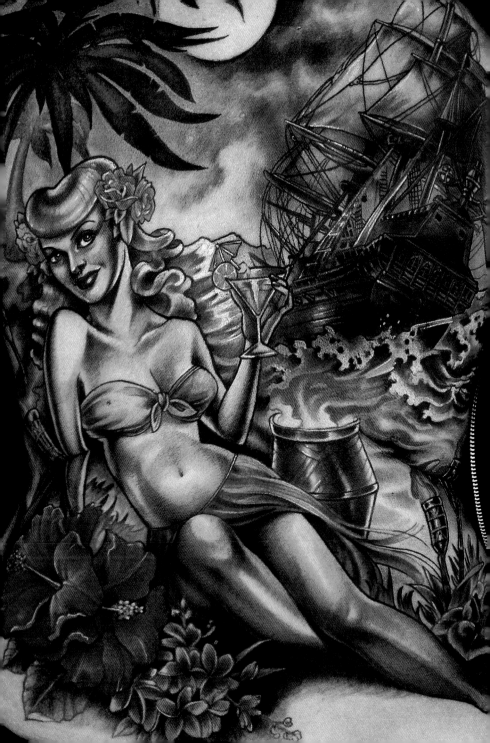

HANNAH AITCHISON

Chicago native Hannah Aitchison loves
to make pretty pictures on people, and
hopes they like wearing them. Currently
splitting her time between the two weather
systems of Chicago and Los Angeles, she
has spent the last 12 years developing a
distinctive artistic style that showcases
elements of classical illustration, mid-
century American propaganda and pin-up
art, and art nouveau. Sometimes there's
even a skull in there somewhere. When
not "dermatologically decorating" other
people, Hannah likes to knit, box, paint,
garden, draw comics, sing, read, cook,
sew, repair vintage cars, travel, attend art
gallery openings and live music events, and
"quantify linear A". Her theory is that
good art comes from good experiences.
She also enjoys long moonlit walks on the
beach, pina coladas, and lawn darts.

Artist picture © Kat Von D.

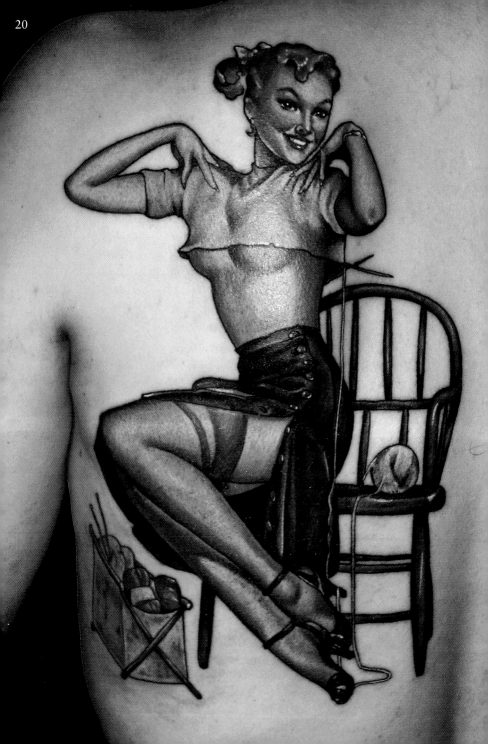

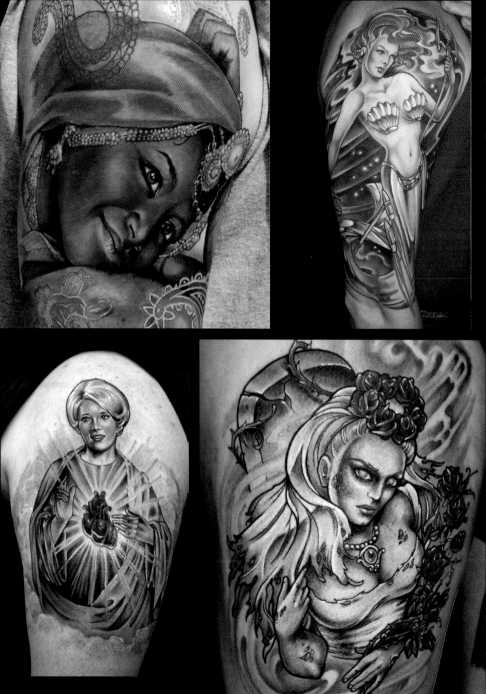

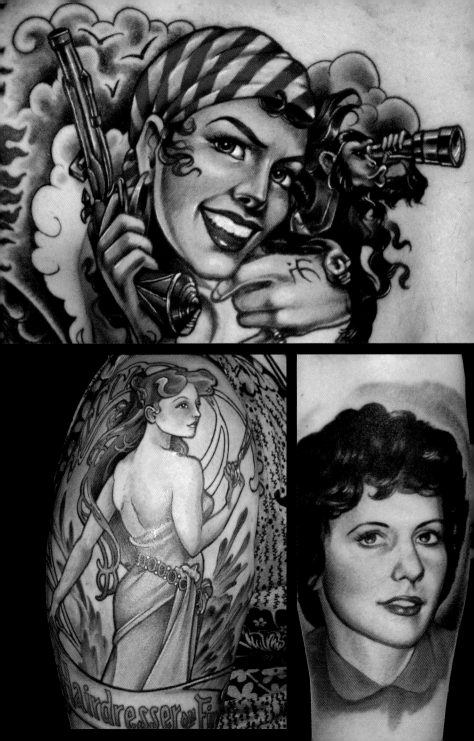

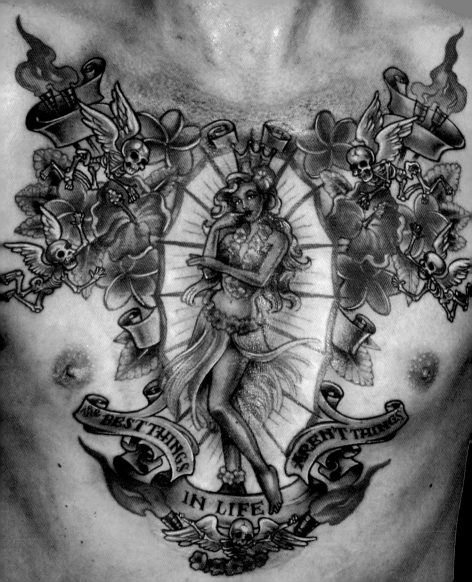

THE BEST THINGS AREN'T THINGS IN LIFE

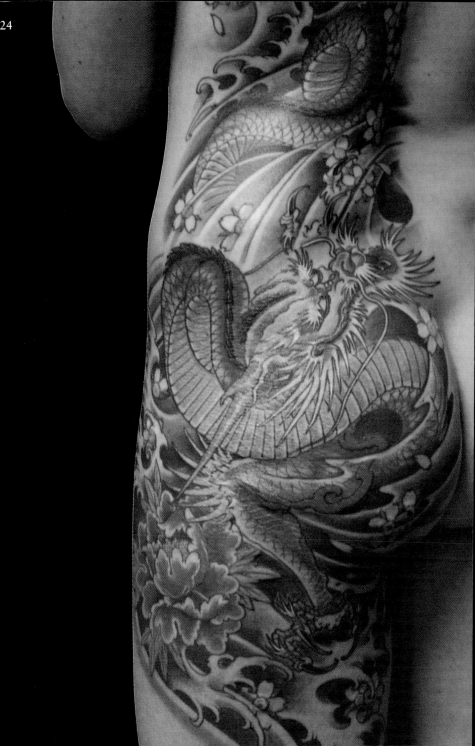

LUKE ATKINSON

Luke Atkinson is RATATTOO. Born in London in 1965, he grew up in Cheltenham, where he just about managed to finish school despite his early interest in tattooing. He has been lucky enough to have met some of the most influential tattooers of the decade who have shared their knowledge with him. He describes himself as eternally grateful for the time they spent with him, which changed his life. He has been working in Checker Demon Tattoos in Stuttgart for 16 years and still loves tattooing. Prior to that he spent seven years on the road gathering information and gaining experience which makes him very content with his present life. He became interested in tattooing because of its magic, and he strives to keep it that way.

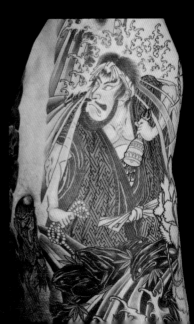

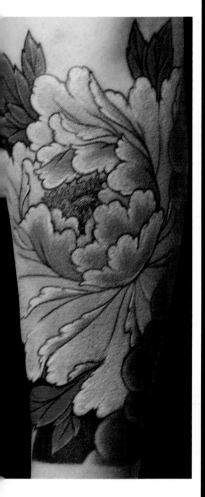

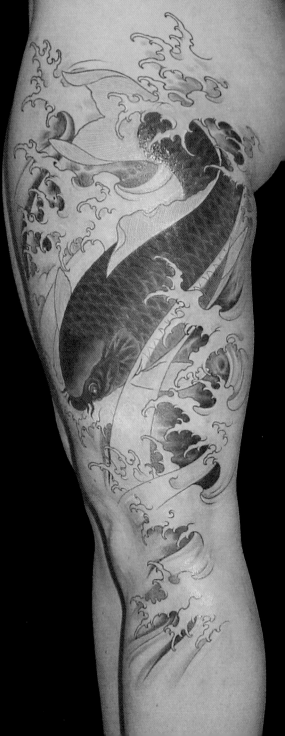

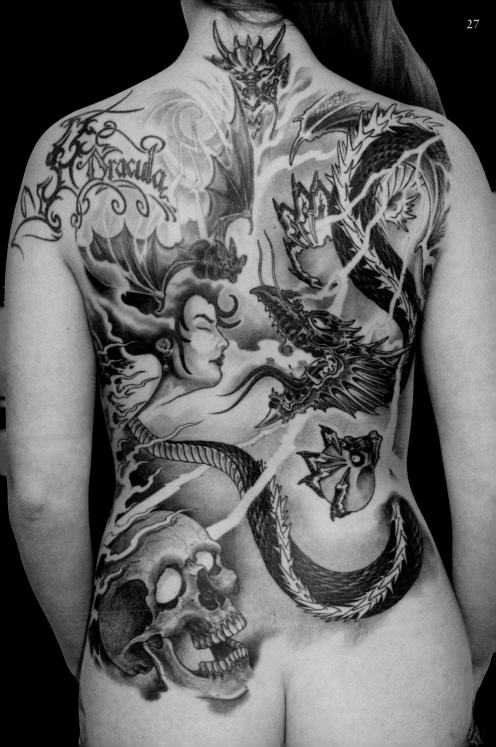

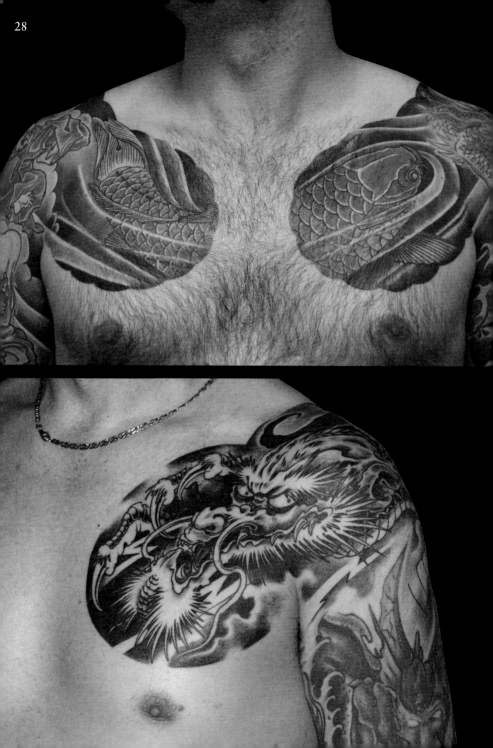

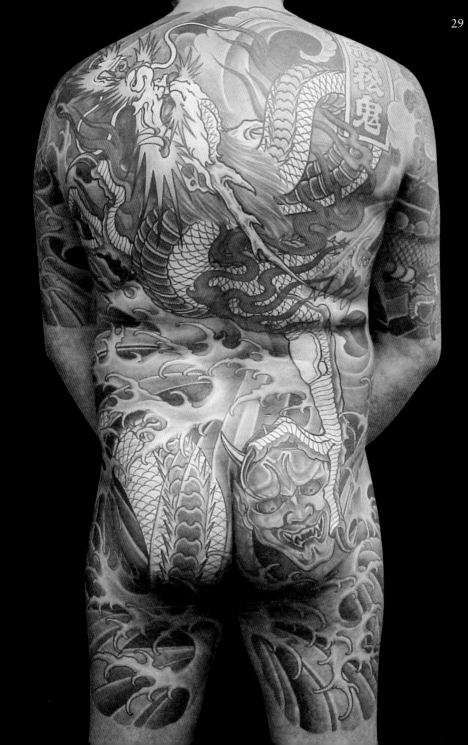

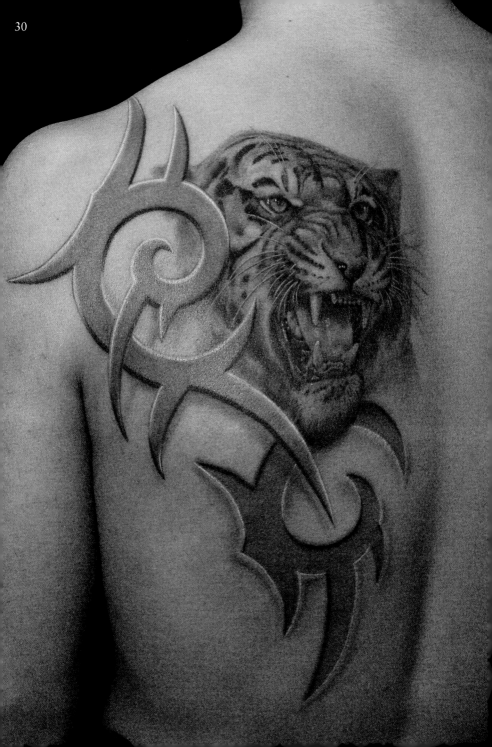

Sergey "George" Bardadim

Sergey Bardadim, known as George, is a Russian artist who did his first tattoo at the age of 17 using an ordinary needle and thread, the primitive method in use in Russia at that time. Following requests from many friends to tattoo them, he created his first tattoo machine out of a "Sputnik" razor and a sharpened guitar string; with this device his career began. In 1993, he and his close collaborator Taras built the first of successive tattoo machines which were to culminate in a professional model. Initially, he worked as a guest artist for studios in Russia, Austria, Germany, and the United Kingdom.
Since 1991 he has been taking part in the bigger European tattoo conventions. He enjoys different styles of tattooing and believes that involving the customer in a detailed discussion of the work is a vitally important part of the tattooing process.

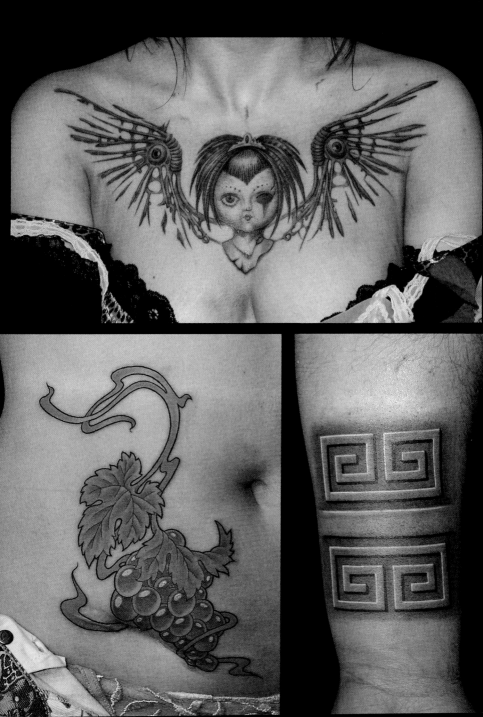

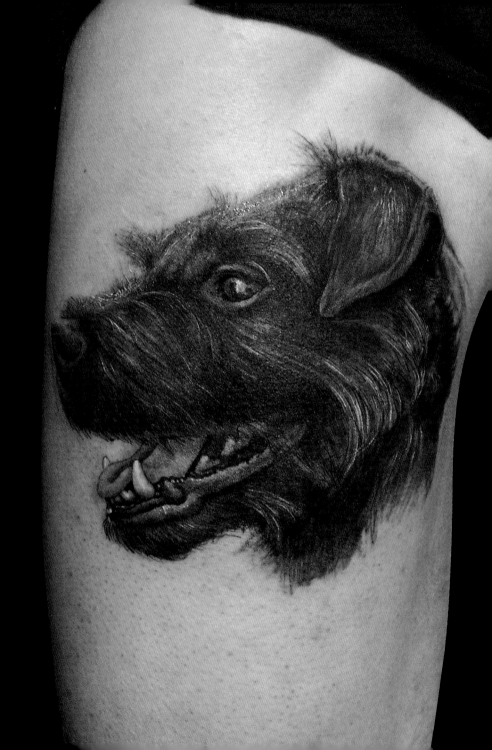

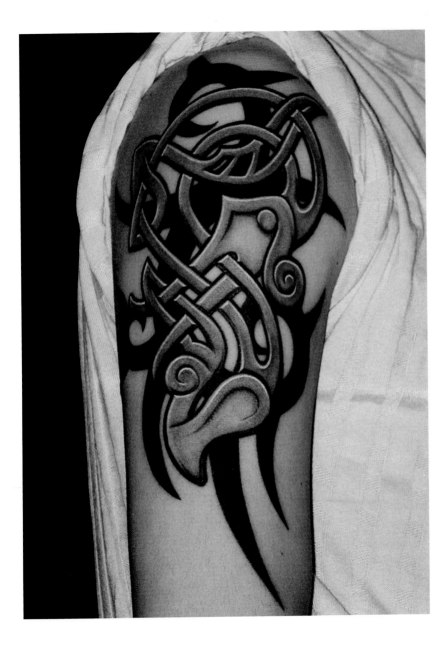

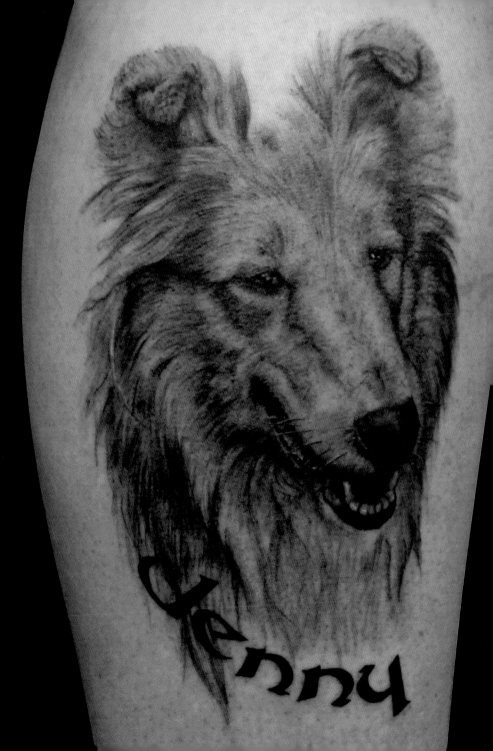

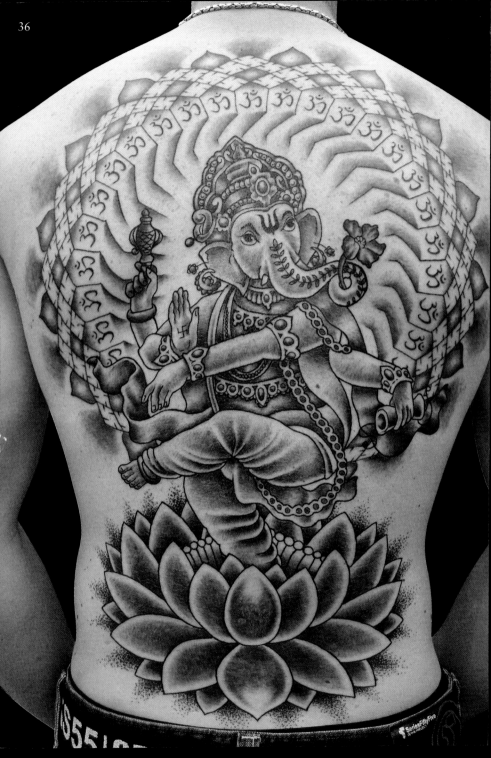

NEIL BASS

Neil Bass was something of
a latecomer in the world of
tattooing, getting his first tattoo at
the age of 27. But just three years
later, in 1998, he set out on the
long road to become a tattooer.
Six years of gaining experience
on his lonesome brought the
opportunity to open his own
studio, Tattoo-fx. Never looking
back, only to the future, has
led the studio from strength to
strength. And rarely turning away
work has enabled Neil to gain
experience in a full range of styles.

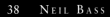

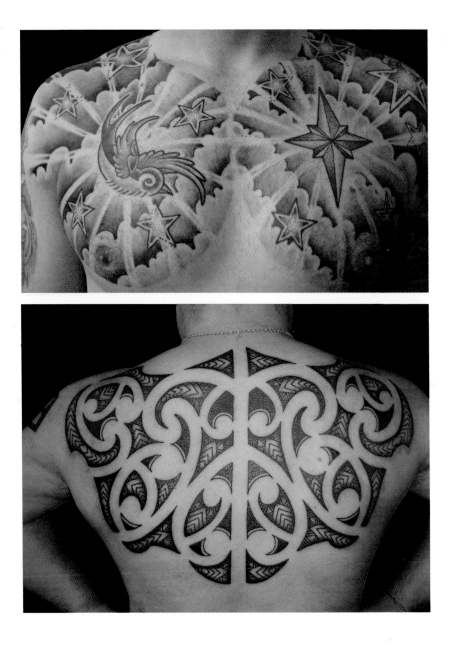

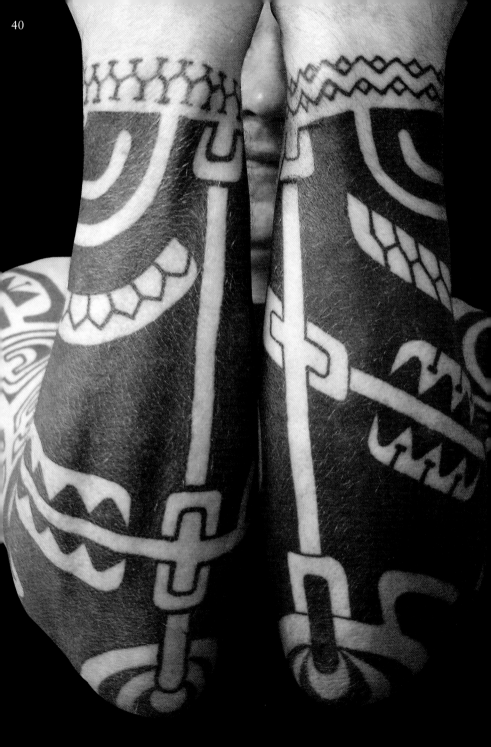

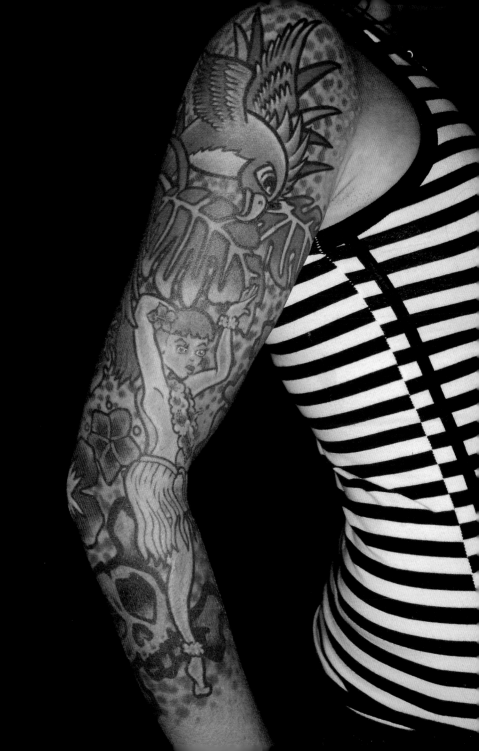

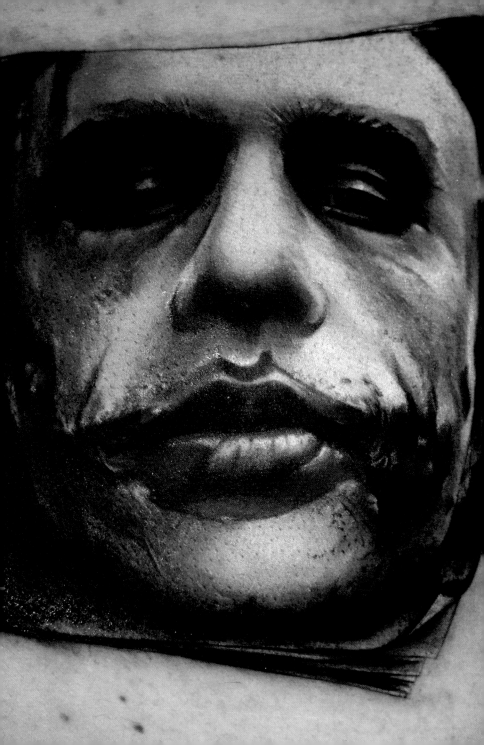

Bez

Bez started tattooing around three years ago, while looking for a new challenge, having worked as an art director in the computer games industry for about 15 years. After trying a few different art-related jobs, he says he "sort of just fell into tattooing", and he hasn't looked back since. In his view it's the best job in the world. It's a lot of hard work, but every day brings a different project to get his head around. He likes most forms of tattooing, but especially realism and high-colour work, though with a bit of black and grey from time to time, too. He also does a lot of Japanese work, under the alias of Mr Woo. Increasingly, he enjoys the contrast with his usual work. Over the next few years he he plans to push the realism side of tattooing a stage further with some "mad and crazy plans".

Artist picture © Katriona Godward.

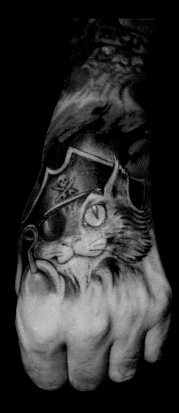

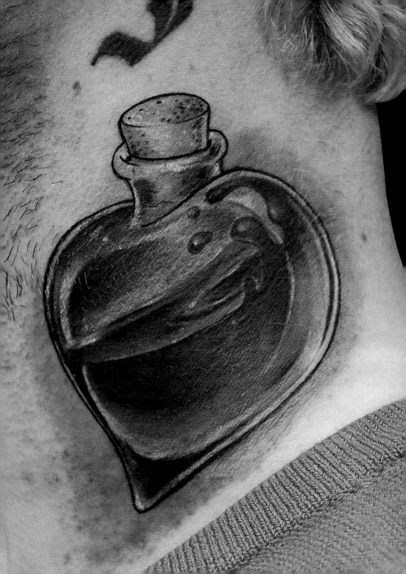

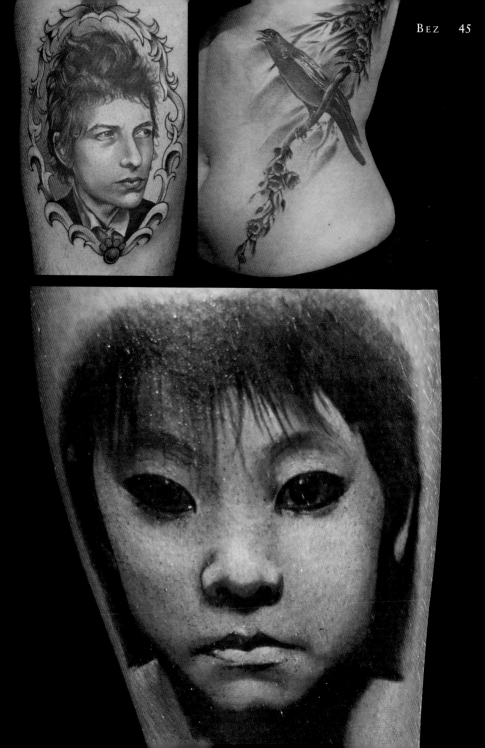

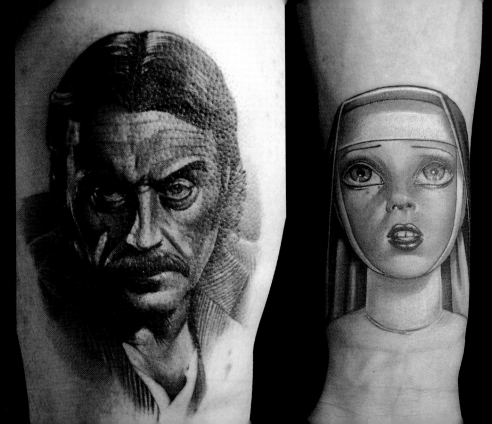

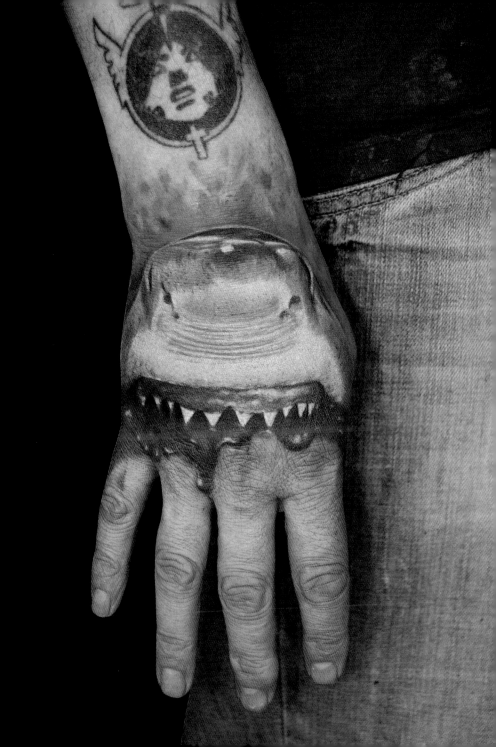

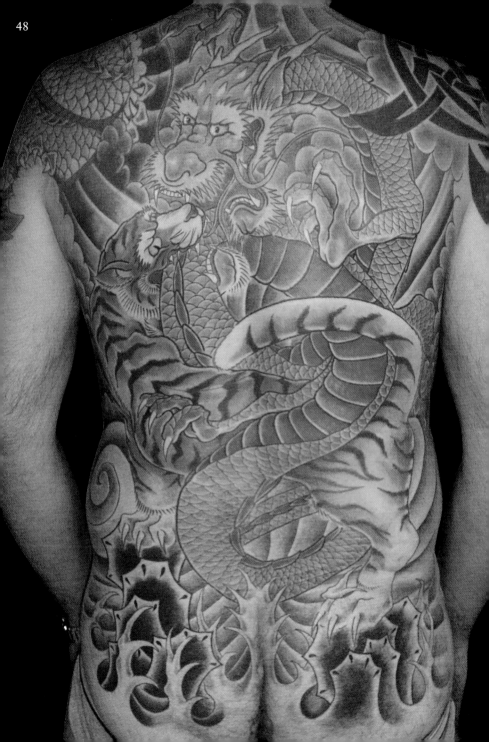

NARESH BHANA

"Tattoo has been a lifelong journey of discovery and adventure, leading me on a merry dance across the globe experiencing tattoo in all its forms and cultural contexts. Collecting tattoos as I went, I found my body transformed into my own personal travelogue, and after 20-odd years of buying just about every tattoo-related book on the planet I finally get to be in one."

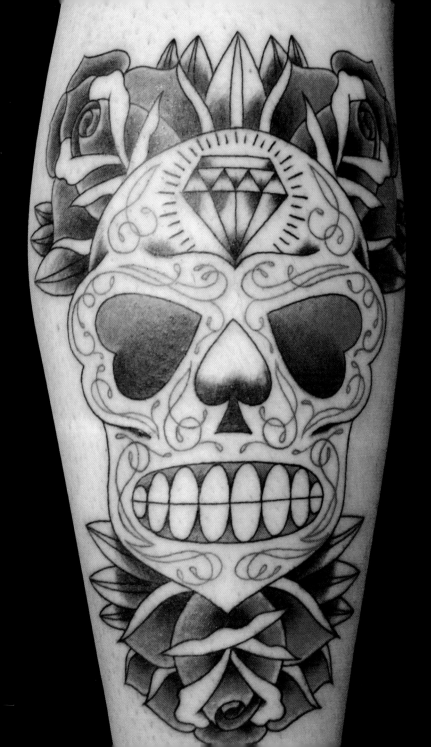

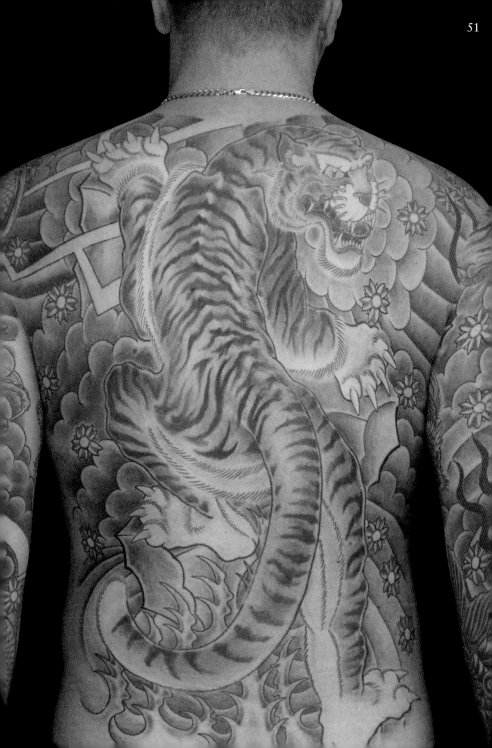

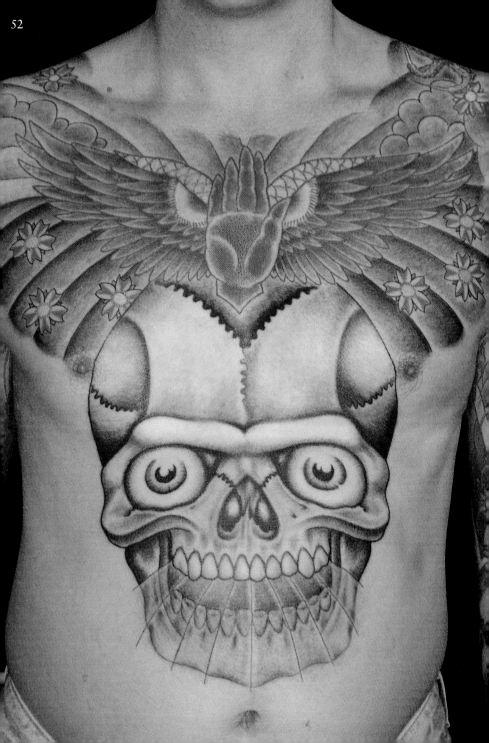

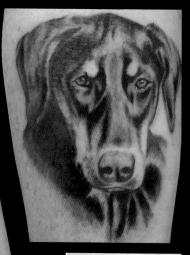

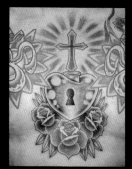

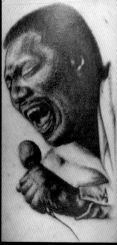

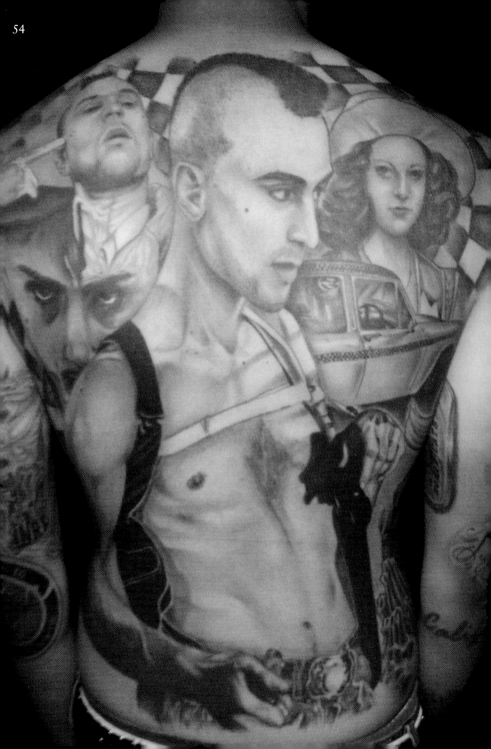

BIG GUS

Big Gus was raised in LA County, California, where he grew up in the streets, drawing and writing on everything he saw until he realized "he could make money off of this". He was airbrushing at 13, tattooing at 14, and working as a professional tattooist by the time he was 22, at Distinctive Ink Tattoo, in Pico Rivera. He learned from watching others, by painting murals in the LA riverbed, on street corners, and down alleys. His mother also helped, by not yelling at him when he wrote on the walls. His favourite style of tattooing is fine-line and black/grey photorealism. He has won well over 100 awards and often had his work published. He believes that you must always keep learning, trying to be original. He says, "I have been blessed and lucky to be part of such an awesome family I call the tattoo world, what else can I ask for?"

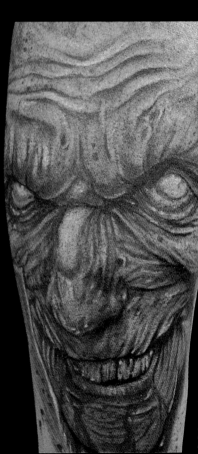

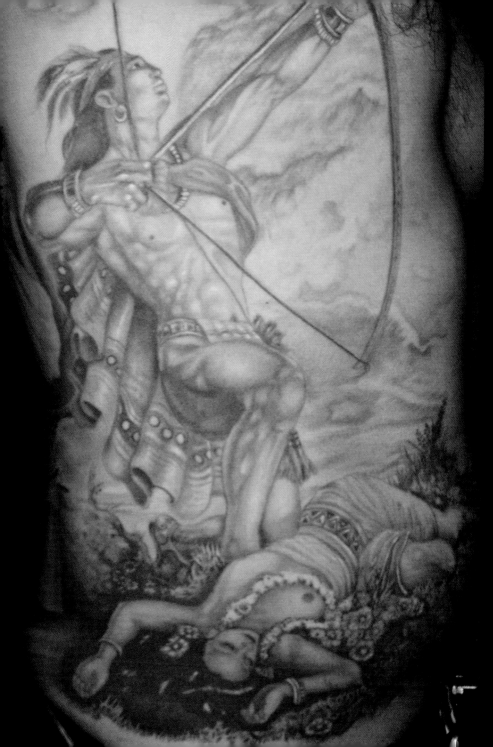

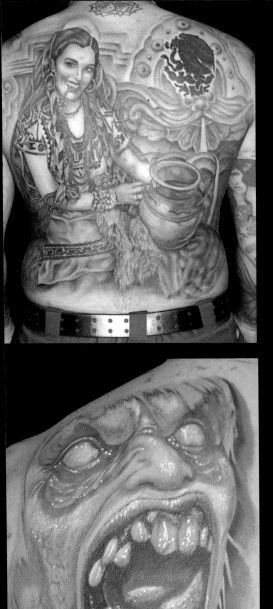

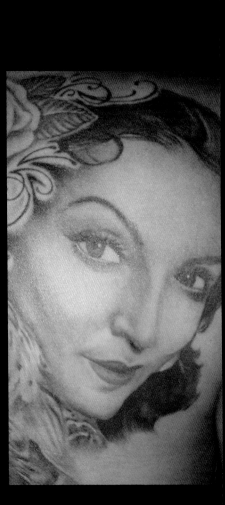

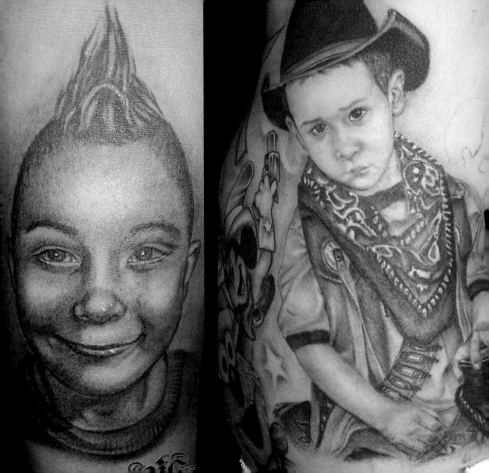

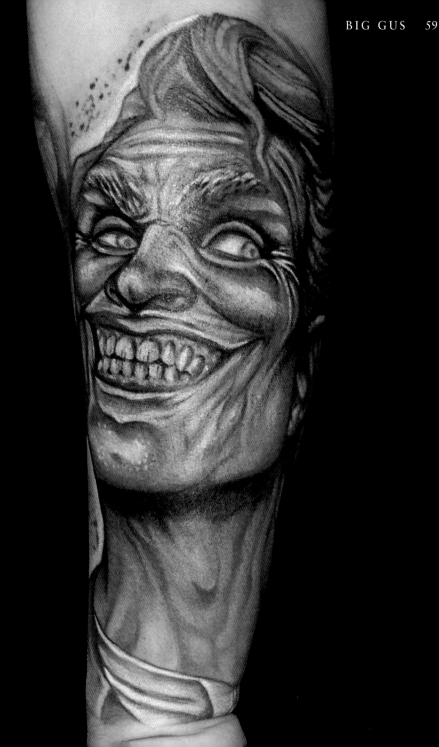

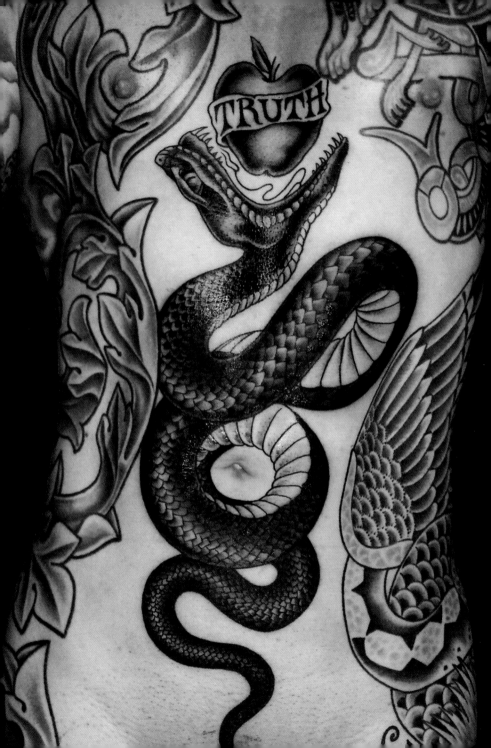

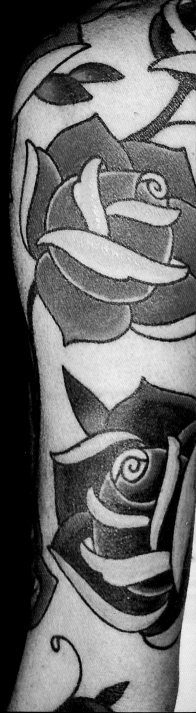

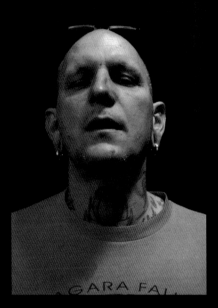

ALEX BINNIE

"Twenty years on and I'm still loving it. Mostly!"

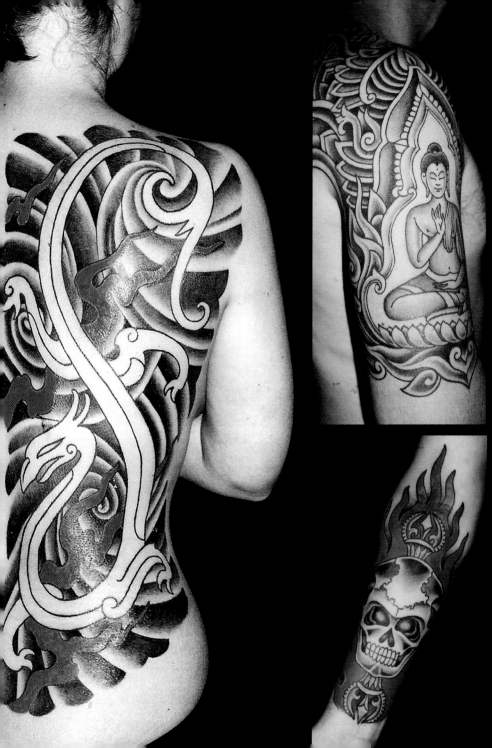

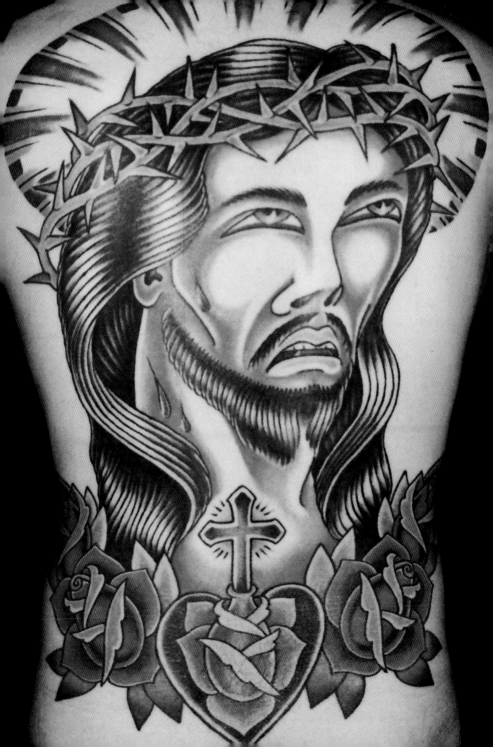

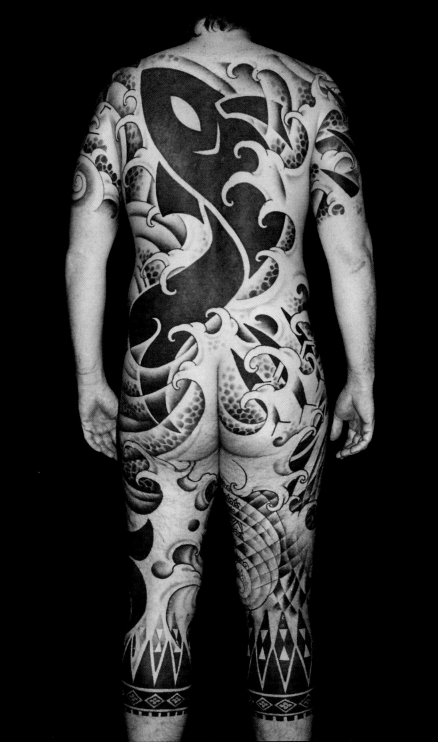

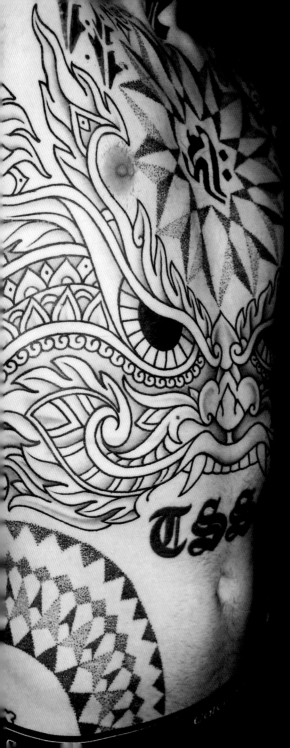

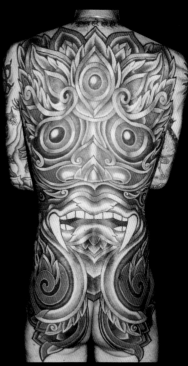

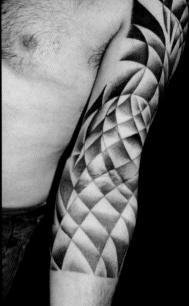

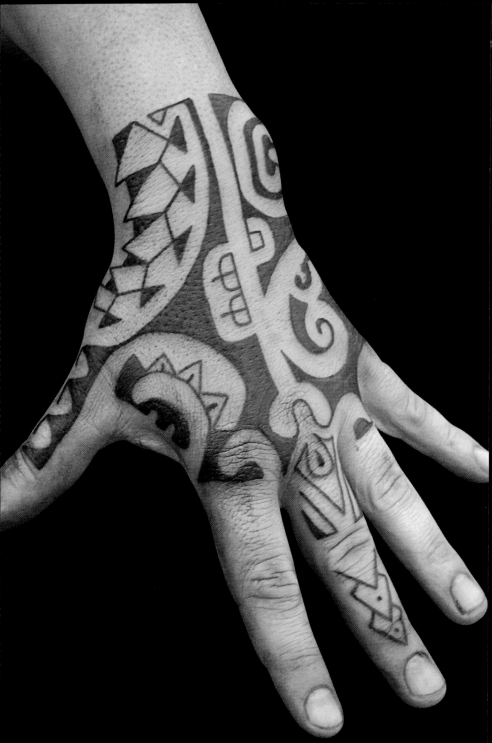

MATT BLACK

Matt Black began tattooing in
Manchester in 2002, where he
worked for two years with Mark
Armstrong at Sacred Art, learning
all the basics, such as how to
make needles and so on. In 2004,
he moved to London where he
worked with Geoff Healy at
BlueFire Tattoo for about three
years. Geoff gave him free rein
to do whatever work he was
interested in taking on, enabling
him to build up a good portfolio
and develop a style of his own.
Matt now works at New Wave
Tattoo. He likes doing neo-tribal,
Polynesian, and dotwork and
his main influences are Curly in
Oxford, Xed le Hed in London,
and Roonui from Tahiti.

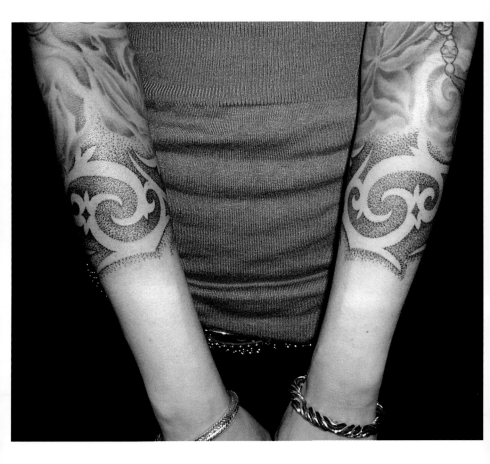

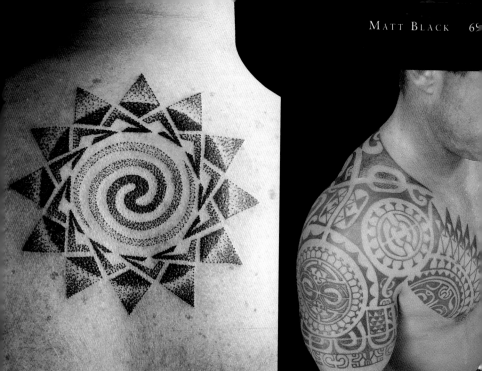

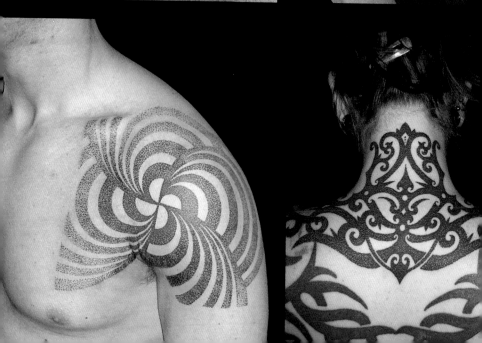

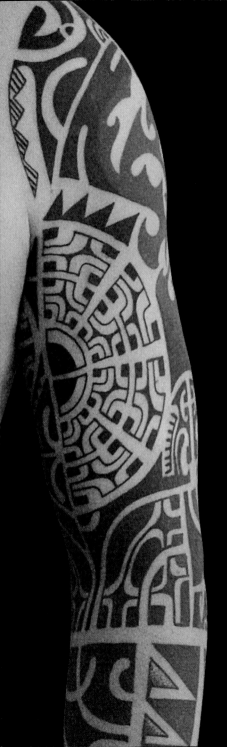

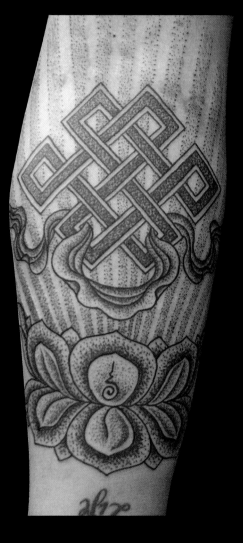

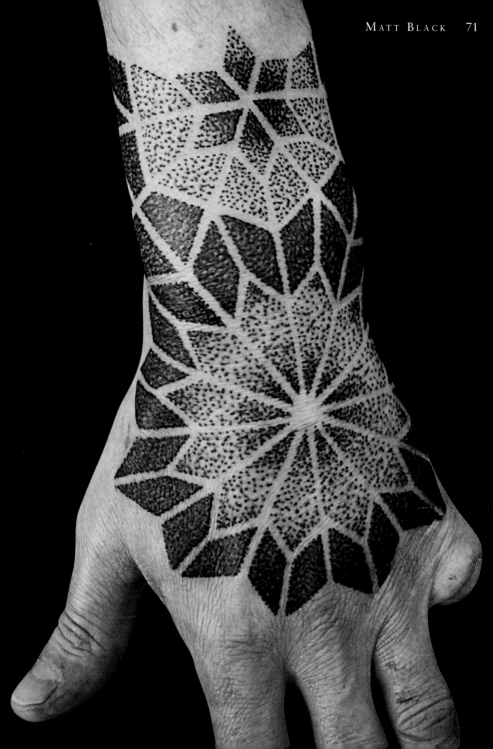

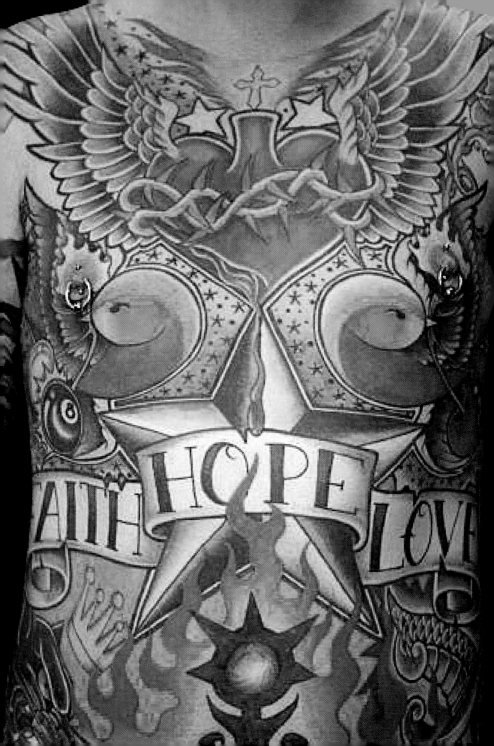

THE BOND FAMILY

Phil Bond: "We have been in the same location for the past 25 years [Phil Bond's Tattoo Studio, in Torquay, England]. I have seen many styles come and go – personally, my favourite style is Japanese. I feel it will never become outdated. Our apprentice, and the youngest member of our team at 15 years old, Spike Bond, works hard and sucks up knowledge like a sponge. One to look out for in the future."

Troy Bond: "I am the eldest of seven children and have worked in our family business for the past 14 years. My personal taste is modern-day old school."

Luke Bond: "I have been tattooing in our studio for the past nine years. Due to walk-in trade we've had to learn to adapt to any style on any given day."

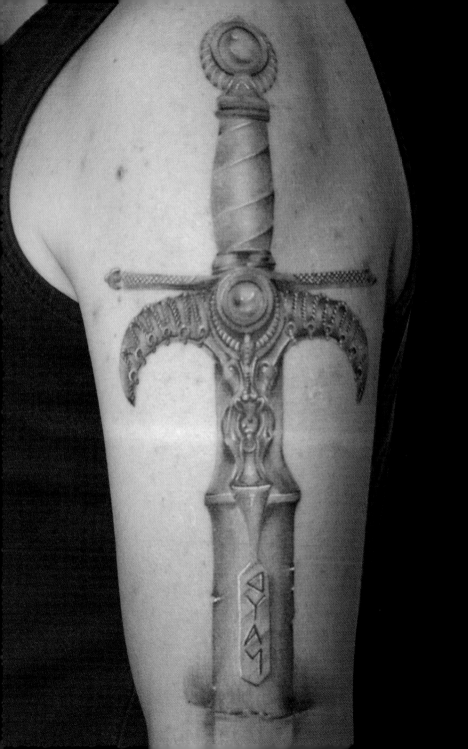

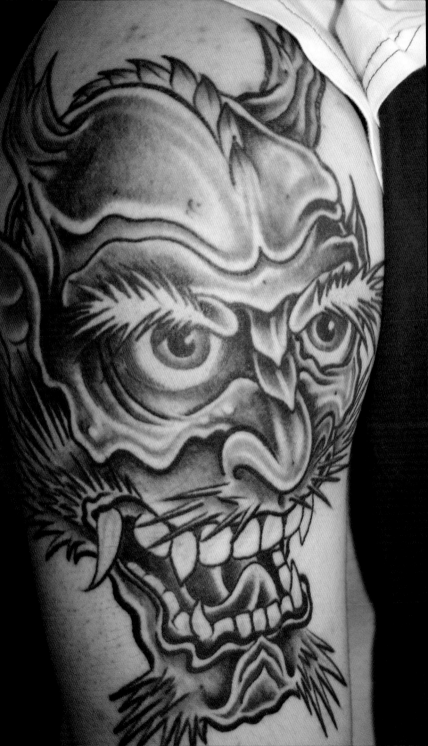

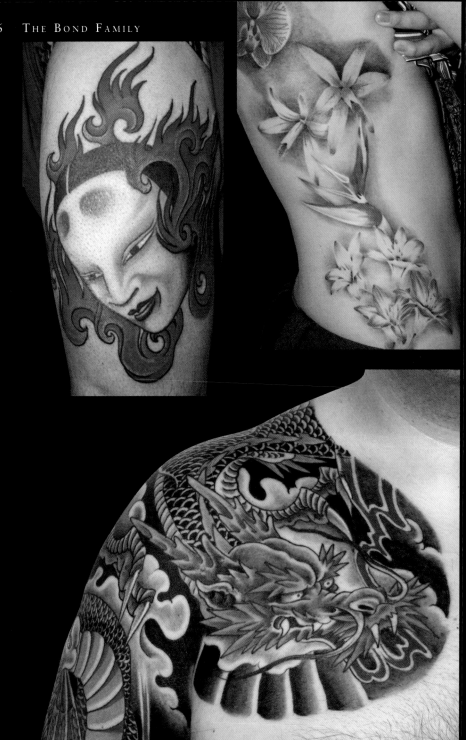

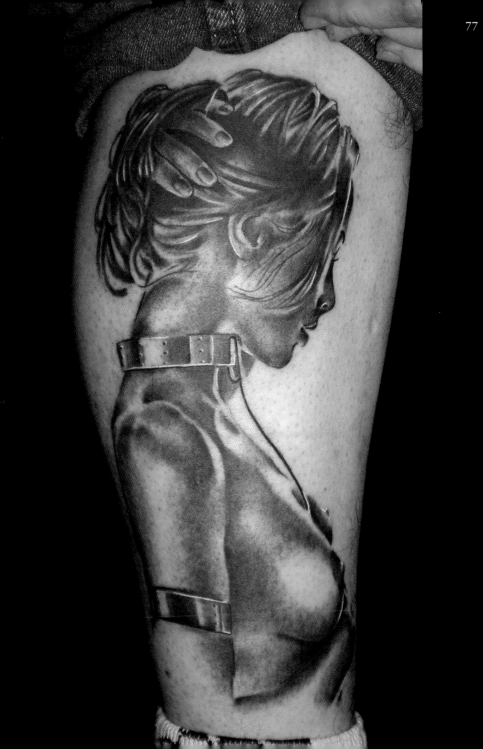

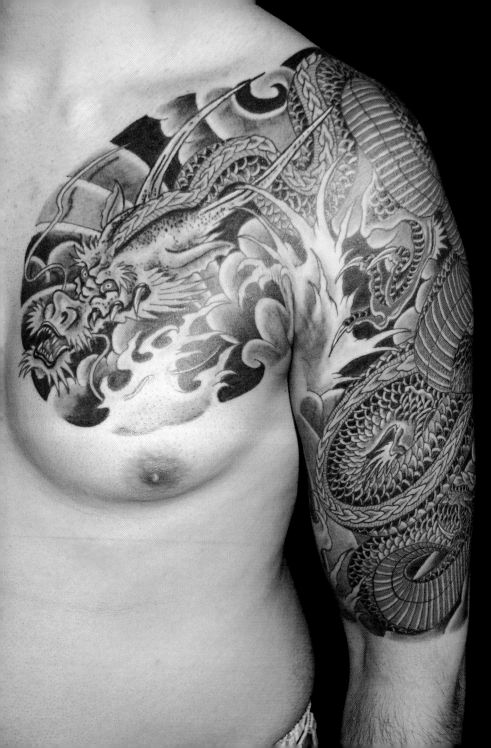

GEORGE BONE

Celebrated at one time in the
Guinness Book of Records for
being Britain's most tattooed man,
George Bone has been tattooing
in his famous studio for the past
36 years. He does most styles of
tattooing, but prefers to do custom
work, Japanese being the most
popular style of tattooing in his
studio.

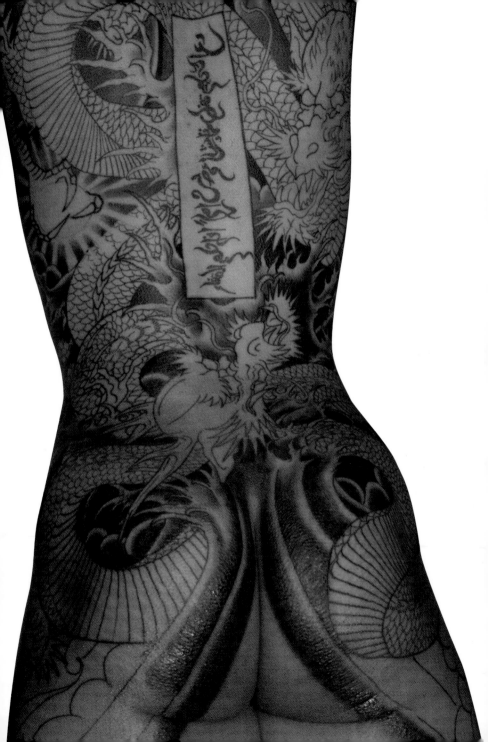

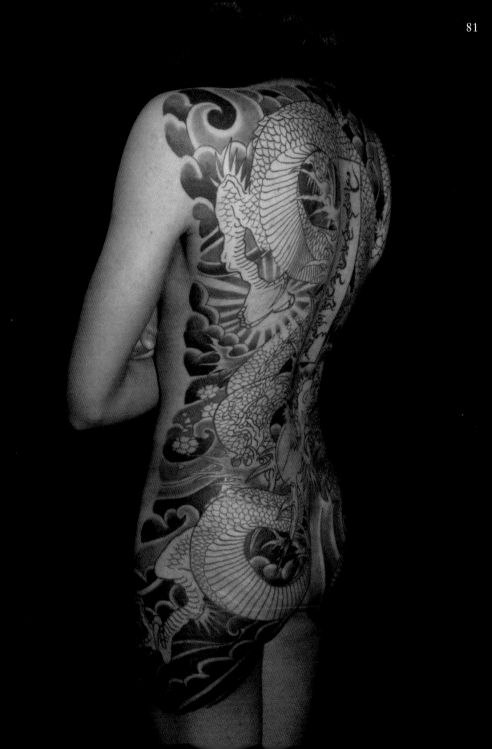

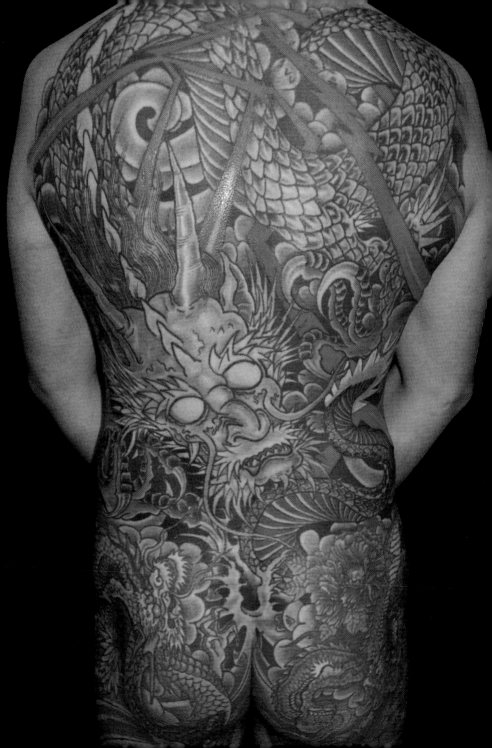

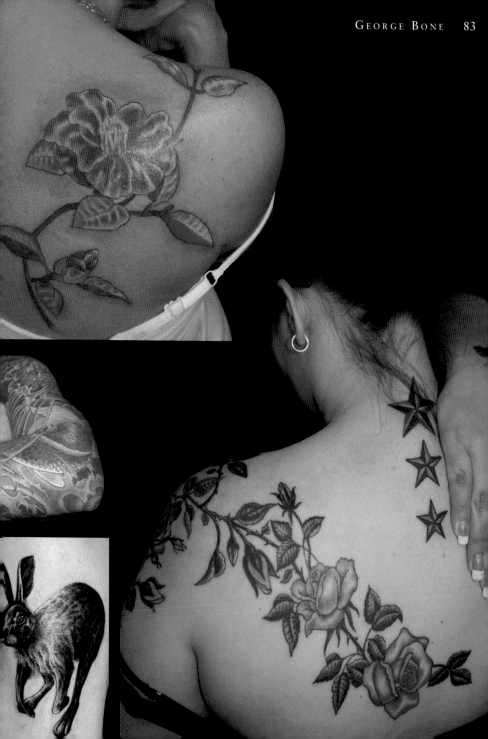

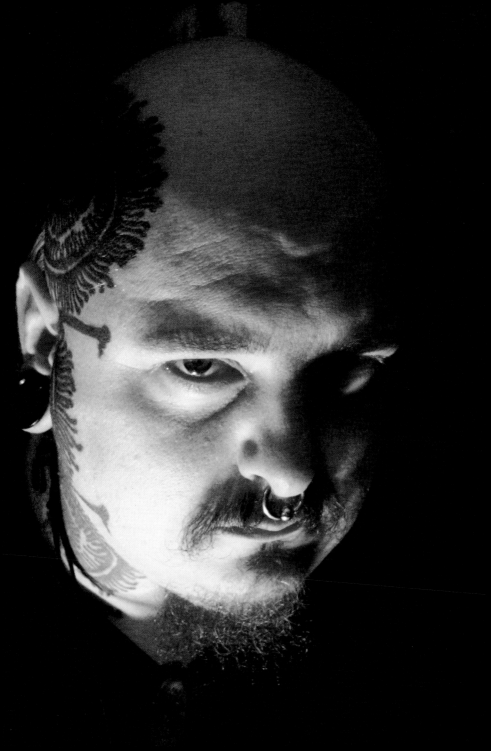

PAUL BOOTH

Paul Booth has been a tattoo artist
for nearly two decades and a painter
before that. Following years of public
appearances and having won numerous
international awards, he is now a
household name with a two-year waiting
list. In 2000, together with the world-
renowned Swiss tattooists Filip and
Titine Leu, he initiated the international
ArtFusion Experiment, bringing together
leading tattoo artists from around the
world to create one-of-a-kind works
of art, also winning an award for his
documentary of the movement. In 2002,
his macabre style and his tattooing
of numerous major metal bands led
Rolling Stone magazine to dub him "the
king of rock tattoos". He is devoted to
the horror genre, and has had a long
relationship with film.

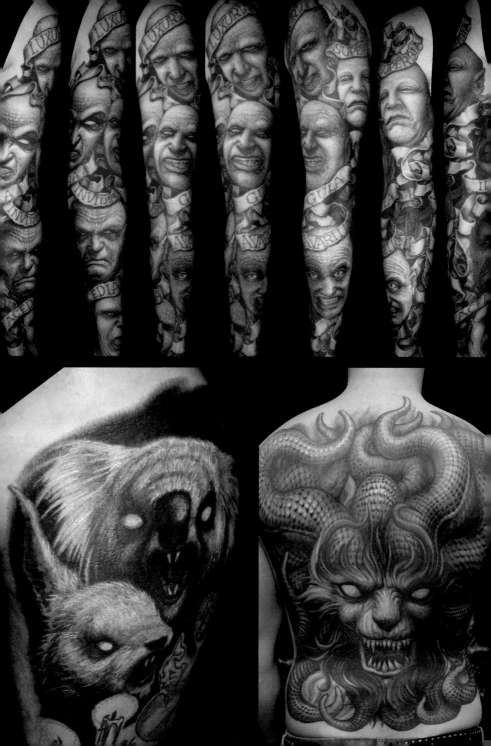

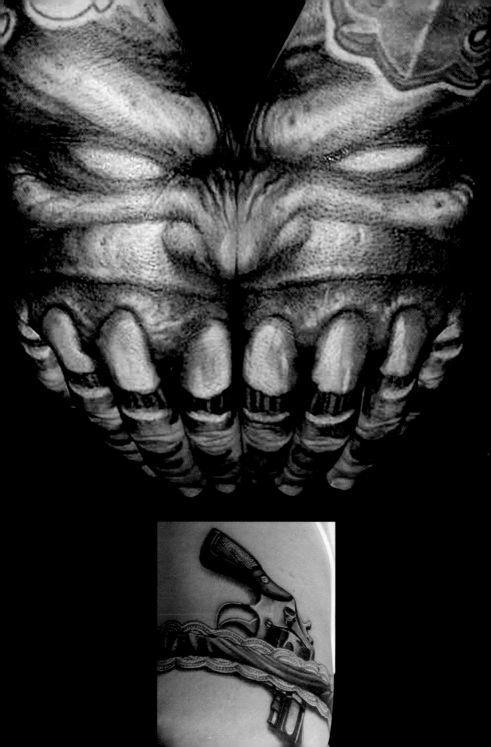

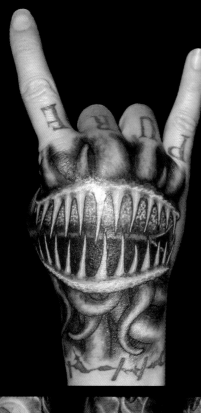
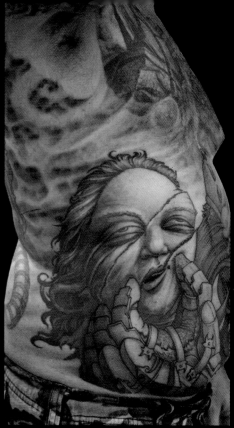
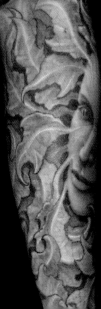
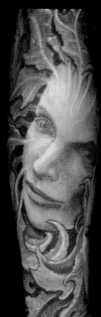
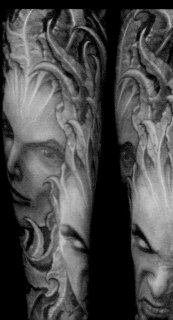

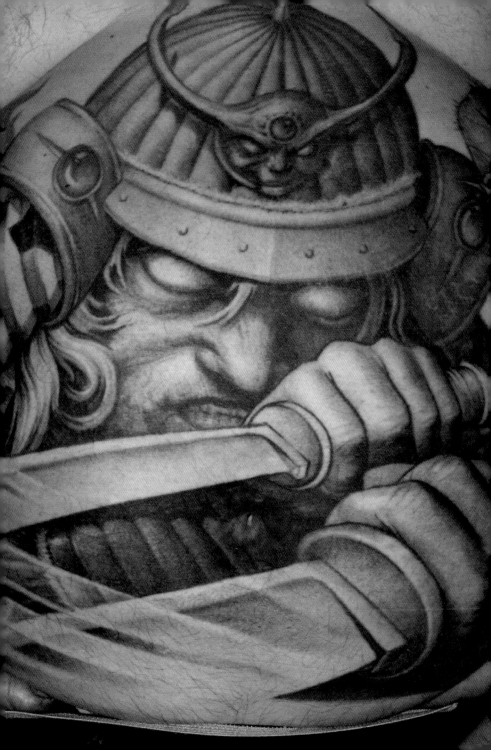

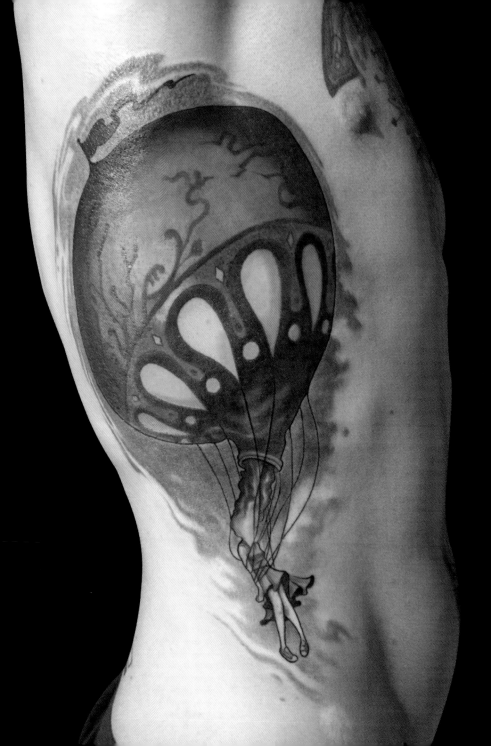

Dave Bryant

Dave Bryant began tattooing in
his native England in early 1999.
After two years tattooing in studios
and feeling that a progressive
environment was eluding him, he
headed for Canada where he spent
the next four years learning from a
multitude of talented artists across
the country, but working for the most
part at Universal, in Victoria, British
Columbia. On returning to England,
he was hired by Evil from the Needle
and worked between London and
Chicago at Deluxe Tattoo, before
settling at Evil from the Needle,
where he has been since 2006. In July
2008, he established the Order of the
Forbidden Donut, an organization
bent on world domination.

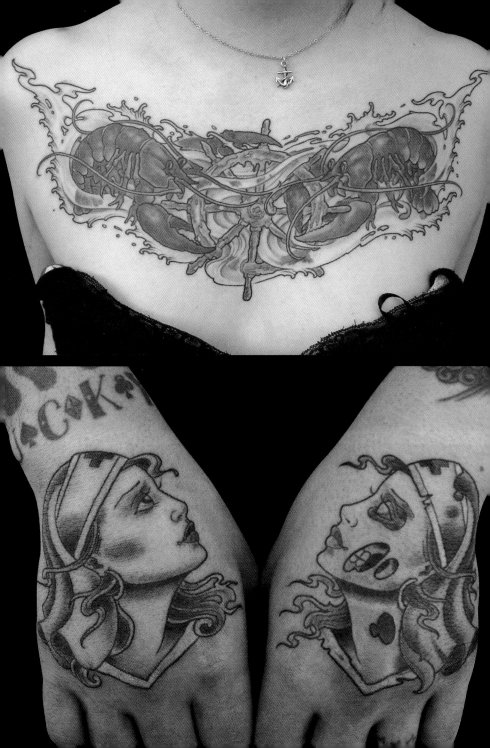

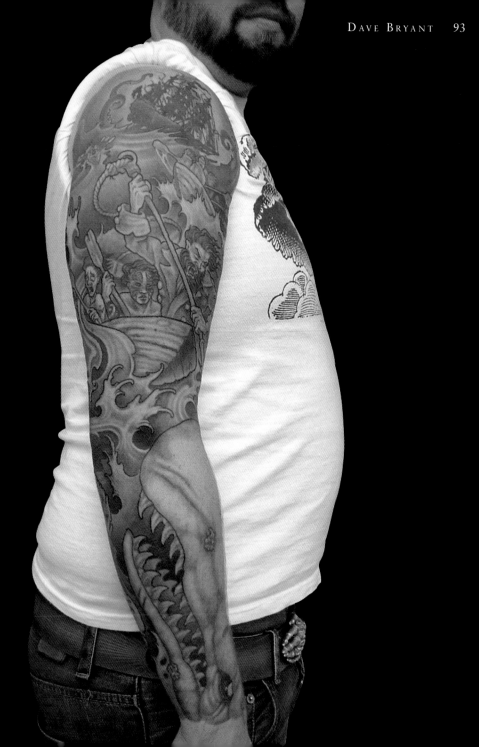

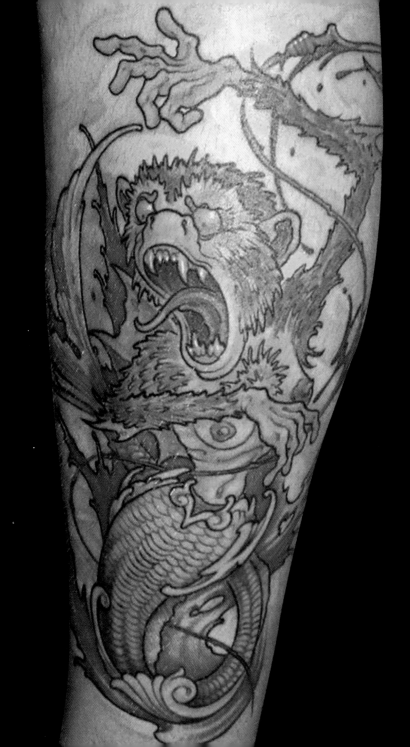

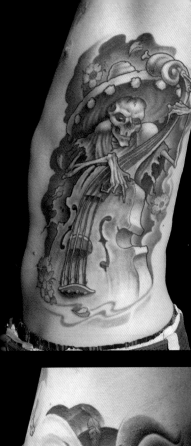

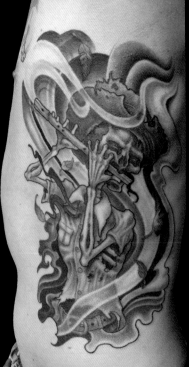

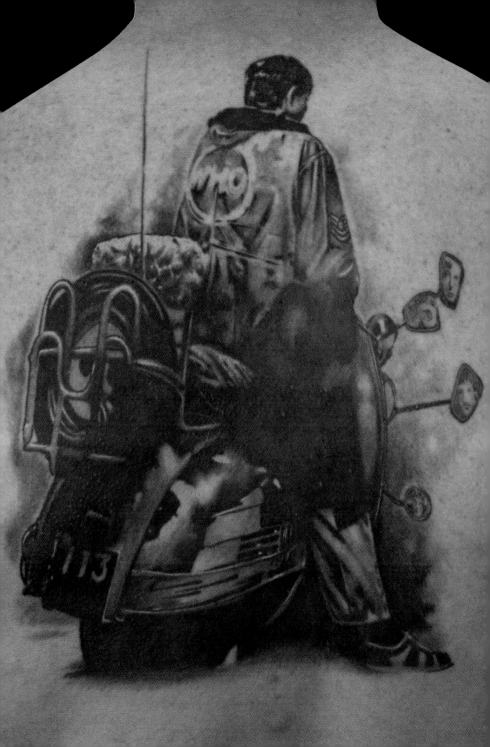

JASON BUTCHER

Jason Butcher grew up in Chelmsford, in the south-east of England, knowing that he wanted to be an artist from a very early age. Although he had no formal art training or tattoo apprenticeship, he started tattooing in 1994, working hard to learn everything he needed to know. He opened his own studio, Immortal Ink, in 1999, and he's been there ever since. His art has always been influenced by his love of horror films, but he likes to tattoo anything photo-realistic or horror-related, and specializes in tattooing in black and grey.

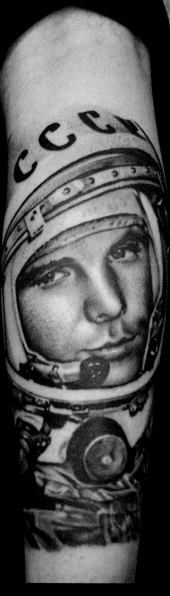
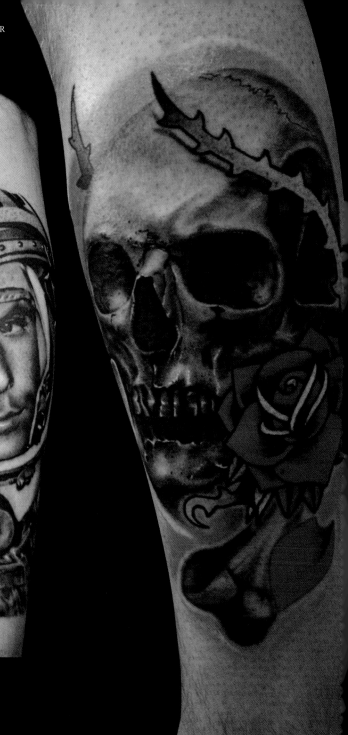

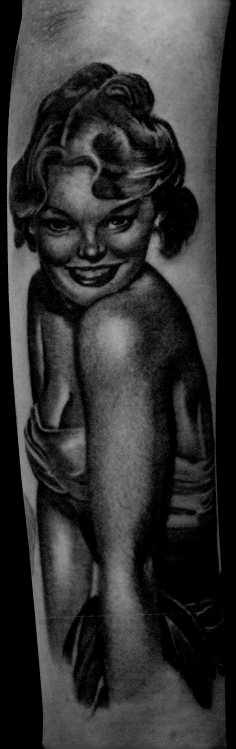
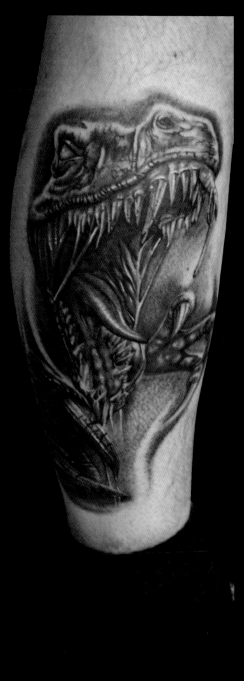

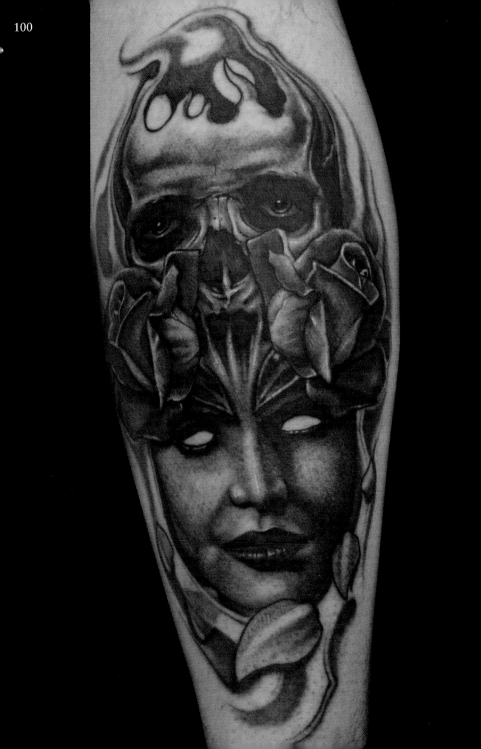

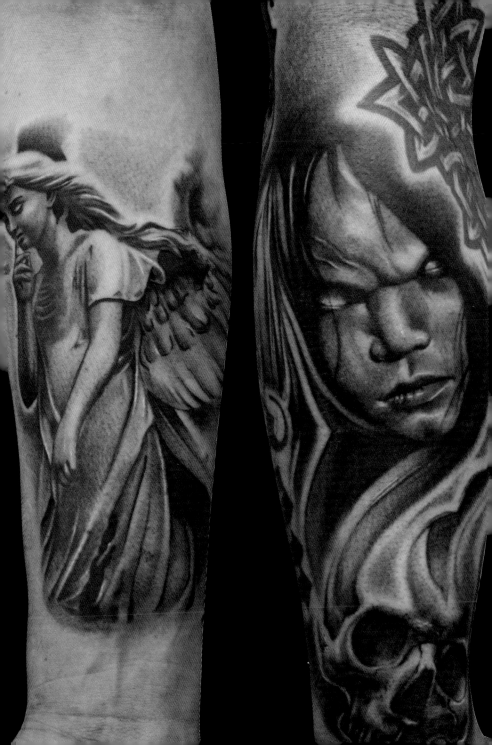

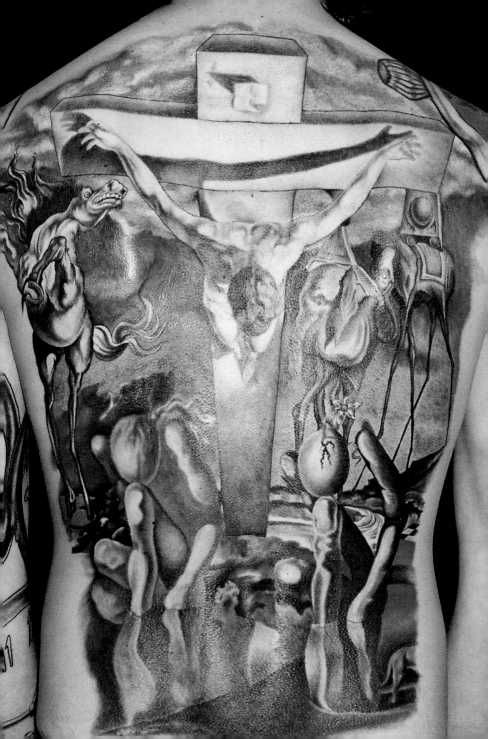

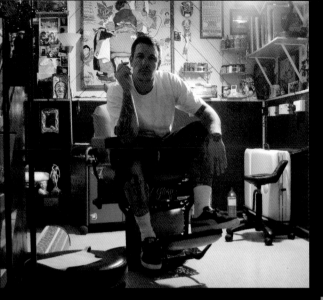

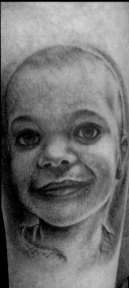

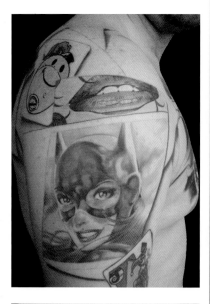

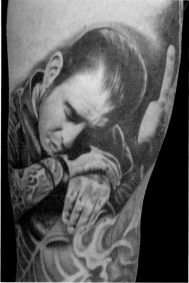

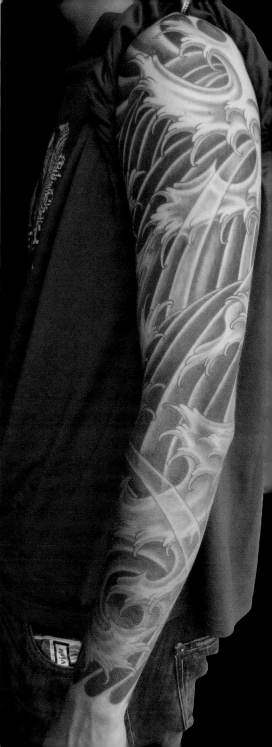

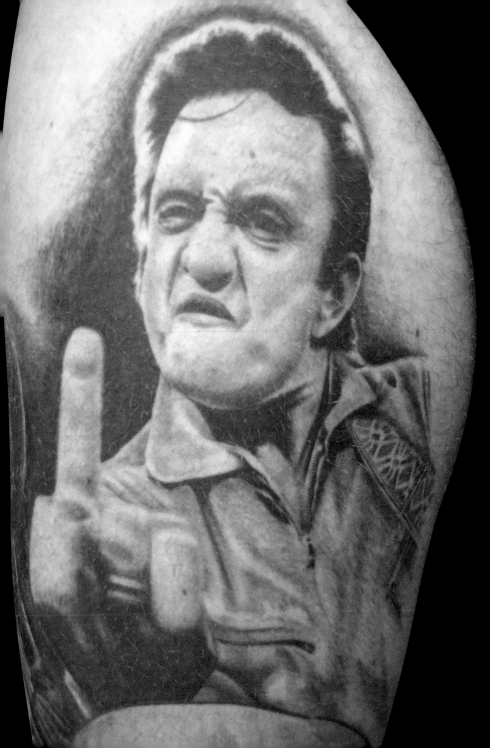

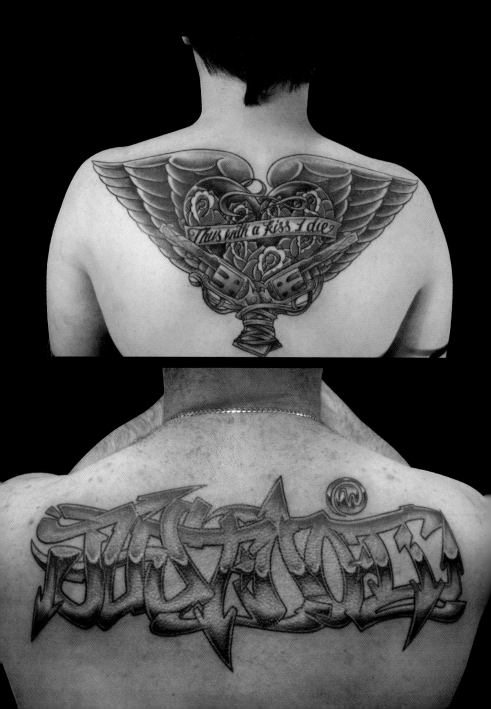

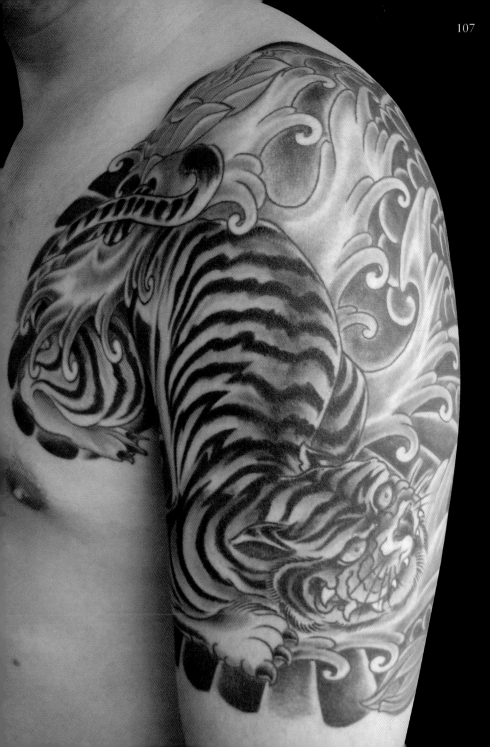

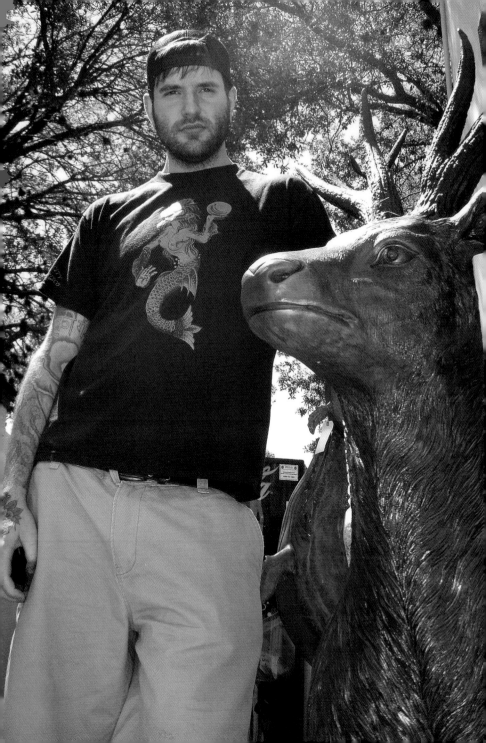

STEVE BYRNE

Steve Byrne was born in Durham, England, in 1978, and has been tattooing professionally since 1998. He has built a strong reputation on his instantly recognizable style with both bold traditional and modern Japanese works in his Name and Blood studio in Leeds, England. He maintains a punishing schedule, not only in Leeds, but all over the world with regular guest spots.

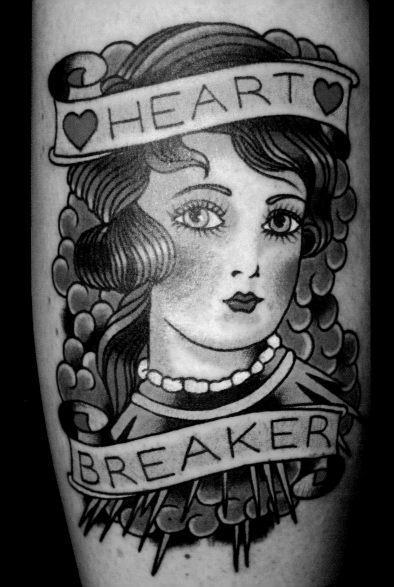

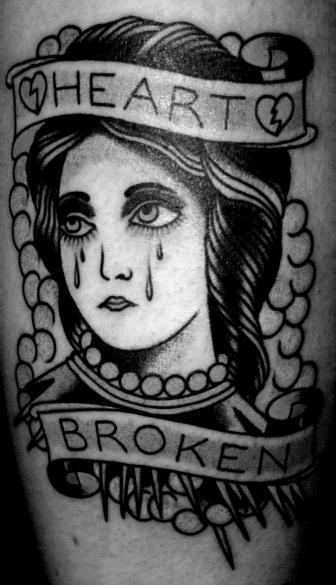

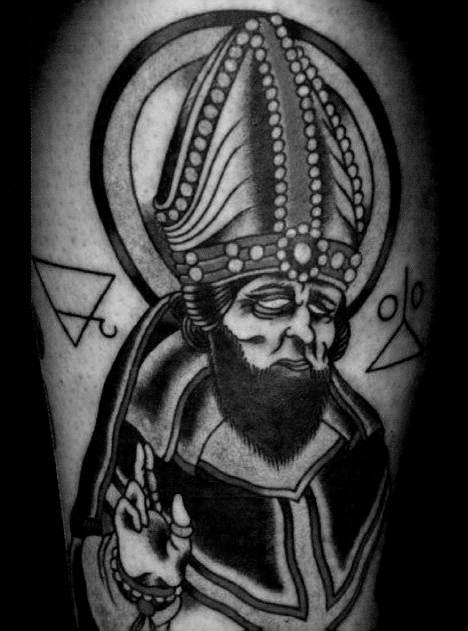

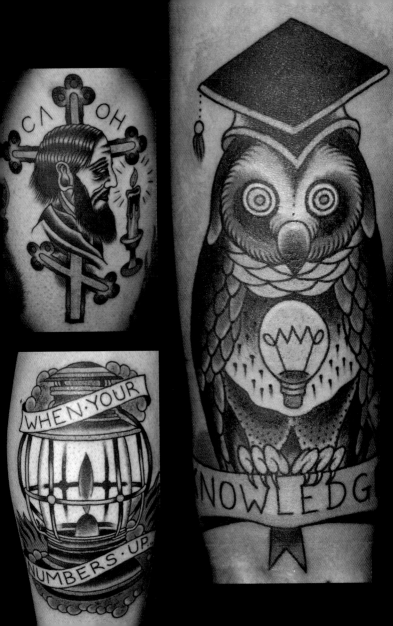

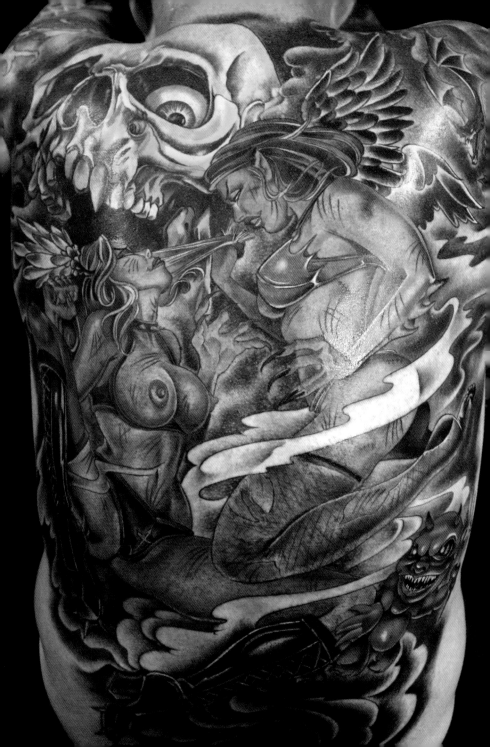

Joe Capobianco

Joe Capobianco got his start on Long Island, New York, where, with the help of fellow artists and a desire to learn as much of the tattooing business as quickly as possible, he flourished. After six years he left New York to further his tattoo education with Cory Kruger in north-eastern Massachusetts. Together, they started Color Box, a small private studio on the border between New Hampshire and Massachusetts, but after two years they went their separate ways. Joe moved to New Haven, Connecticut, where he founded Hope Gallery alongside Julio Rodriguez and Eric Merrill – together, they truly left their mark on the north-east. Joe has also published a number of bestselling sketch books. He currently lives in New Haven, Connecticut, with his lovely wife Alethea and their cute little French bulldog, Molly, but "keep your eye on the sky because who knows where he'll end up next".

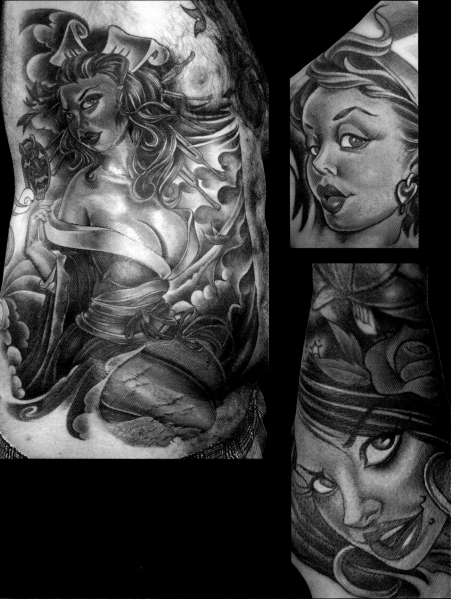

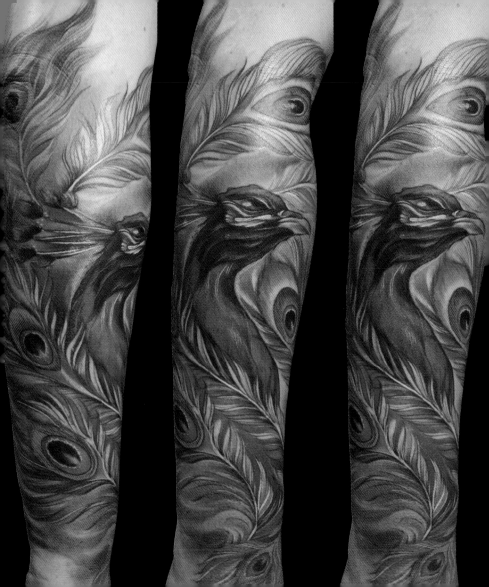

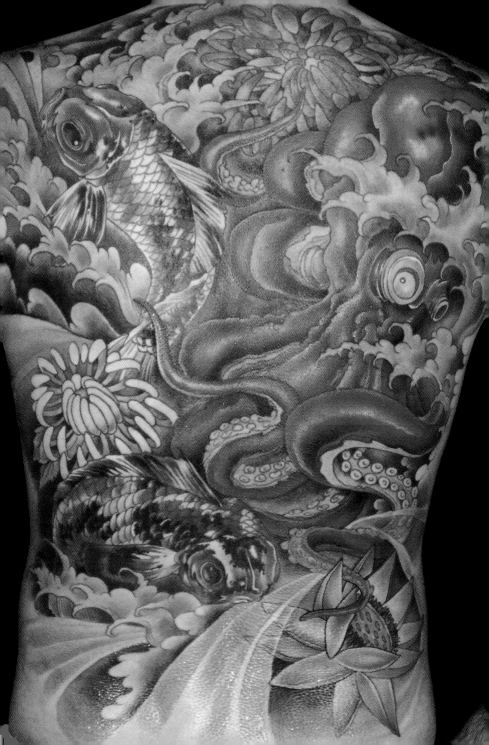

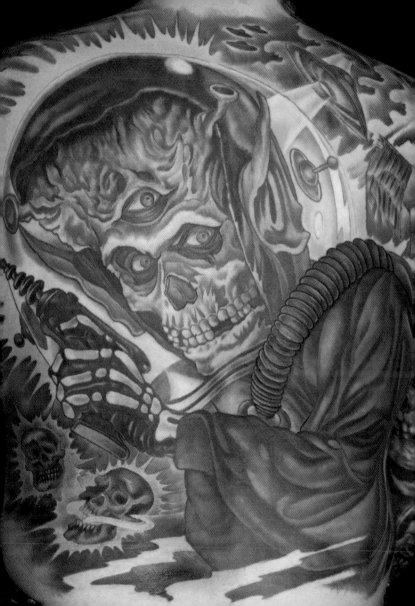

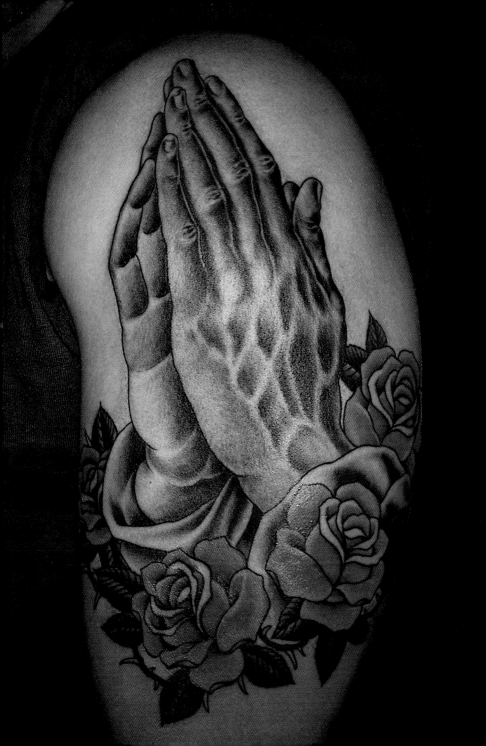

Marco Cerretelli

Marco Cerretelli was born and raised in Florence, Italy. His first
encounter with tattooing came while he was in the Italian Army where he
built his first tattoo machine out of an old Walkman, a toothbrush, and a
pen. From 1998 to 2002, when he graduated from the Academy of Art in
Florence, he worked for Maurizio Fiorini, "Il Maestro", the oldest living
Italian tattoo artist. After participating in a few tattoo conventions and
art shows and working in a couple of tattoo shops around Italy, he felt
he needed to travel to America to learn more about the art of tattooing.
After a year spent working in New York, he moved to Los Angeles,
California, in 2003 where he now works for the legendary Bob Roberts
at Spotlight Tattoo, alongside other great artists.

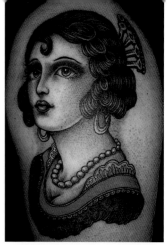

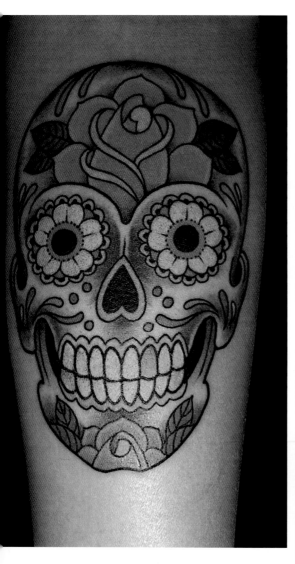

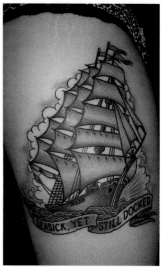

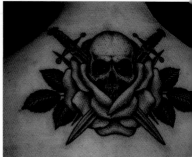

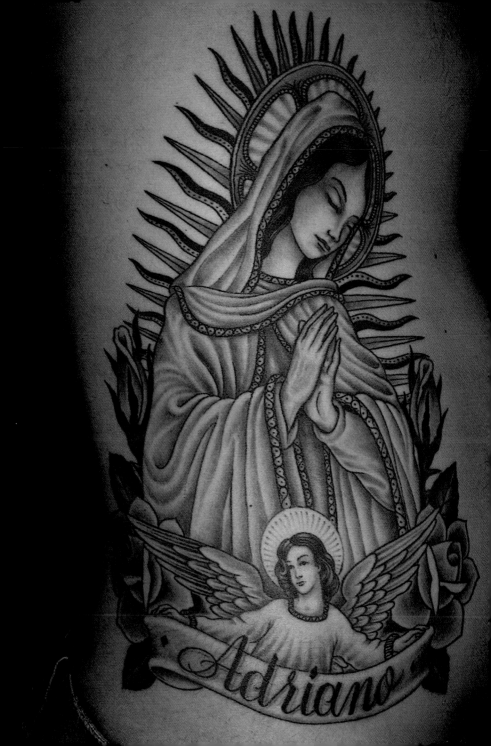

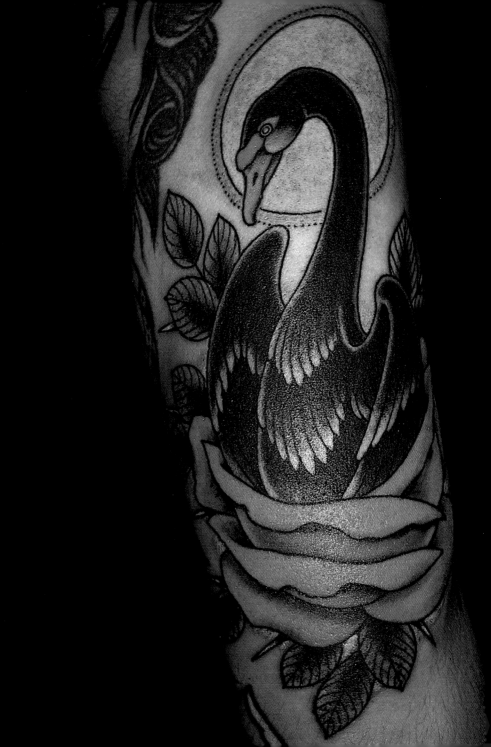

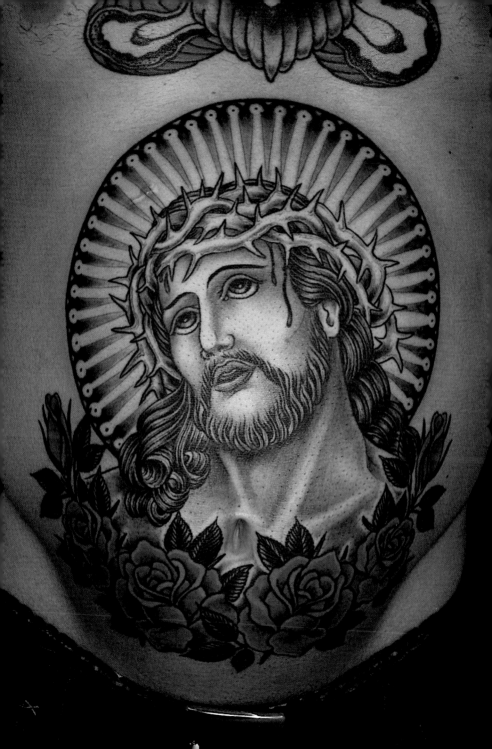

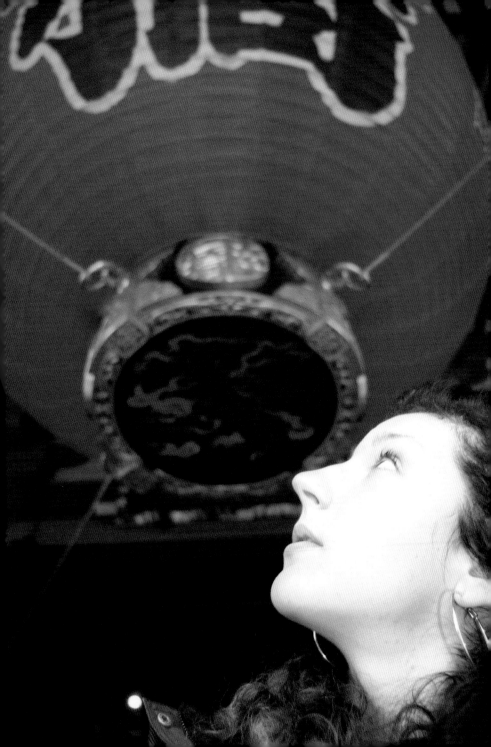

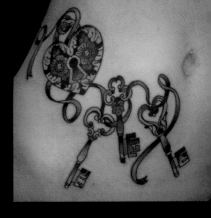

CLAUDIA

Claudia De Rossi, a.k.a. Sabe, was born in Italy in 1980. She started tattooing from home, in 2004, with the help of some tattooist friends, but her career really took off when she had her sleeves tattooed by Ian Flower at Into You, in London. She showed him her sketch-book and he offered her a job at his studio in Surrey. Before taking up the job, she worked for six months at Andy Tattoos in Rovigo, Italy. Since then she has worked at Frith Street Tattoo, in London, and New Skool Tattoo, in Surrey. Her favourite styles are traditional Japanese, Old School, and graffiti-related, but she also enjoys "whatever comes through the door". She is inspired by a number of different sources such as jewellery, fashion, old pictures, architecture, and sculpture. For Claudia tattooing is all about shapes and flow; she is a graffiti writer and loves her Italian heritage.

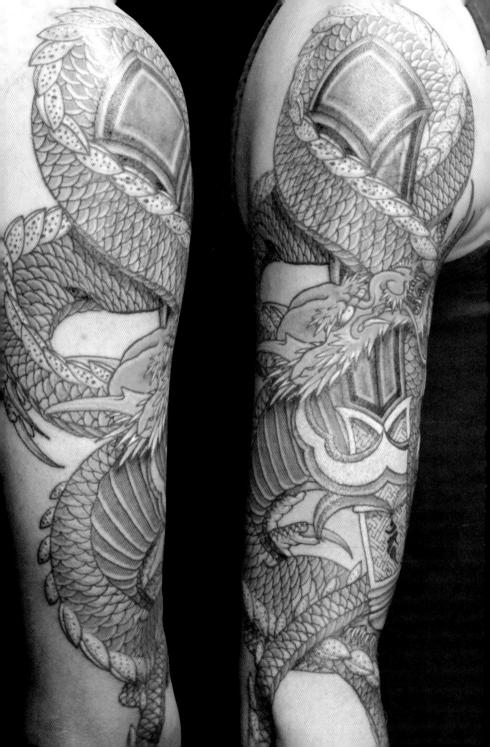

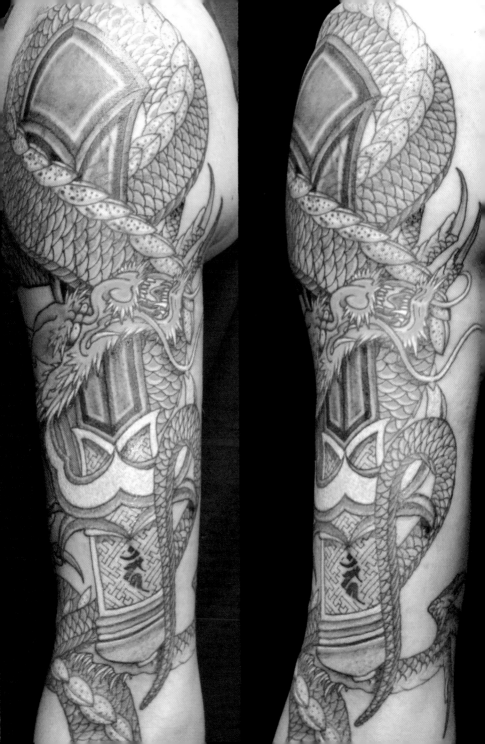

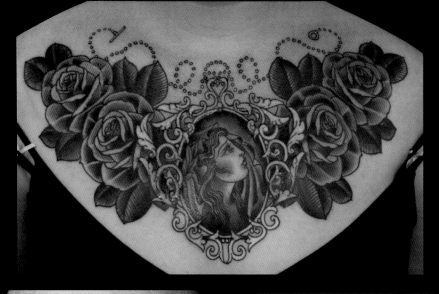

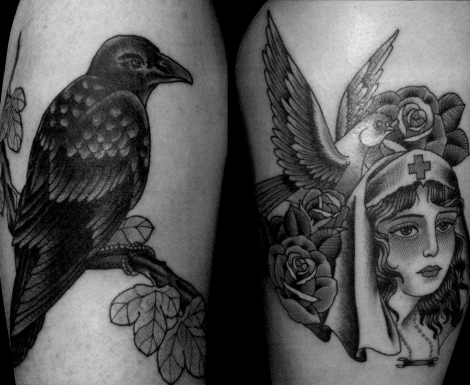

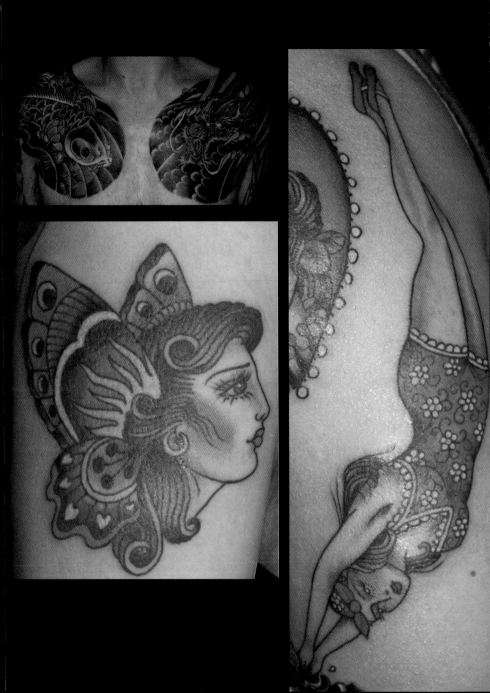

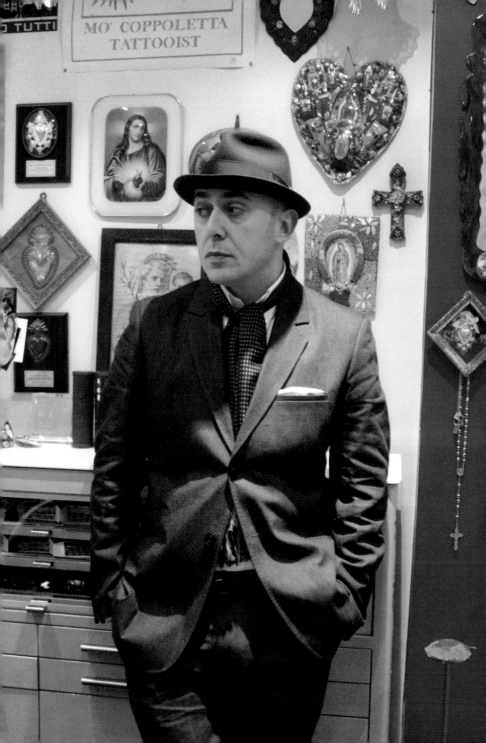

Mo Coppoletta

Mo Coppoletta started tattooing in 1997 after several years spent running around the world visiting his favourite artists and collecting tattoos. Those were the days of the "Great Tattoo Renaissance" with a flood of mind-blowing tattoos from all over the world – Japan, Europe, America – the like of which the world had never seen before. As he puts it, "How many times did I hear, 'This is it . . . it can't get any bigger . . .'? And I felt I got into it a bit late. Well, we were all wrong. The magic world of tattooing has grown bigger and better than any of us could ever have expected. I feel very fortunate to belong to such a world and to have made my passion my everyday profession."

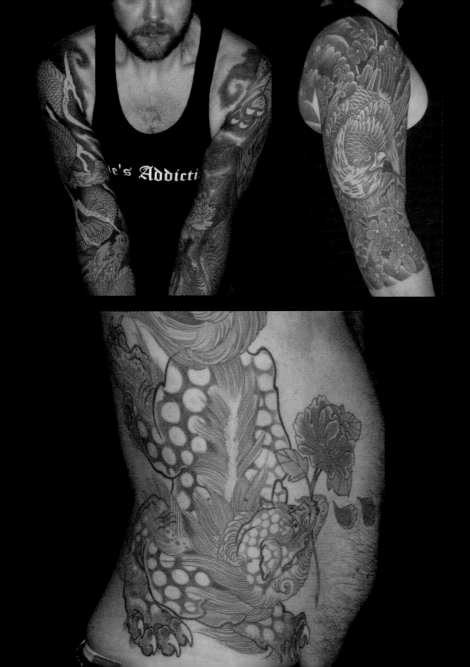

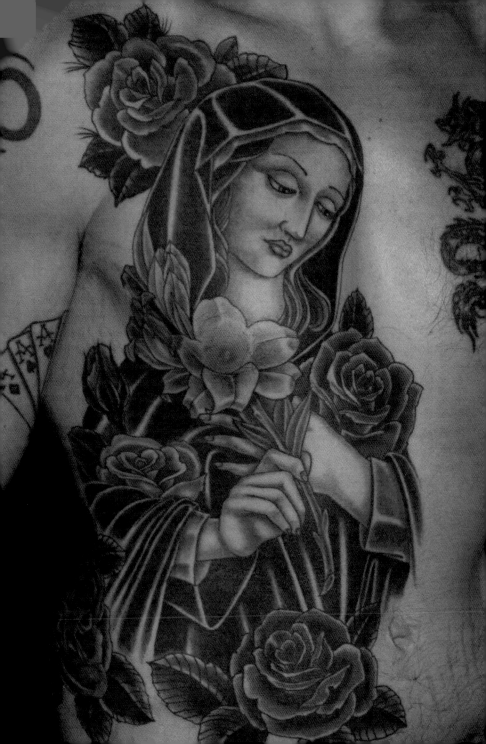

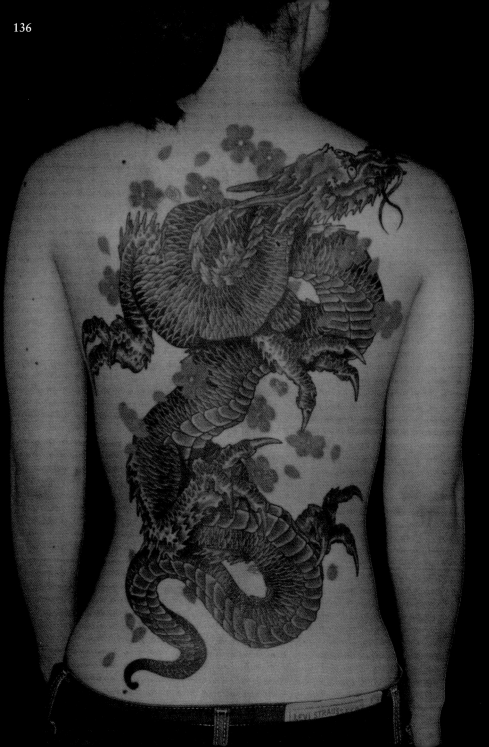

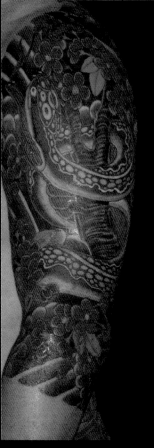

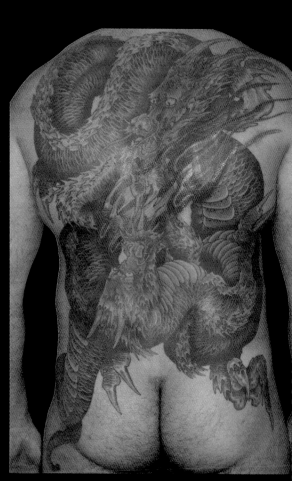

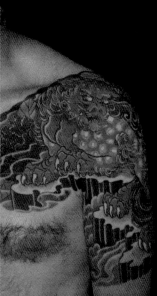

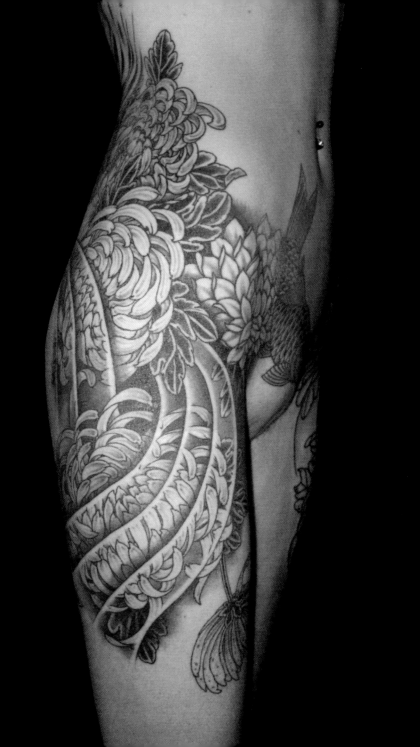

WIDO DE MARVAL

Wido de Marval started tattooing in 1999 in a studio in Lausanne, Switzerland, his home town. Two years later, he was invited to work with the prestigious Leu Family's Family Iron, where he "enjoyed working for six years with one of the most generous and talented artists [he has] ever met." For many years he has been collecting Japanese antiques with his father, who is a renowned collector, and he now specializes in traditional Japanese tattooing. He also travels twice a year to Japan with his friend Alex Reinke to visit his main influence and idol, Horiyoshi III. Wido tries through his work to pay respect to the great masters who did so much for tattooing before he was born.

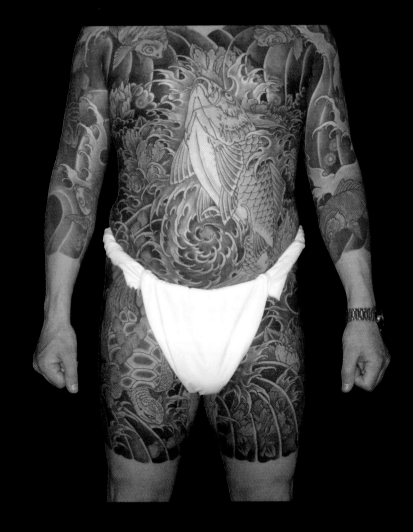

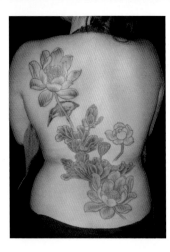

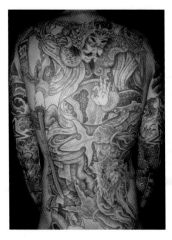

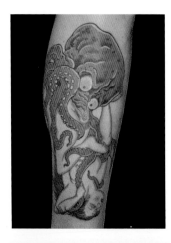

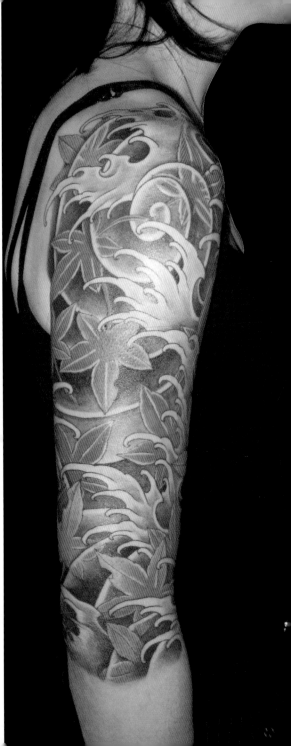

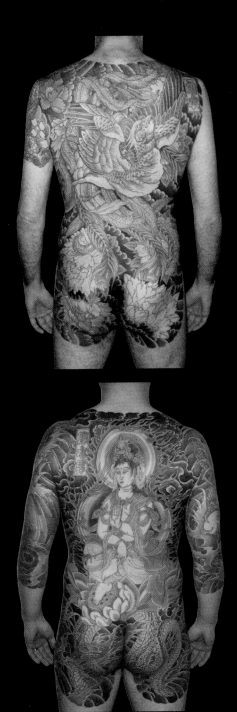

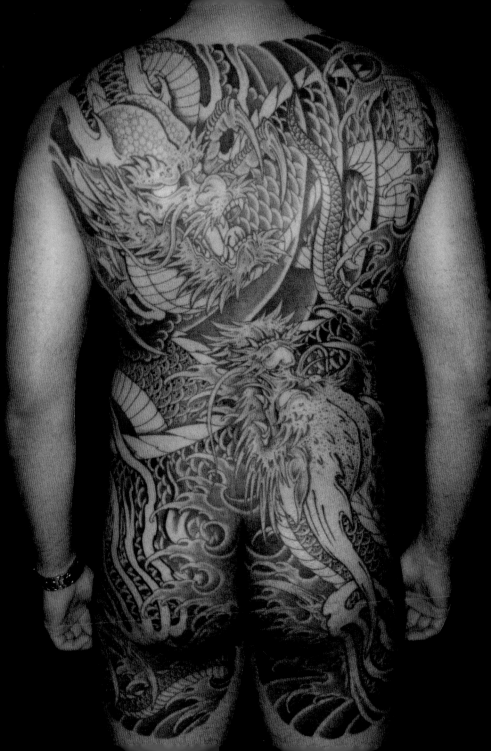

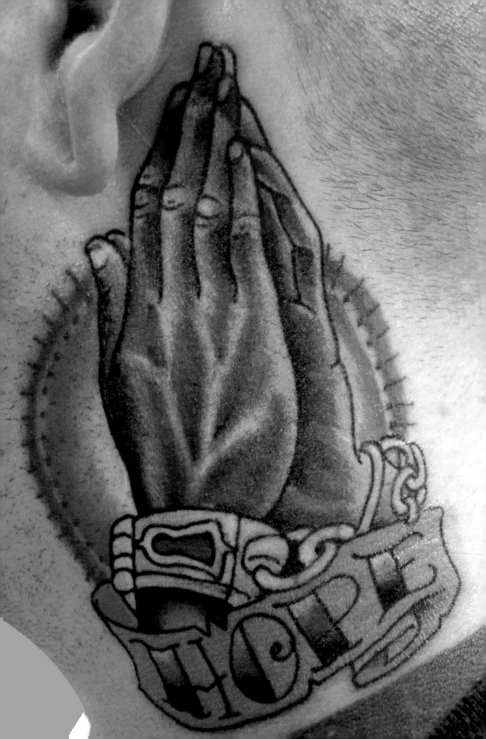

Rob Doubtfire

Rob Doubtfire was born in
Sarawak, Borneo, where his father
was stationed with the British
Army. In 1968 he returned to
England where he grew up in
Skipton, Yorkshire. His interest in
tattoos was sparked by his father's
tattooed arms and, at the age of
11, he began practising on school
mates with a bottle of Indian ink
and a pin. Being a "colourful" lad
he ended up in various institutions
where his tattooing really took
off and he realized it was going
to be his life's work and passion.
Twenty-five years later Rob is
going stronger than ever and his
character remains as loud and
colourful as his artwork

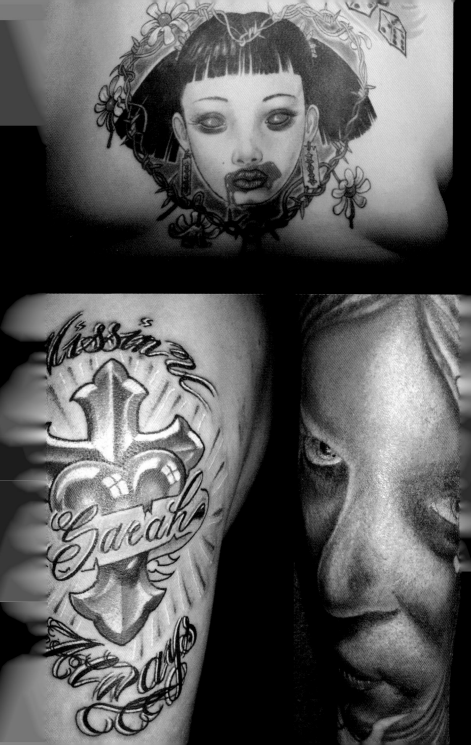

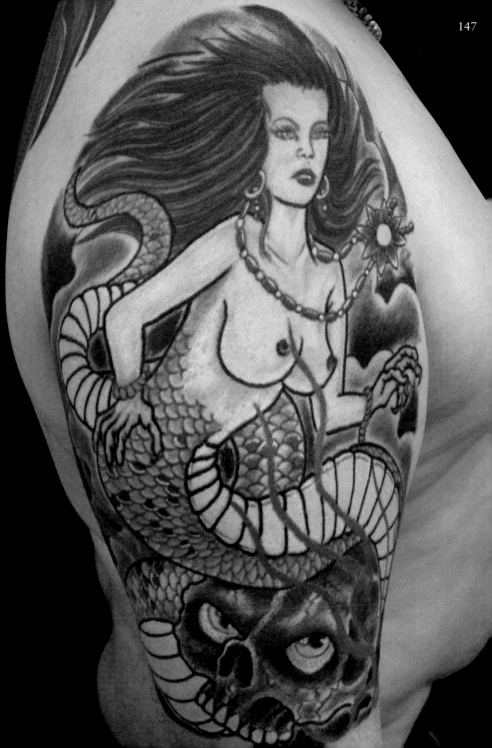

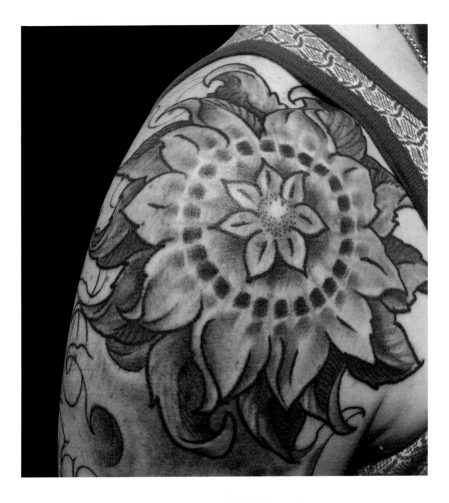

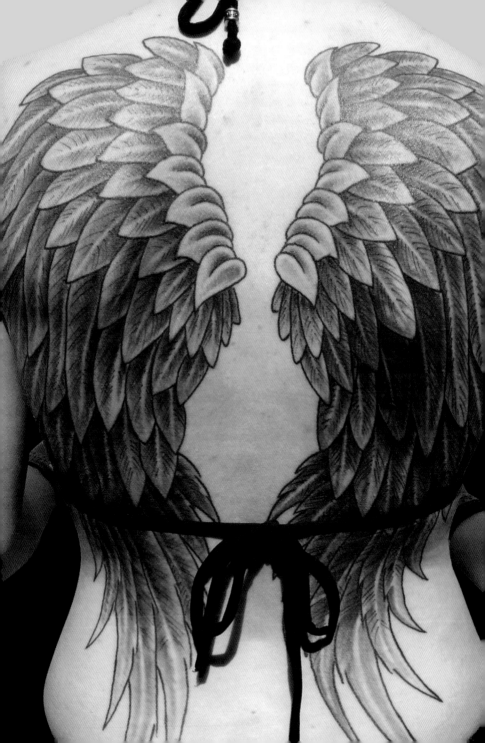

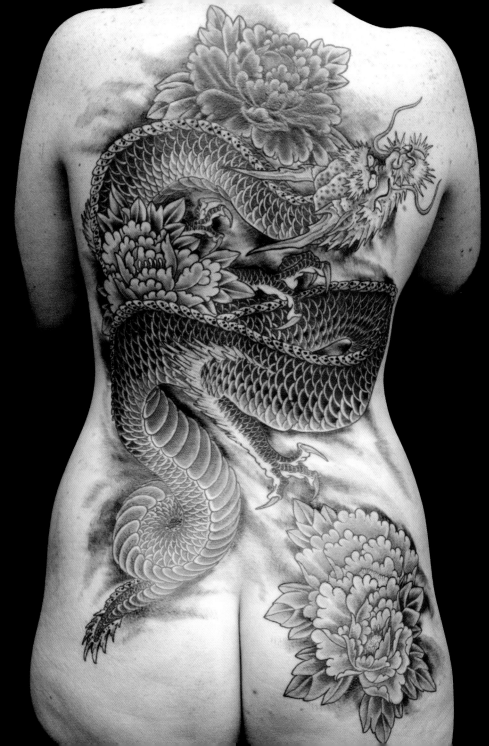

Kian Forreal

Kian Forreal began studying, researching, drawing, and getting tattooed in 1986 and has been tattooing professionally since 1993. Originally from Canada, he has lived in Europe for many years. Naturally drawn to travel, he has worked with and learned from some of the best tattoo artists living today. Sometimes it was small things he learned – such as how to make a better needle, or shade a dragon in a particular way to suggest more volume – but sometimes it was a life-changing drawing technique which altered his whole approach to his art. He is forever indebted to them for their guidance and kindness. Kian's own personal philosophy towards tattooing has evolved over the last few years; what began as a desire simply to tattoo people with any design they chose has been transformed into a drive to tattoo art with aesthetic appeal, power, meaning, and depth.

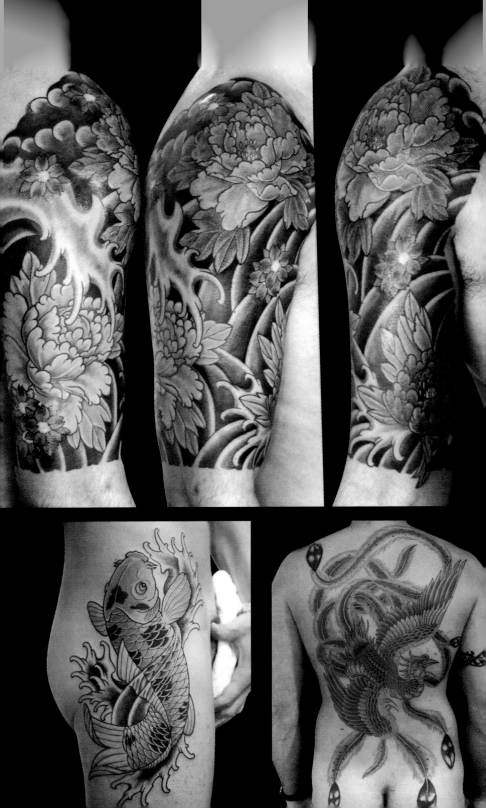

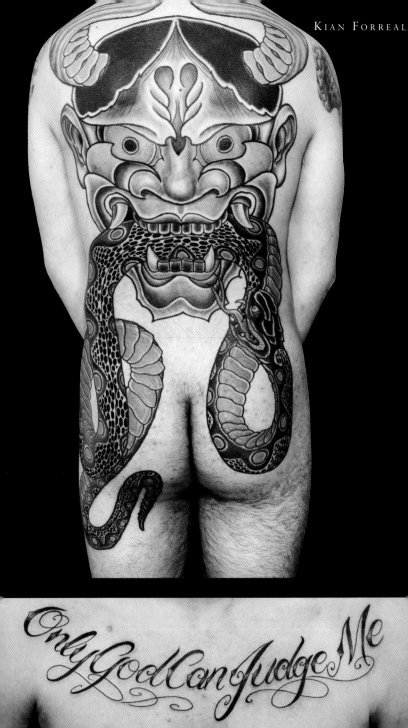

KIAN FORREAL

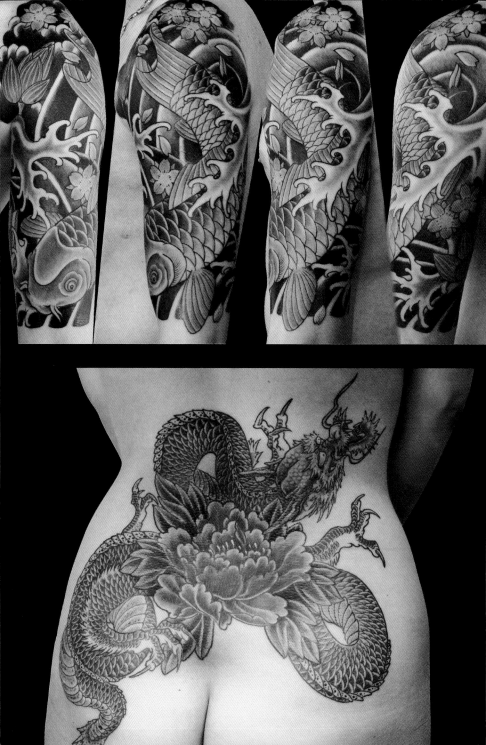

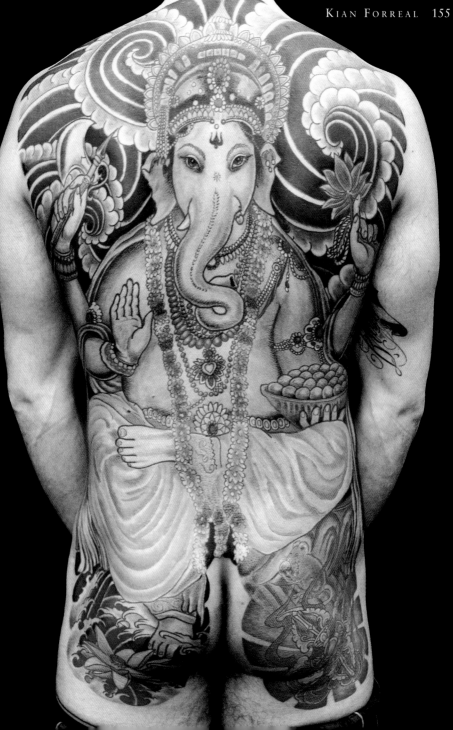

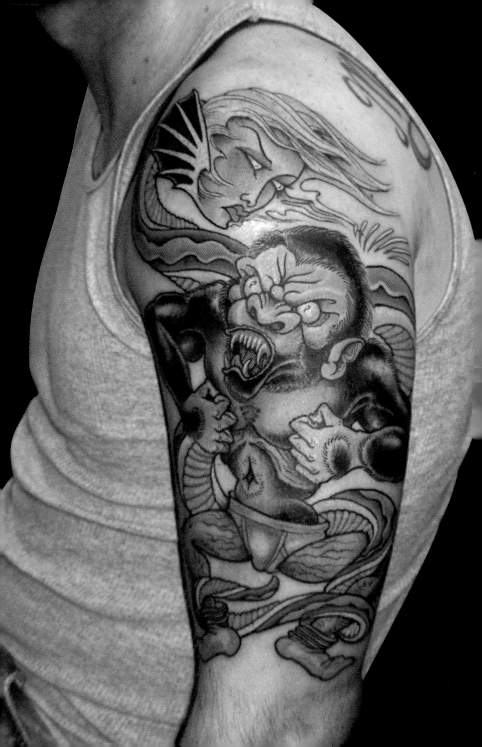

Dave Fox

Before becoming a tattooist, Dave Fox did a lot of other stuff. He rode BMX freestyle as a kid, touring the United States with the Schwinn Freestyle Team when he was 15 in the summer of 1988. He also published a BMX/skateboarding 'zine in the 80s called *Stylin' Zine*. Back in those pre-Internet days, Dave had to save his pennies and photocopy the things he had to say, put stamps on the envelopes, and then mail them out – "Craziness!" as he puts it. After that he started playing guitar with various metal, hardcore, and punk bands. Finally, he began tattooing, drawing and painting for years until he felt like he'd learned something, all the while tattooing and tattooing. Now, he plays in a metal band, the Dark Lords of Stonehurst, but "the band's old so it's not really going anywhere". He is still tattooing, though, in Philadelphia, at Studio One Tattoo, supporting his wife and cats.

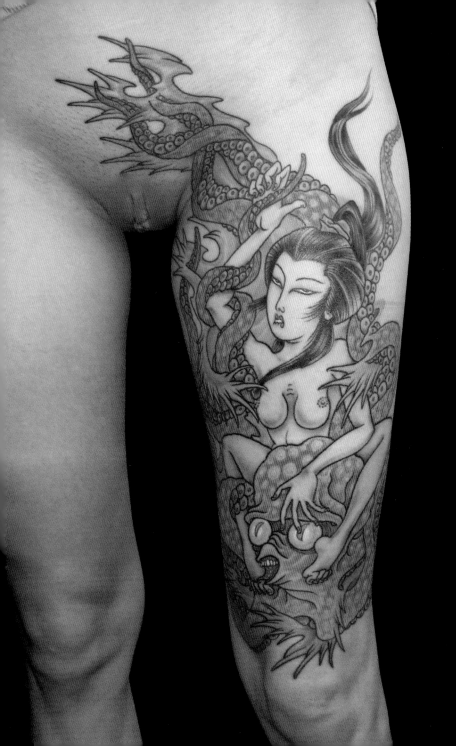

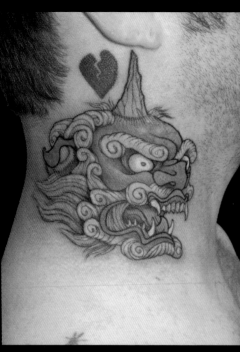

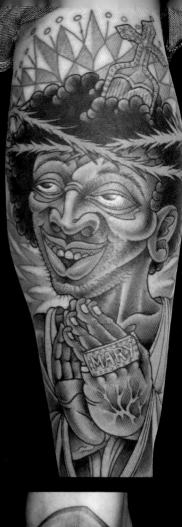

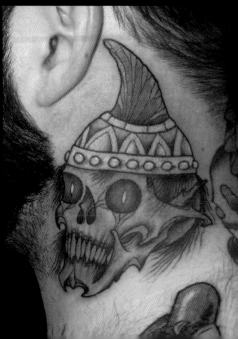

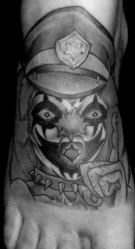

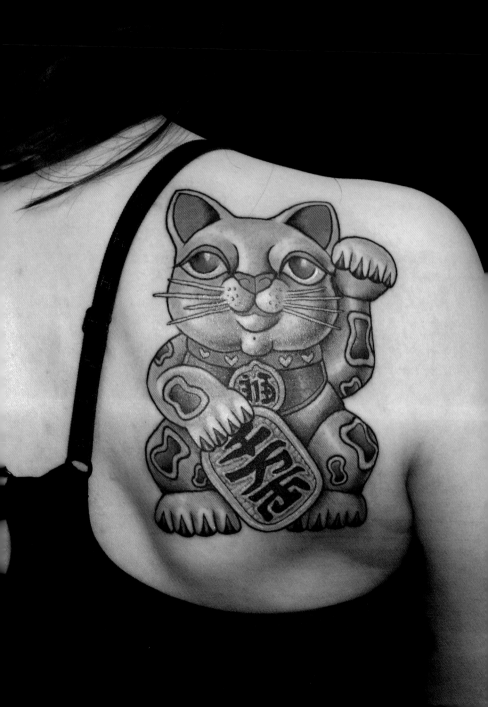

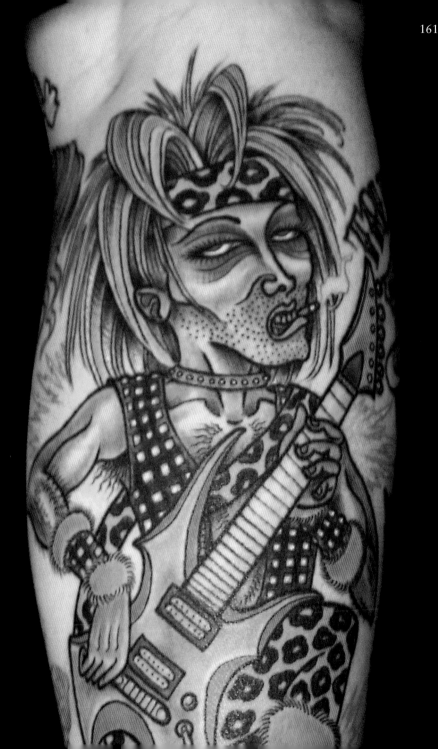

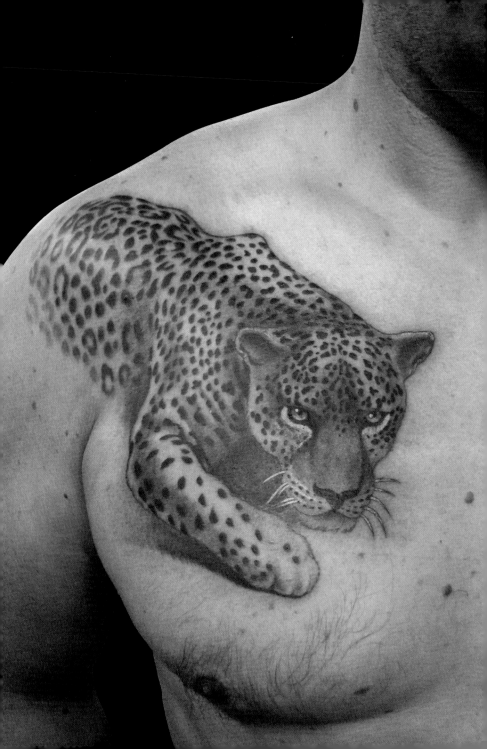

CHRIS GARVER

"I would like to thank everyone that I have tattooed for letting me mak
a living doing what I love."

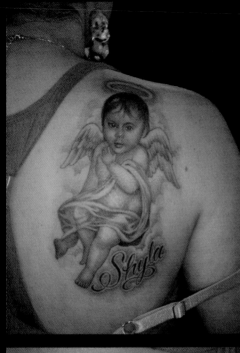

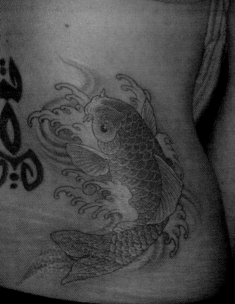

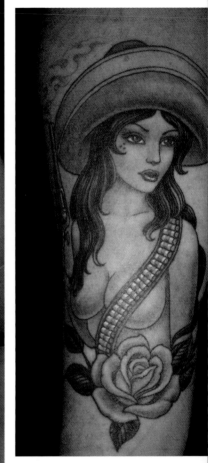

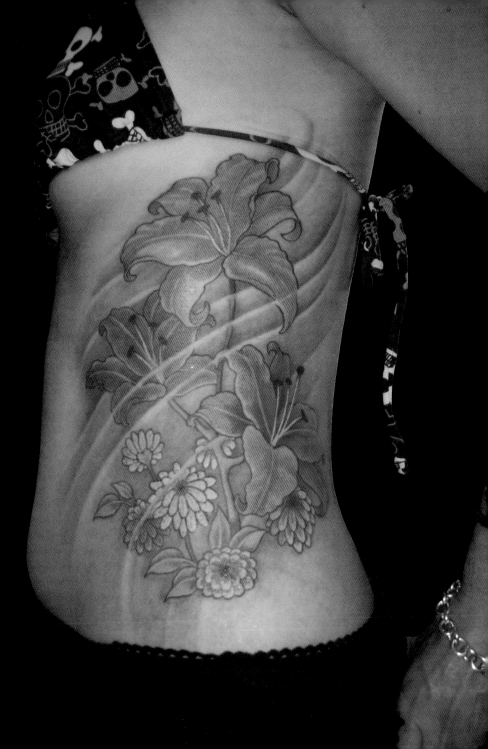

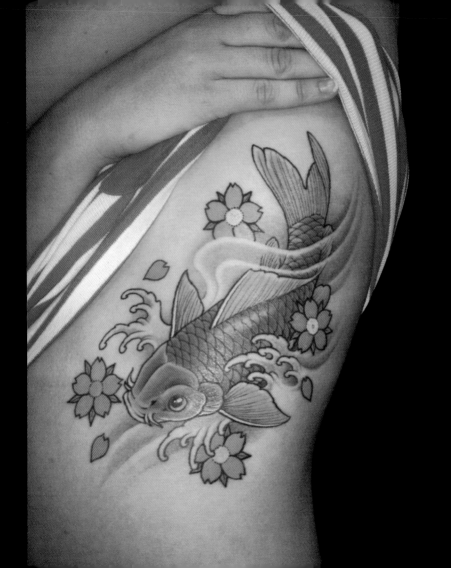

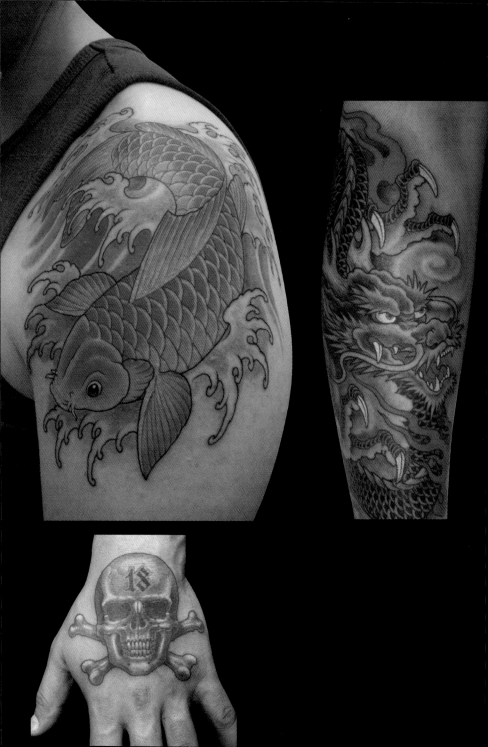

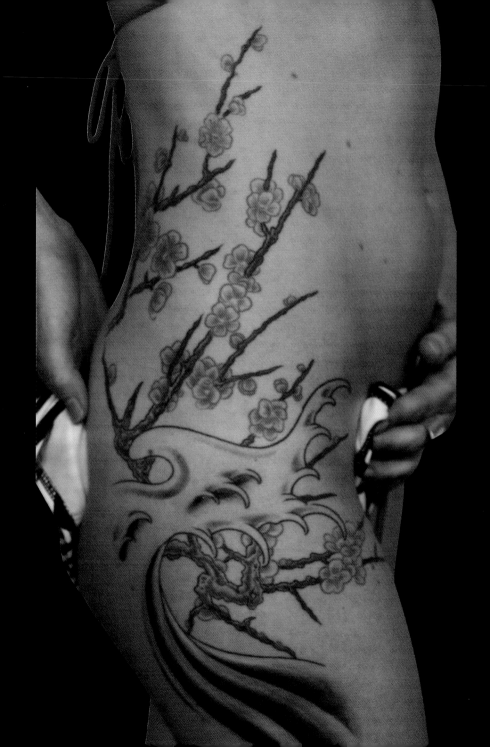

RHYS GORDON

Rhys Gordon began tattooing in Melbourne, Australia, in 1990. He spent the better part of eight years travelling and working in many leading studios in London, elsewhere in Europe, and Asia before settling in Innervision Tattoo in Sydney, Australia. His preferred styles are traditional, Japanese, and script lettering, but, being schooled in the "street shop" way, he can turn his hand to all styles.

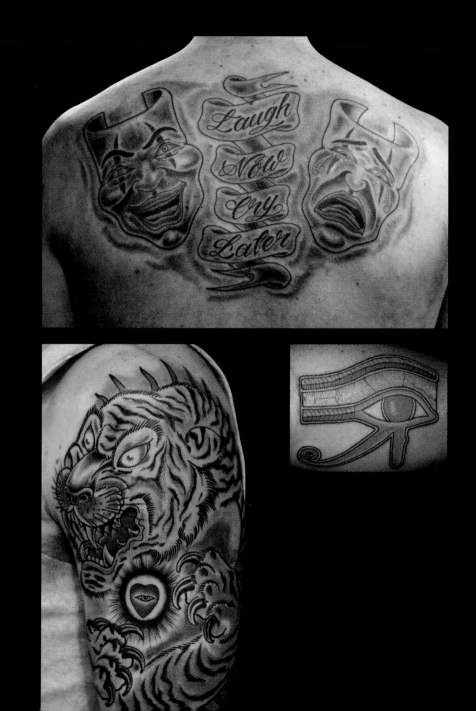

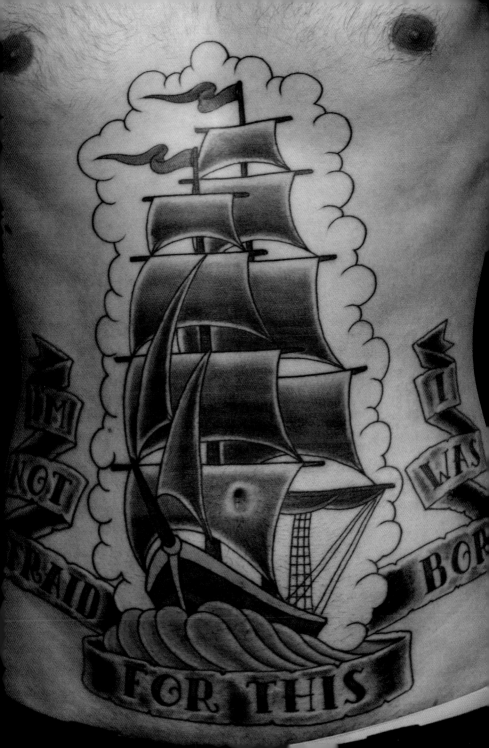

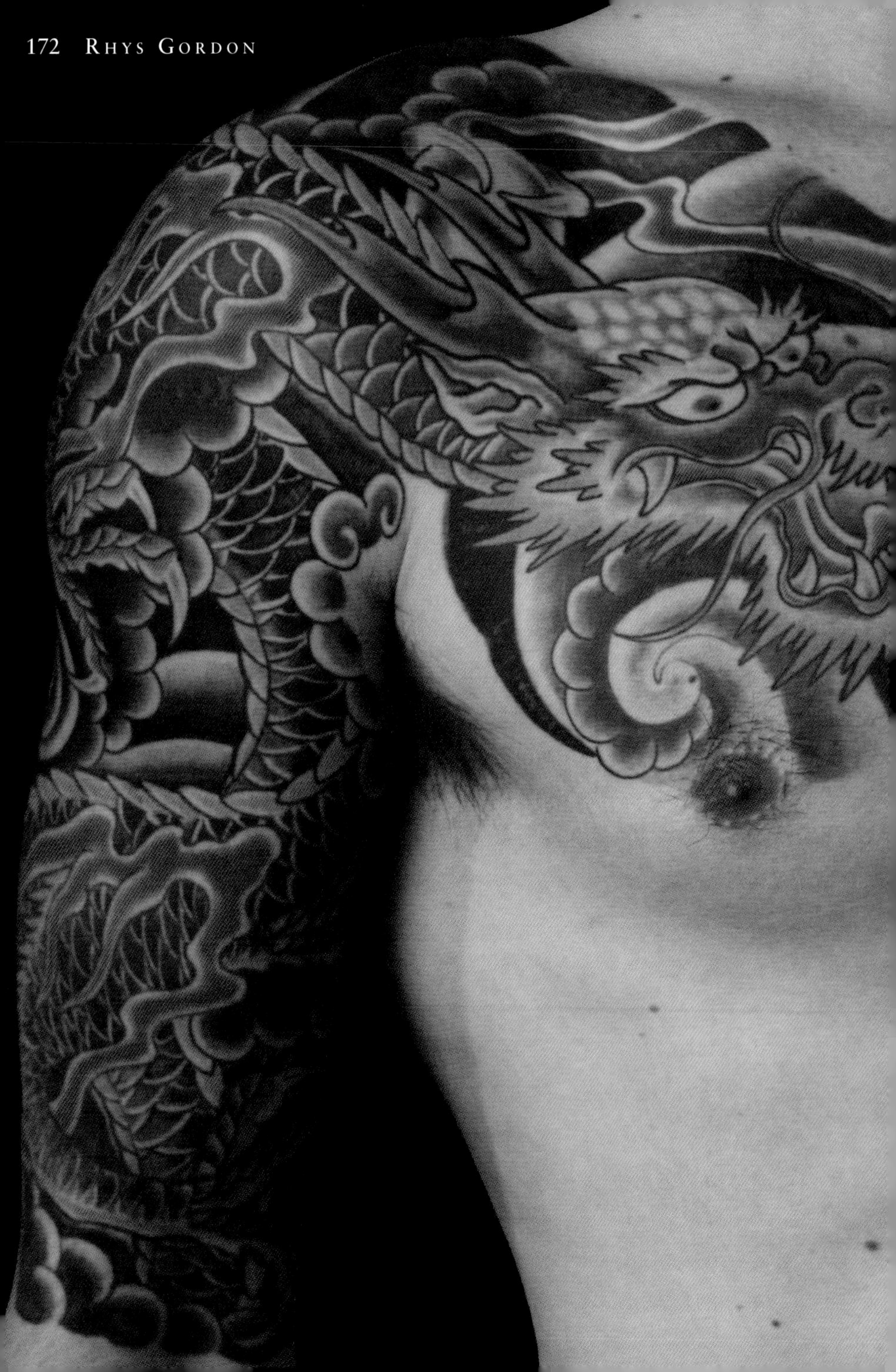

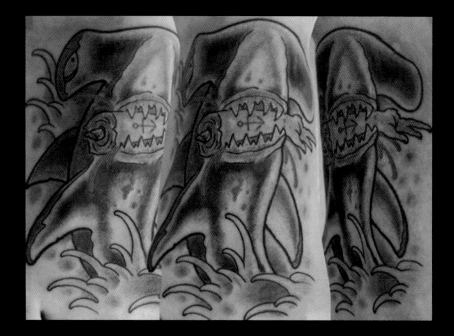

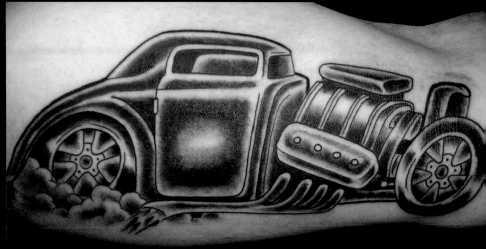

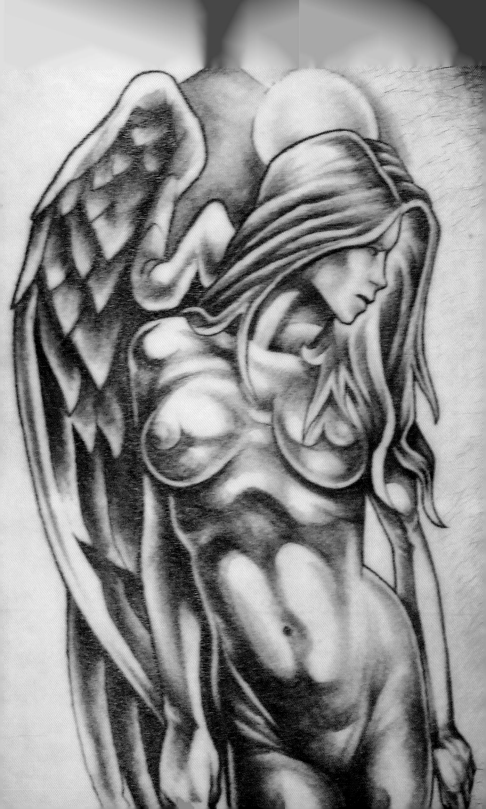

WAYNE GRACE

Wayne Grace was born on 26 April 1972 in London. From an early age he was always interested in art, watching his father paint, and he has never wanted to do anything other than draw for his living. His first real passion in art was graffiti, starting in the early 80s, an influence which has continued to this day. Wayne started tattooing in 1998 at Primitive Origins in Hammersmith, west London. He worked there for eight years before moving to north London to work at New Wave Tattoo.

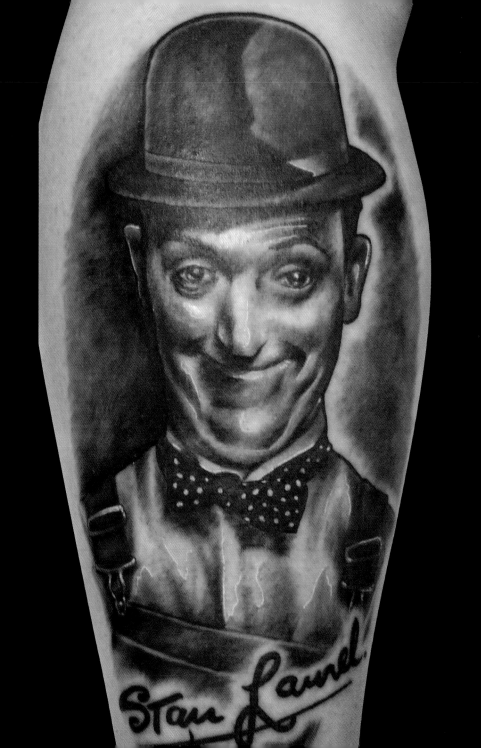

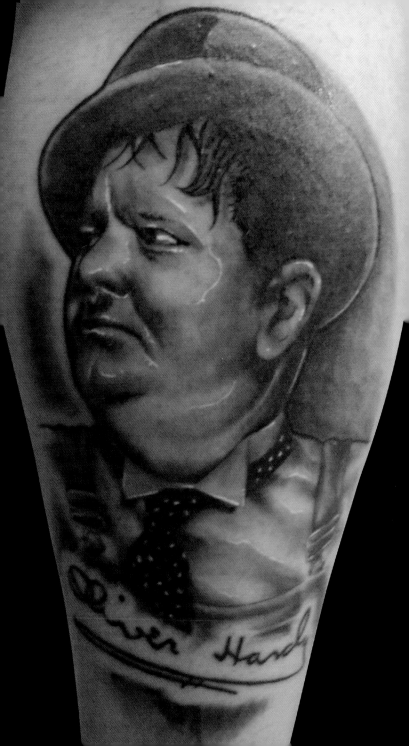

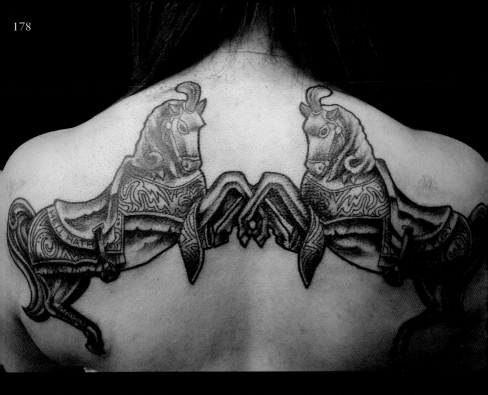

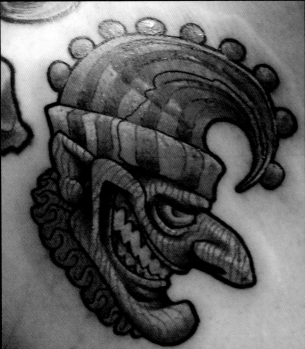

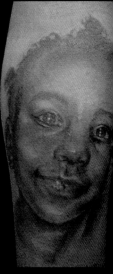

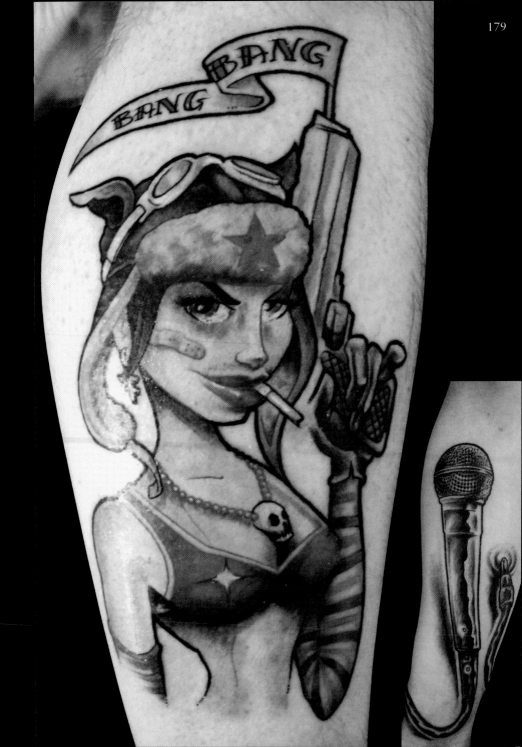

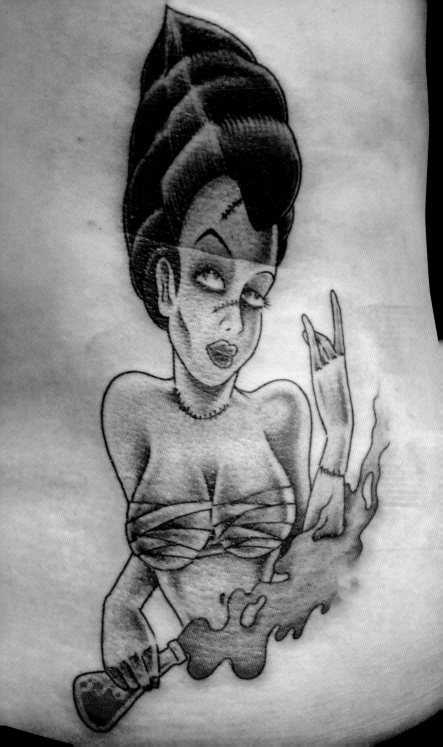

ALLAN GRAVES

Allen Graves always wanted to have tattoos, but didn't think about becoming a tattooist. When he was a kid he wanted badly to become a comic book illustrator, but after attending a few different arts schools he realized that the career of comics was "kinda slow". Then, after getting his first tattoo, he discovered that there was a lot of art in it. He has been tattooing for eight years now and is really looking forward to doing it for a long time yet. His main inspirations are horror and American culture. While Haunted is closed, he can be found at Jolie Rouge on Caledonian Road in London.

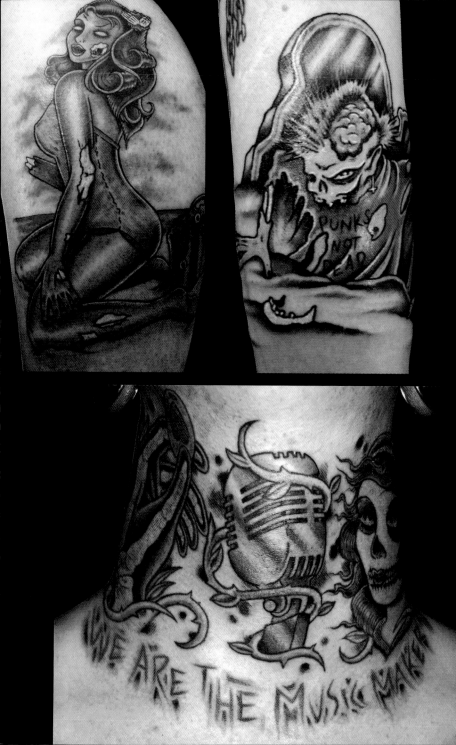

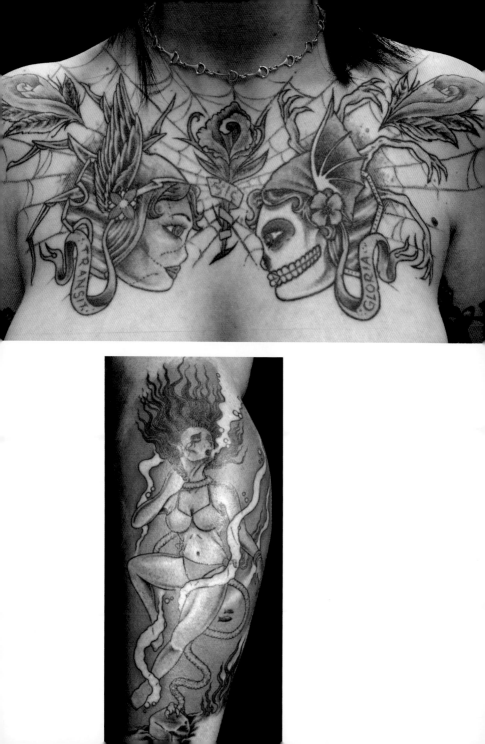

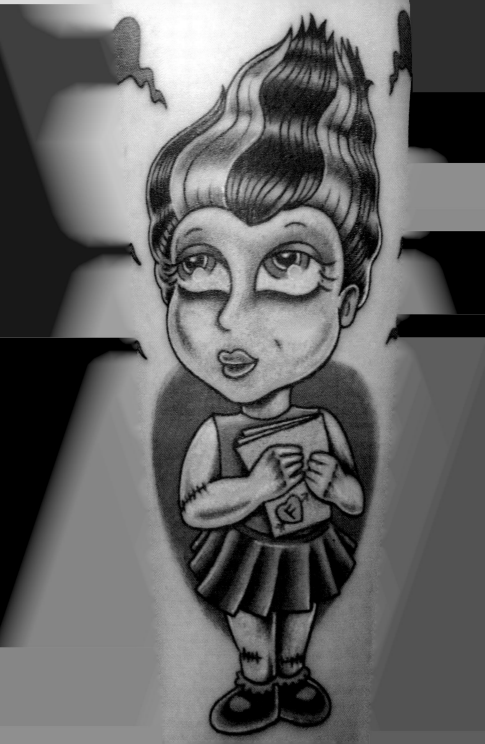

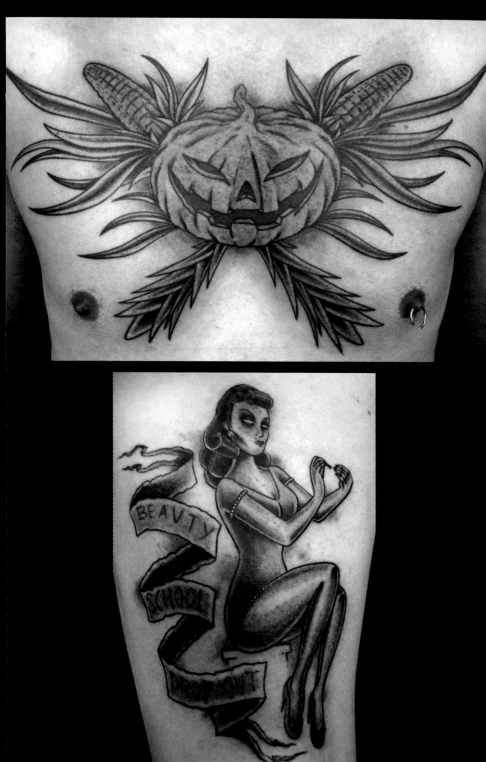

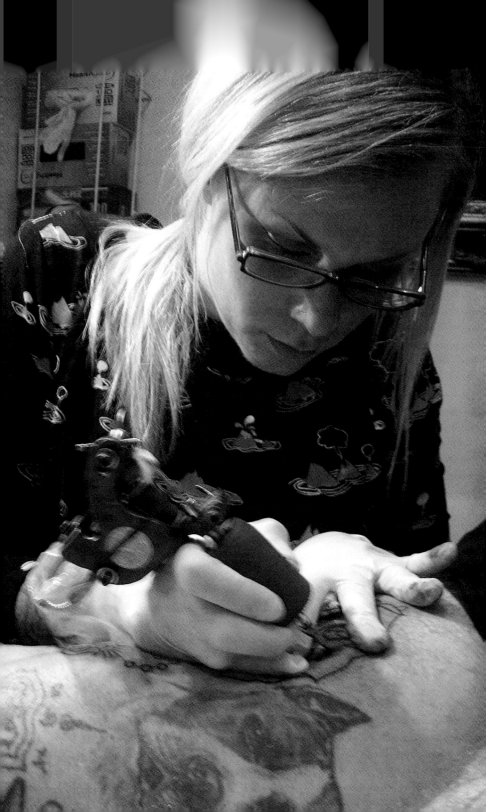

ROSE HARDY

Rose Hardy started tattooing in
2000 in Auckland, New Zealand.
After working with Adam Craft,
Dean Sacred, and Dan Anderson,
and seeing work by people
like Chris Conn and Sabado,
she started to focus on more
illustrative, custom designs. She
paid more attention to doing clean,
single-weight line work with less
colour and more black, developing
her immediately recognizable style.
She says, "Tattooing has allowed
me to travel the world and work
in amazing studios and make
great friends who I have learnt
a lot from. I can't imagine doing
anything else."

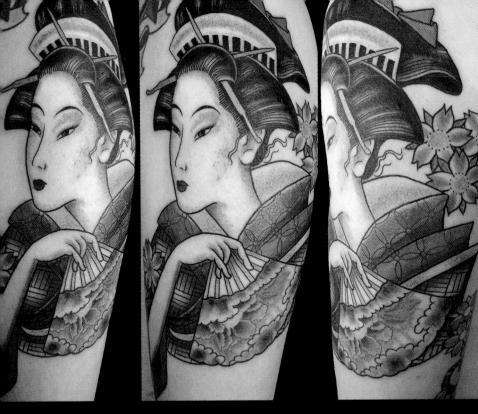

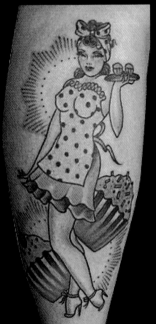

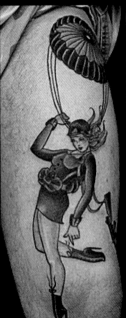

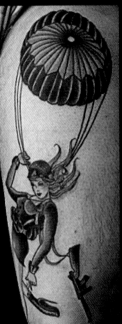

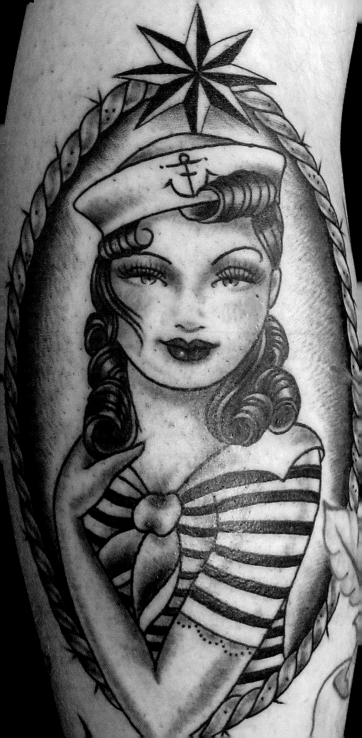

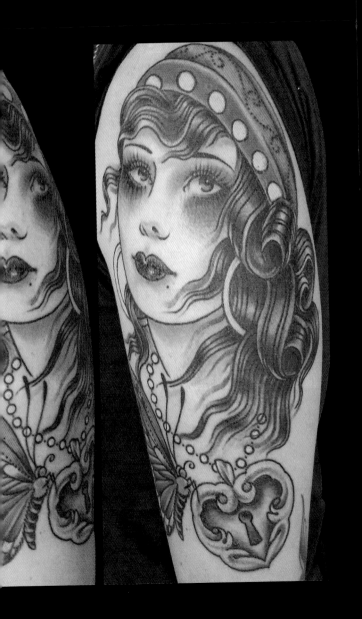

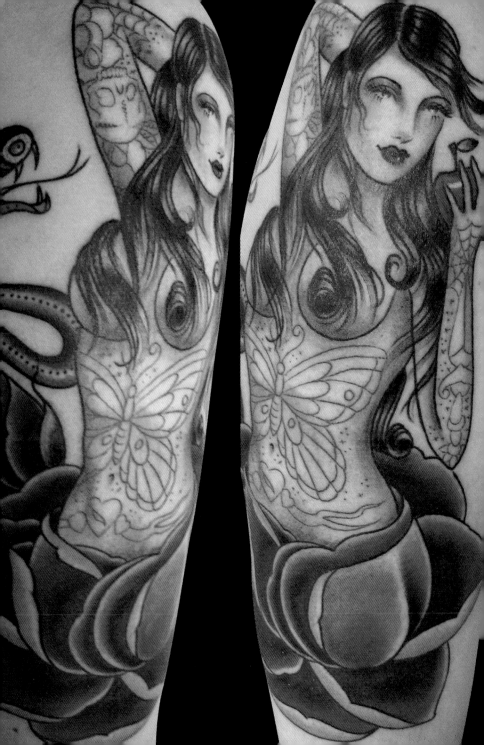

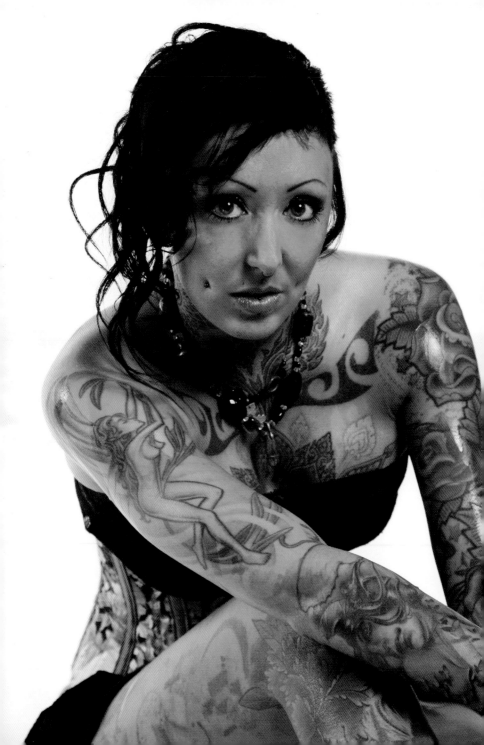

Jo Harrison

Born in 1976, Jo Harrison
was raised on the outskirts of
Birmingham, England. She fell in
love with tattoos when she first
noticed them on all the punks in
the late 70s and early 90s. While
studying for a degree in textiles,
she worked at Kev Shercliff's
Midland Tattoo Centre, in
Staffordshire, where, although not
apprenticed, she learned about
tattooing. At that time she started
to get tattooed by Fiona Long, a
strong influence and a great help
at the beginning of Jo's career. In
1999, with her business partner,
she opened her own shop, but,
realizing that she always felt most
inspired at conventions, she set
off on a "Sweet Sting" world tour,
working 22 conventions and doing
20 guest spots in one year. She
plans to continue travelling, but
also to find more time to paint,
surf, and scuba dive – to enjoy life
as well as do the job she loves.

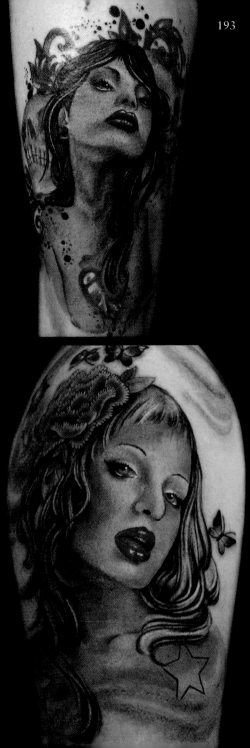

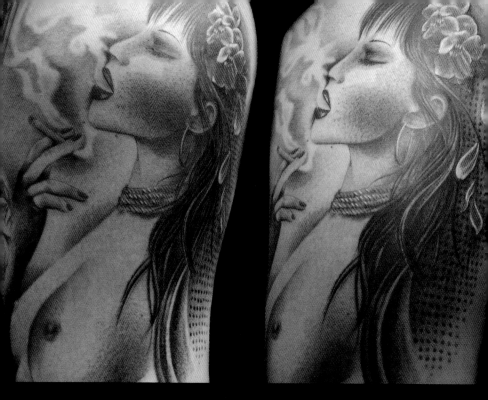
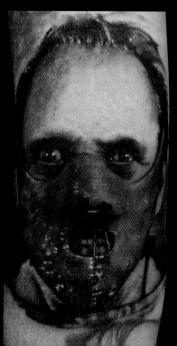

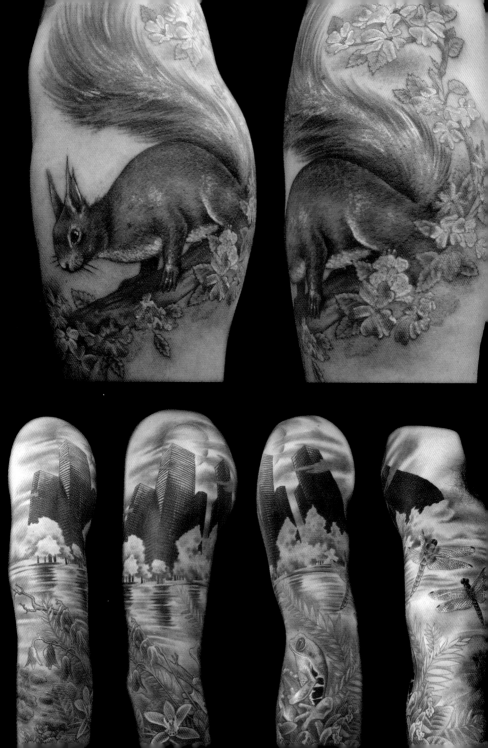

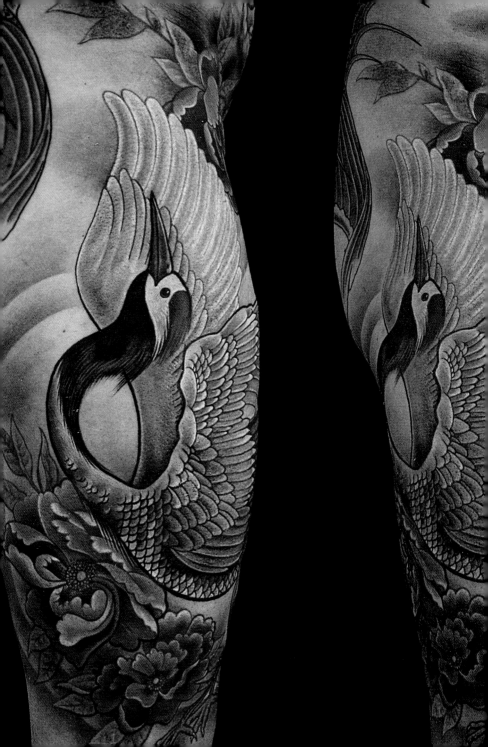

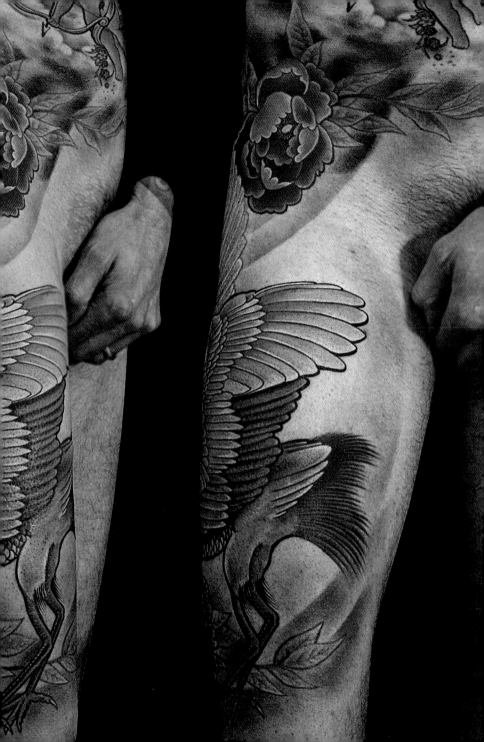

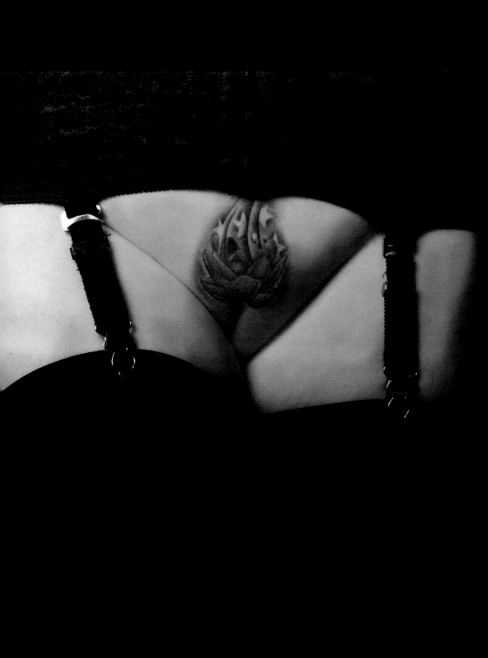

HARRY AND ELY

It was obvious to Harry from the embryonic stages of trying to understand the tattooing process and all that goes with it that he was leading himself down a path that would bring him a great deal of frustration and heartache, but that would also ultimately prove to be one of the most challenging and rewarding decisions he would ever make. From a background of having been a formal gardener and an art student he begged and pestered a local studio into letting him do all the usual apprenticeship jobs. He owes his beginnings and love of the timeless art of tattooing to David Notley.

Ely feels she's lucky to be a tattooist, allowed to live a life lacking in responsibility, travel about and do a job she loves. As she puts it, "I meet cool people, have a chat and do a bit of drawing on their skin all day long. What more could a girl ask for? Oh, and I can take my dogs to work so that's cool, too."

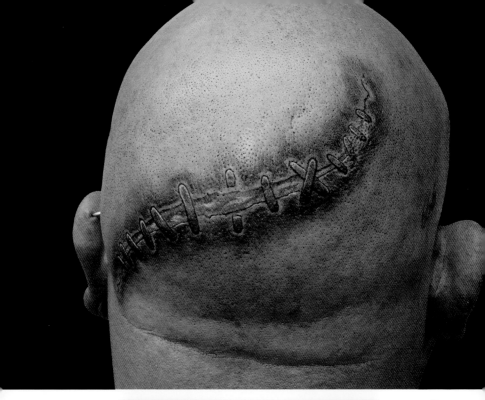

Harry

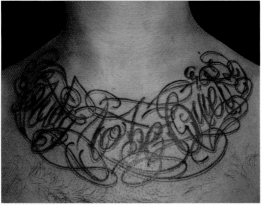

Ely

Facing page: Ely

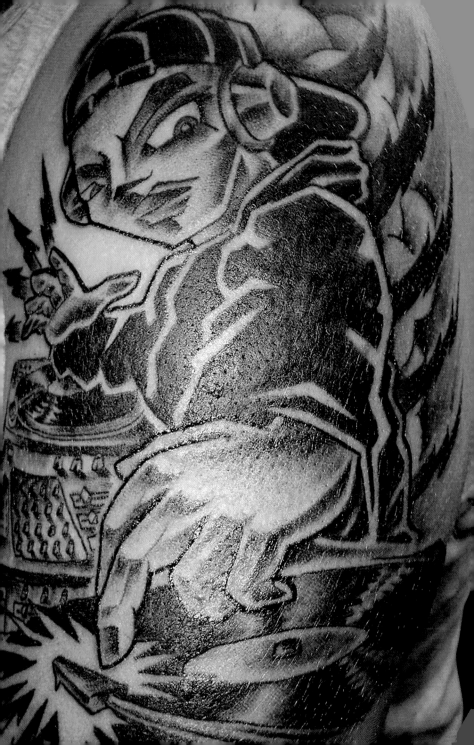

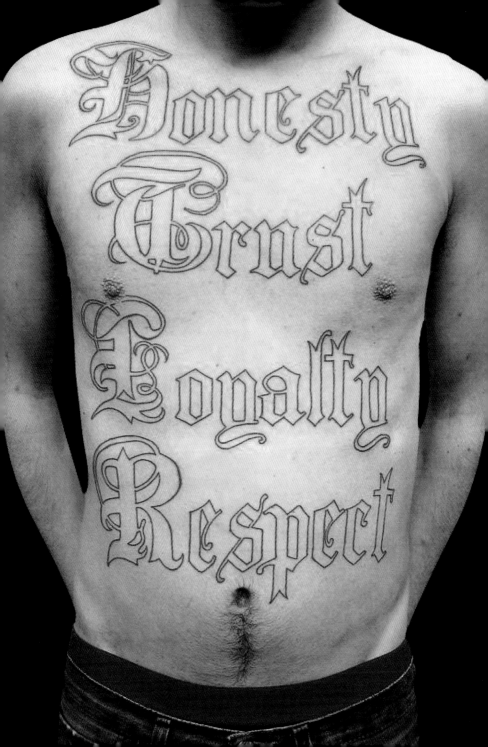

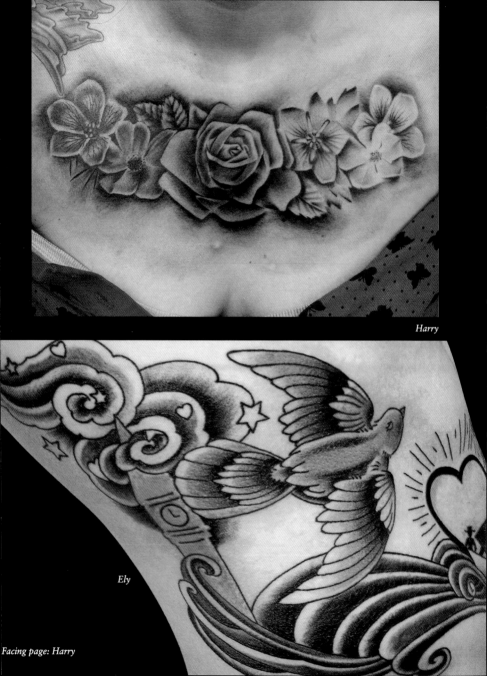

Harry

Ely

Facing page: Harry

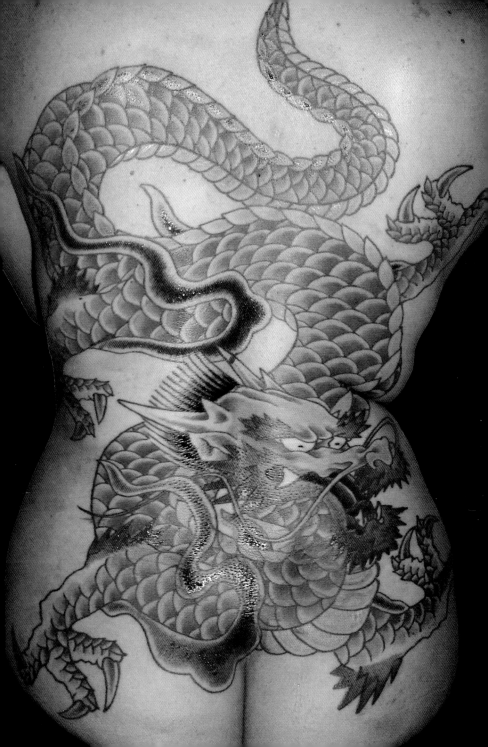

HERCOLY

Hercoly lives in São Paulo, Brazil, where he runs a private studio. There he creates many large, one-off tattoos. He also travels each year to Europe where he works in the studios of various friends, doing smaller pieces on walk-in customers. He likes to spend time at the beach and partying. He also has a great love of nature and enjoys studying flora and fauna, particularly birds. He loves dogs and owns a whippet.

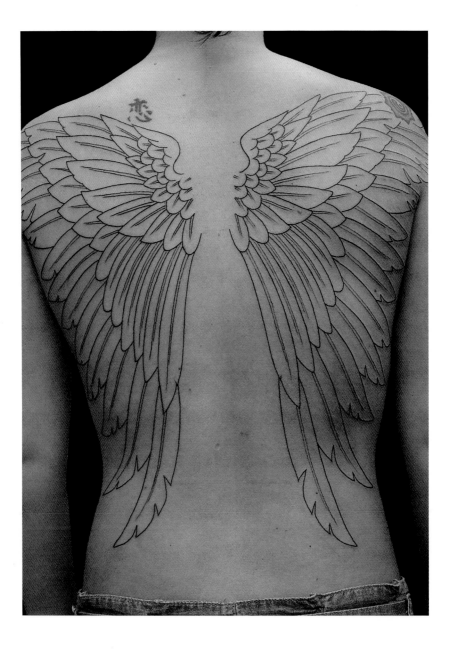

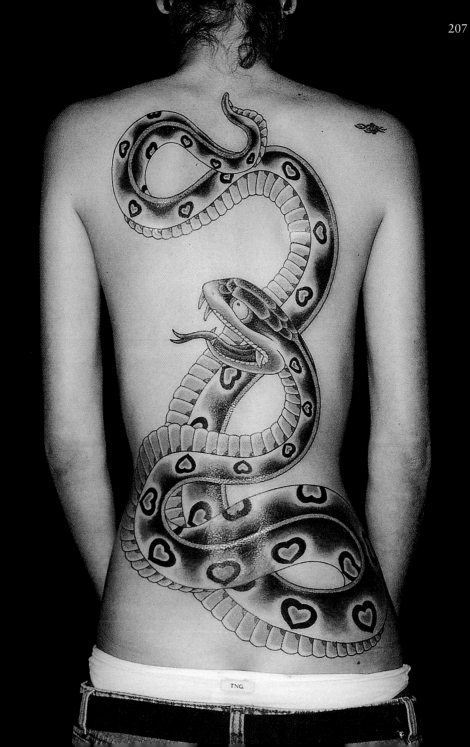

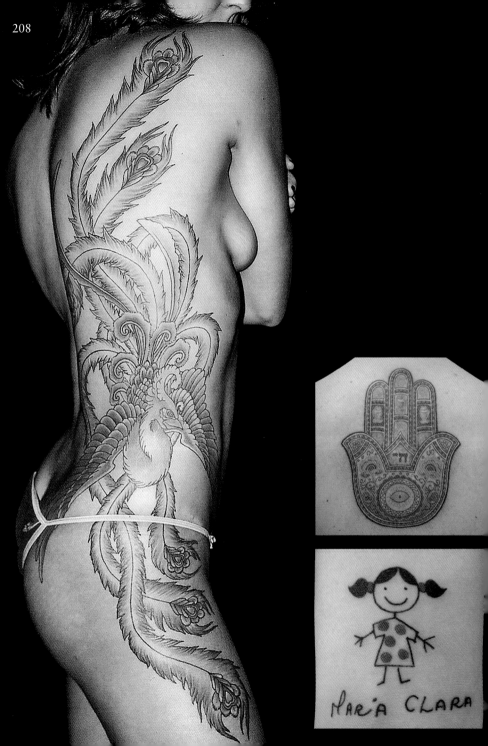

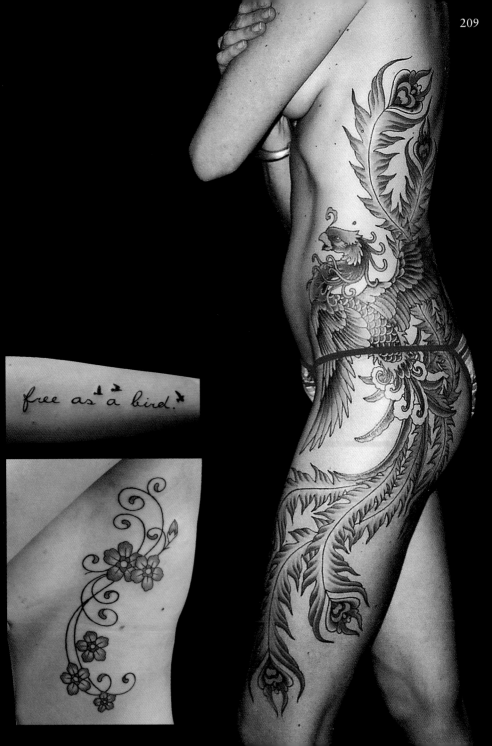

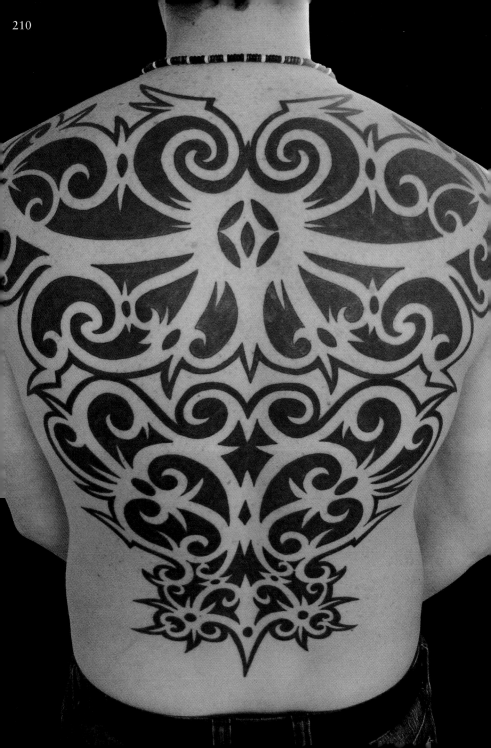

CHRIS HIGGINS

Chris Higgins was born in 1971 and got his first tattoo at the age of 21. At the age of 23 he had his arms tattooed by Curly at Into You, an experience which inspired him to tattoo himself and his friends by hand. In 2000, he left his job at Barclays Bank to pursue a full-time career in tattooing. Since then he has worked in a variety of studios from Burgess Hill to Barcelona, and from London to Brighton. He is currently working at Tattoo-fx, in Burgess Hill, and Into You, also in London, continuing to improve his understanding and practice of traditional styles of tattooing. He specializes in traditional tribal tattooing.

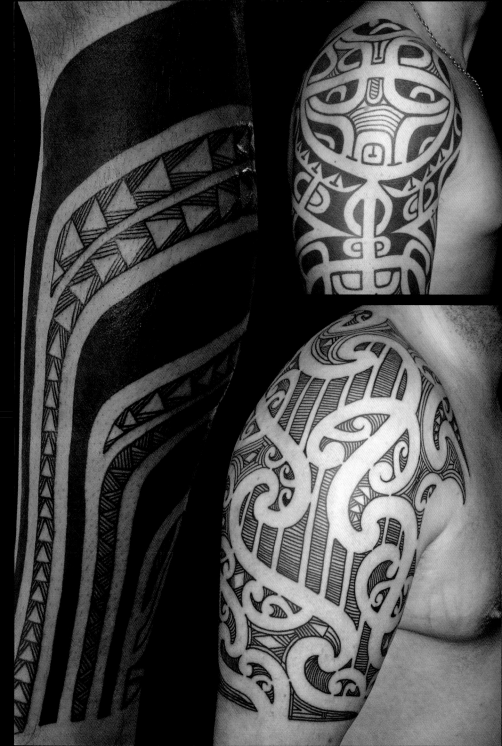

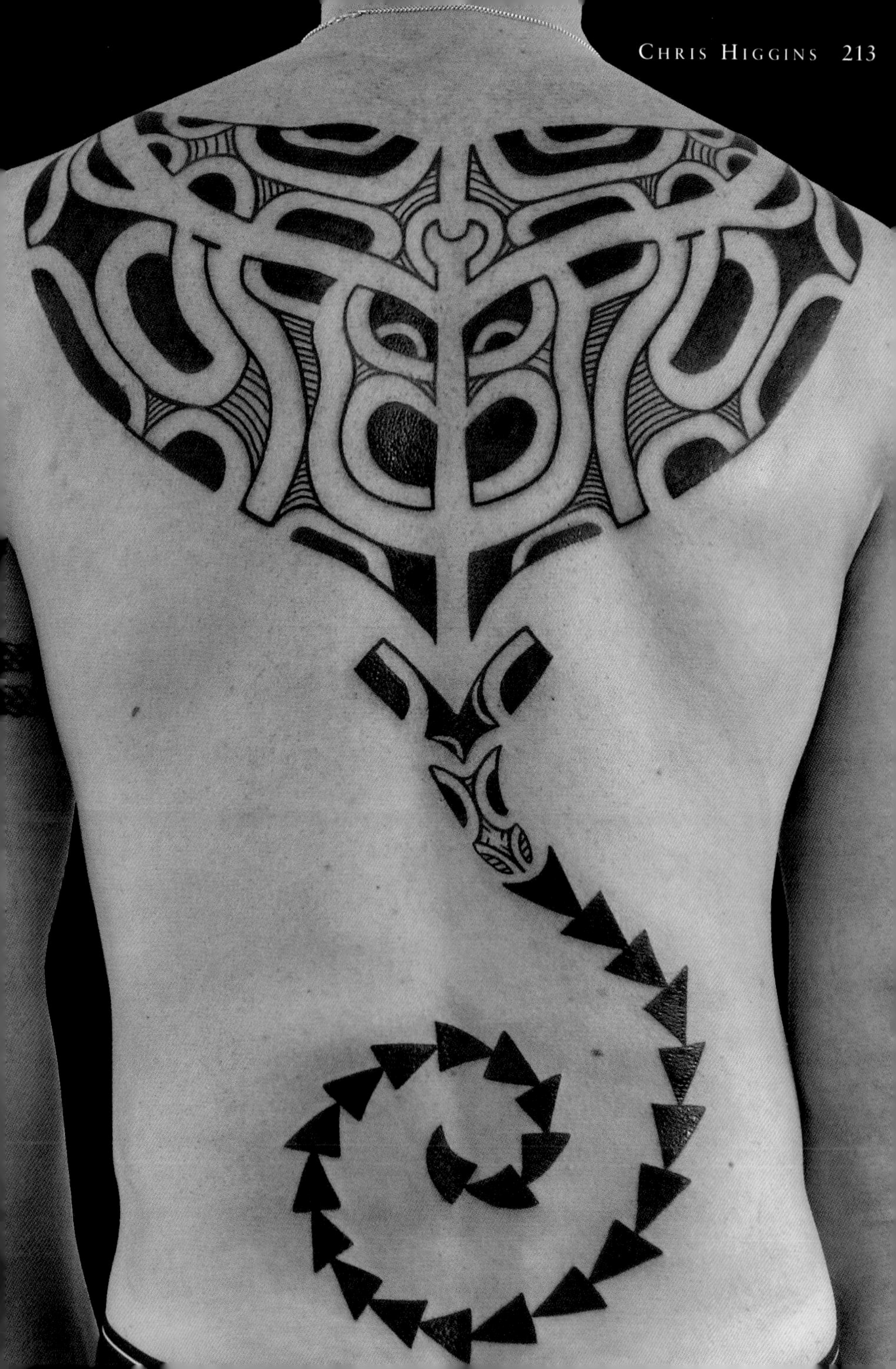

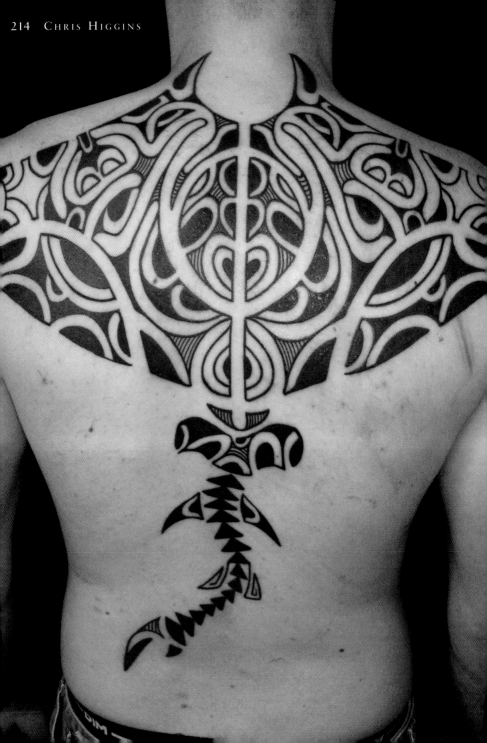

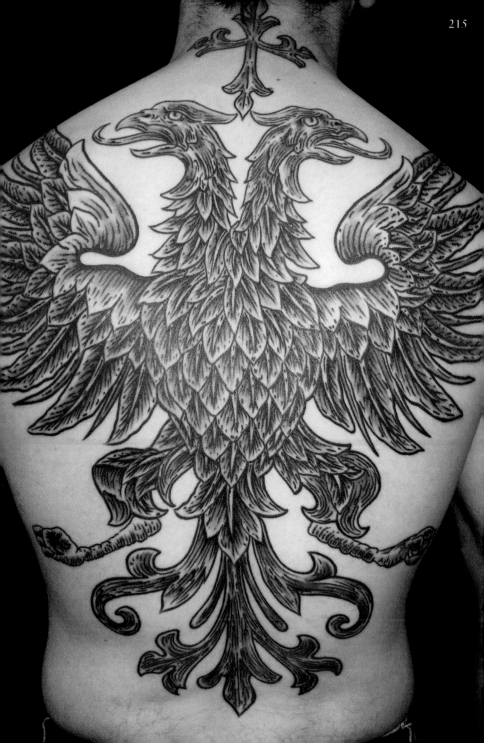

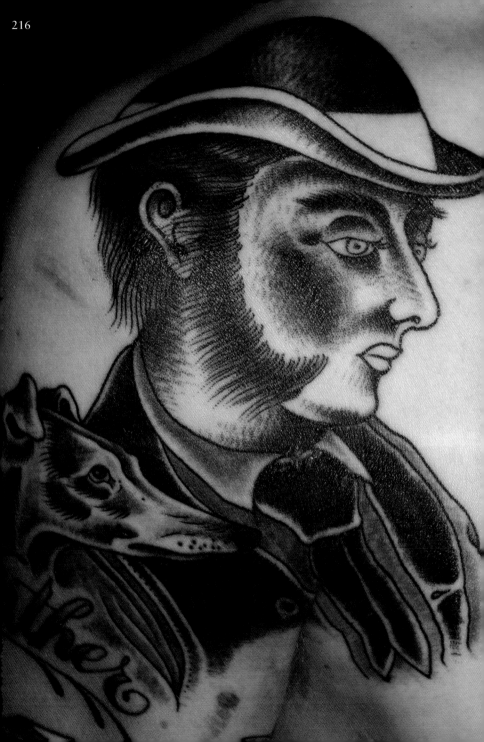

Thomas Hooper

Born in Hastings, in East Sussex, England, Thomas Hooper now lives in New York City where he works at New York Adorned. He has worked for Jim Macairt, Alex Binnie, and Dante Dimassa. He's extremely grateful to have such good friends from all over the world in his life, and to have been given the opportunity to tattoo such loyal customers.

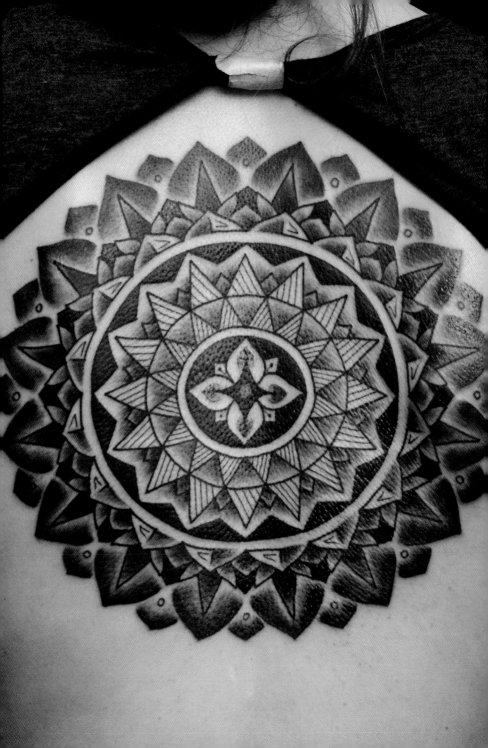

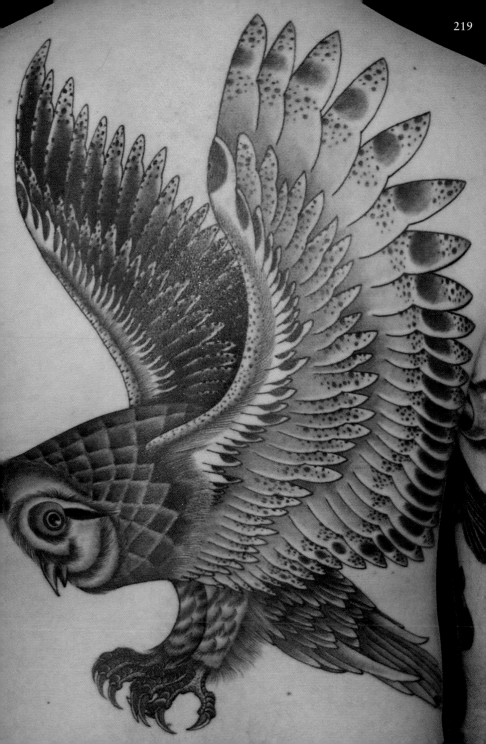

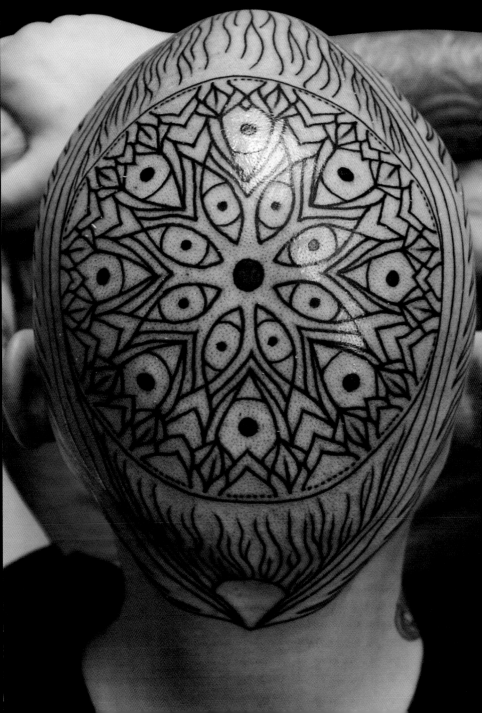

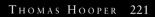

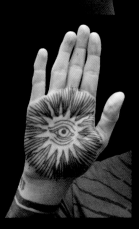

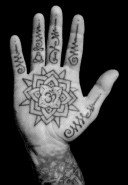

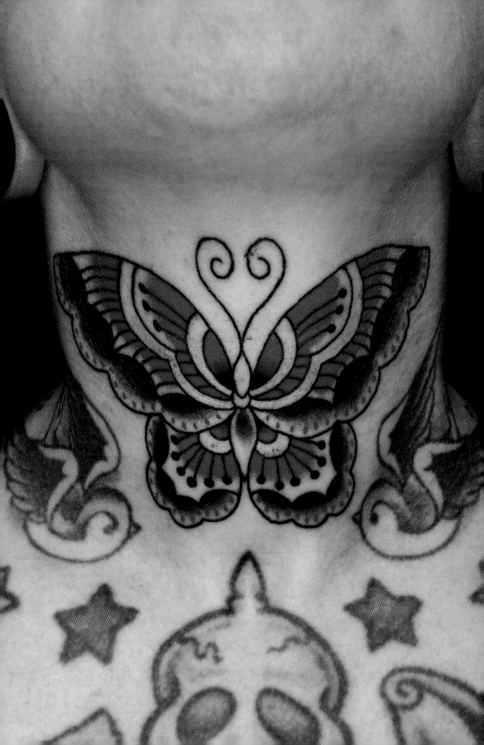

SAIRA HUNJAN

Saira Hunjan was born in Balham, south London. Growing up, her
natural talent and passion for drawing and her hunger for creativity led
to a school work placement at The House of Living Art, in Earlsfield,
London. Little did she know that this was where her tattooing career
would begin. In 1998, she served an apprenticeship at New Skool Tattoo,
in Surrey. At the age of 23, having graduated in Fine Art and with five
years of hands-on tattoo training, she landed a job at Soho's Frith Street
Tattoo Studio (formerly Angelic Hell). Since 2004 Saira has worked at
the Family Business, in Exmouth Market, London. Her work reveals her
love of Indian and Mexican art, but she also creates old American Sailor
tattoos and beautiful gypsy goddesses. In 2008, Saira launched her own
Gypsy Devi label, branching out into items such as silk scarves, murals,
and even coffins.

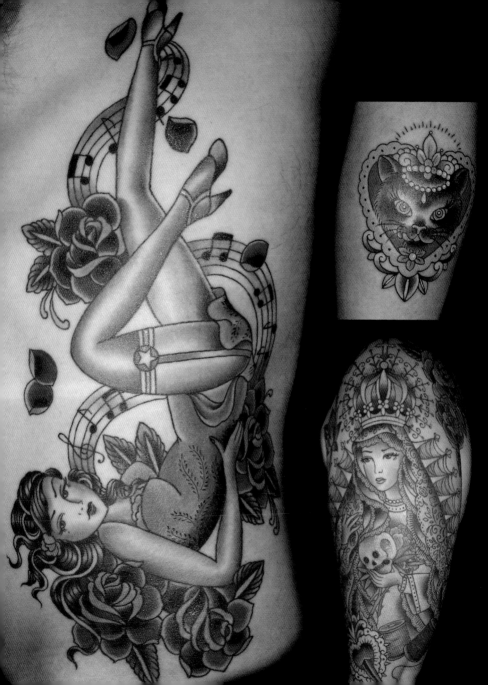

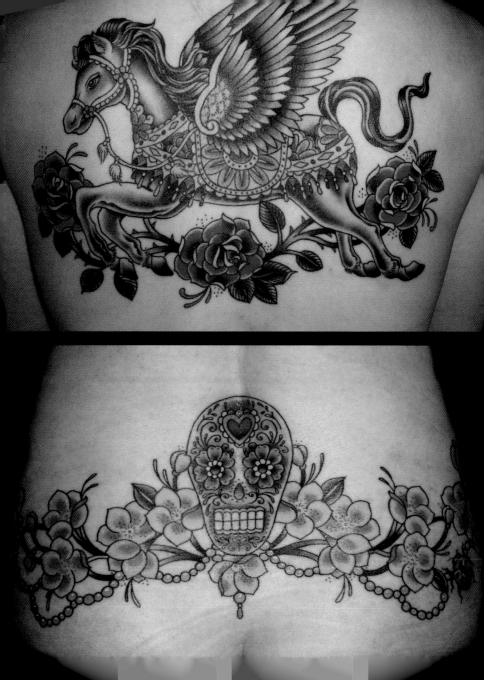

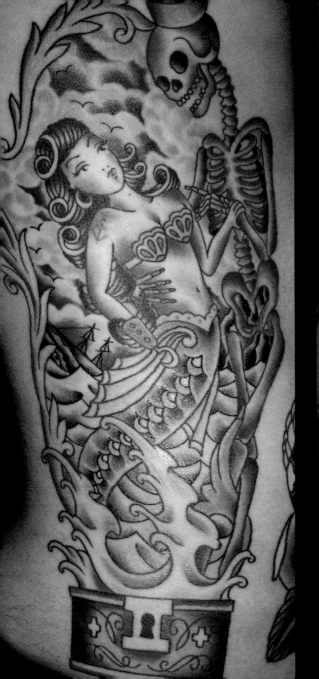
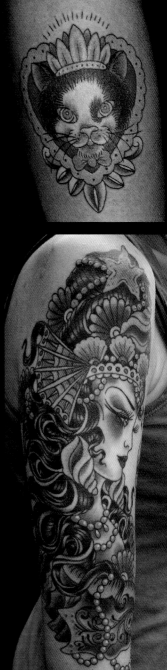

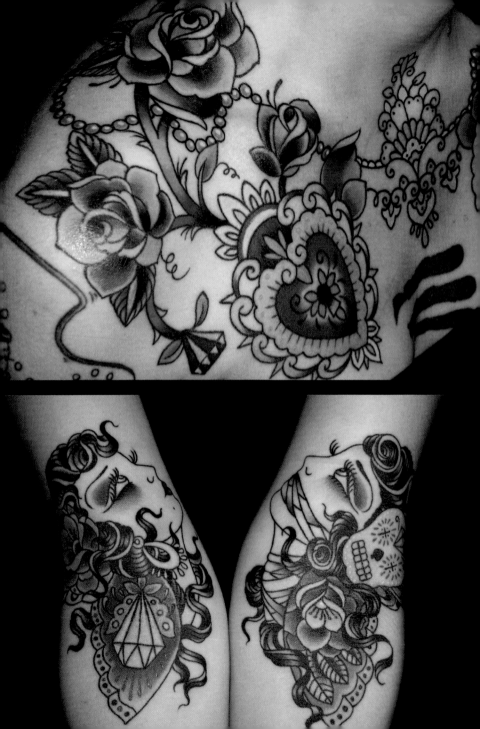

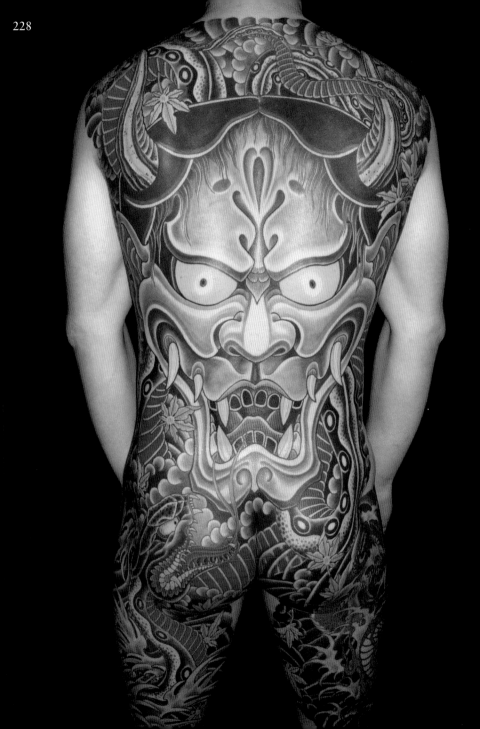

228

Henning Jorgensen

Henning Jorgensen started
tattooing in 1979, in the red light
district of Copenhagen, Denmark.
In 1982 he moved to Nyhavn to
work with the late Tattoo Ole
and a year later he opened Royal
Tattoo in Helsingør, which has just
celebrated its 25th anniversary.
In 2004, together with Mike
Rubendall, he started Tattoo Elite
International, selling Flash artwork
from top artists around the world.

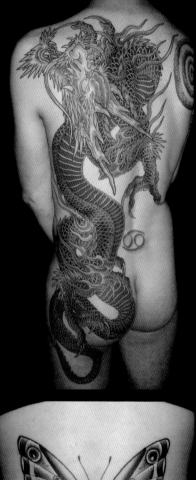
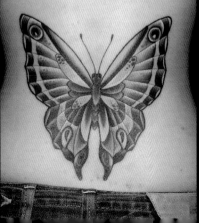
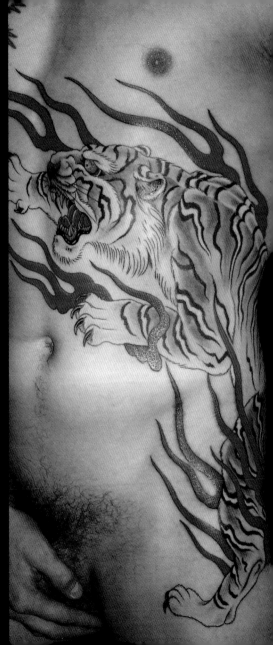

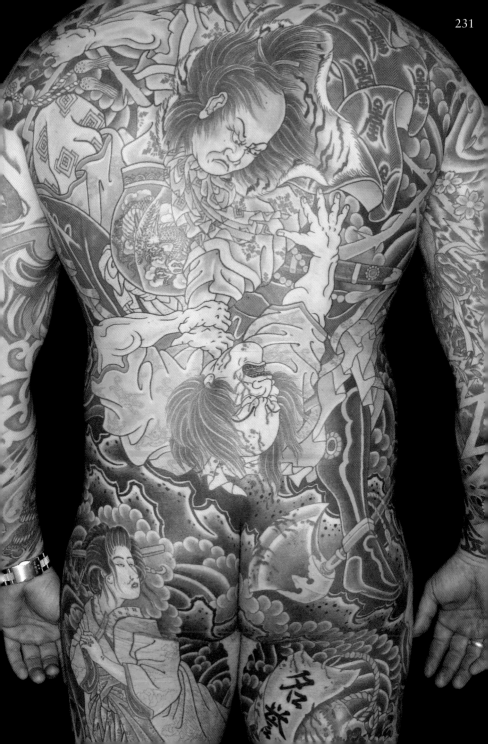

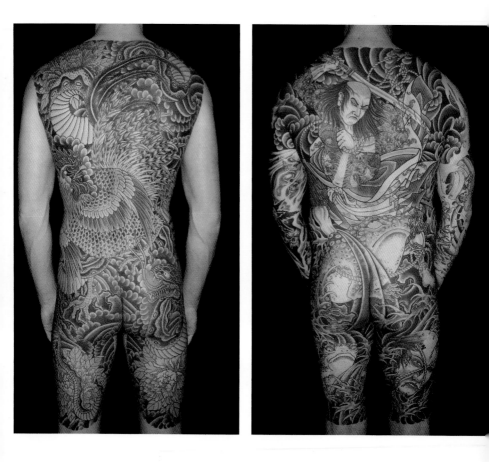

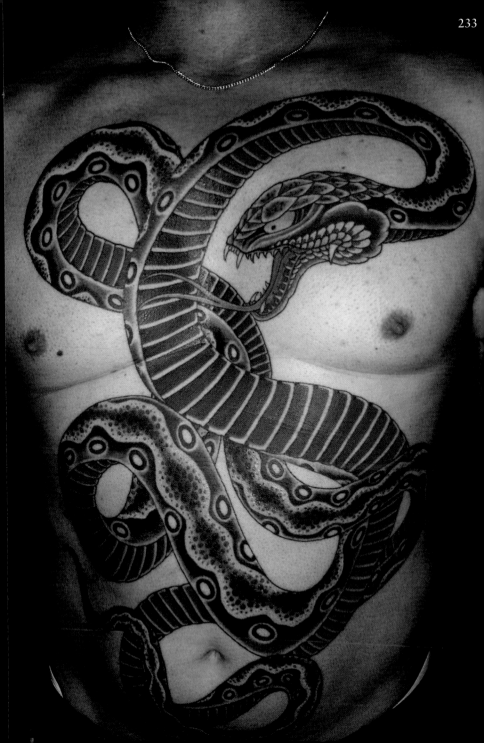

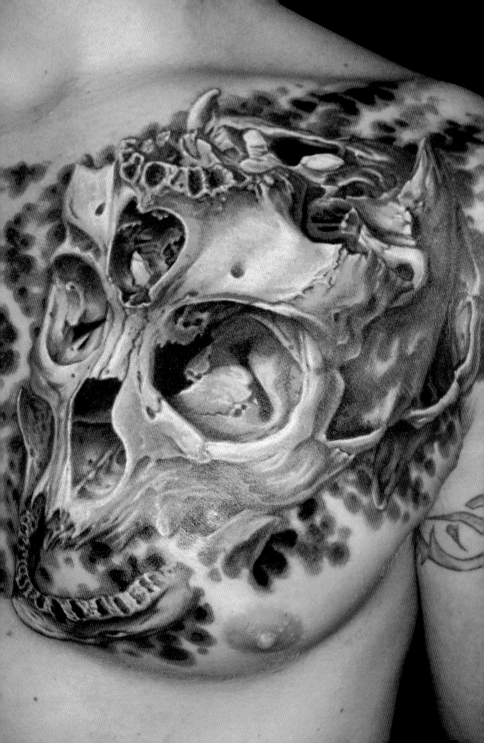

TIM KERN

n his own words: "Tim Kern is a rotten, carny bastard. A seventh-generation twin, he was born in a state of Misery, half-cooked and with a lazy eye. Over the years he has developed a passion for human oddities, prestidigitation, and serial killers. Tim has been a tattoo artist for 13 years, and works at Tribulation Tattoo in NYC. If seen, do not approach, and shoot on sight."

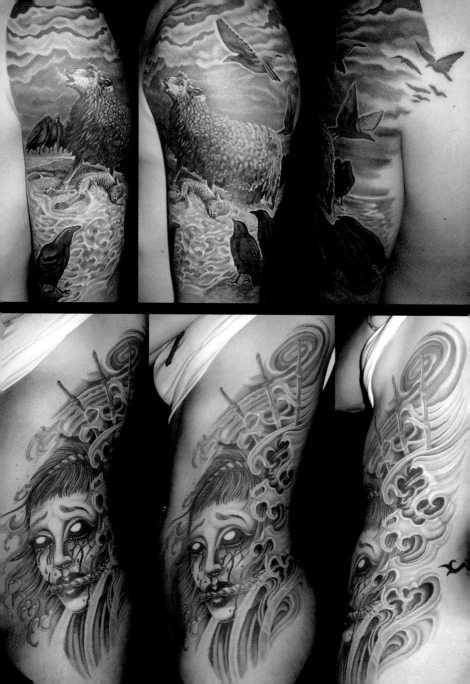

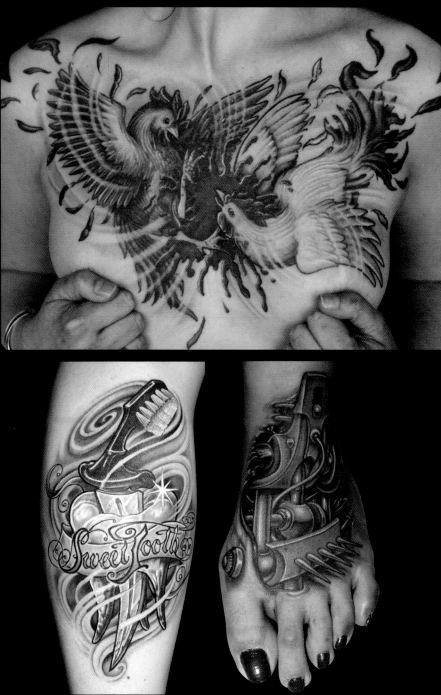

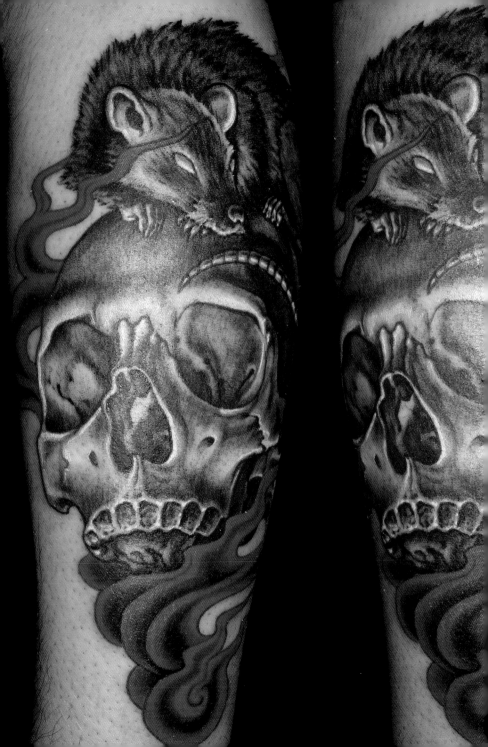

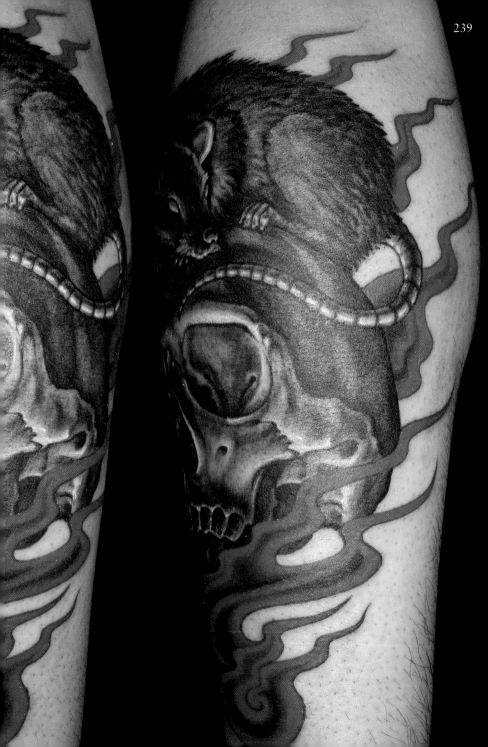

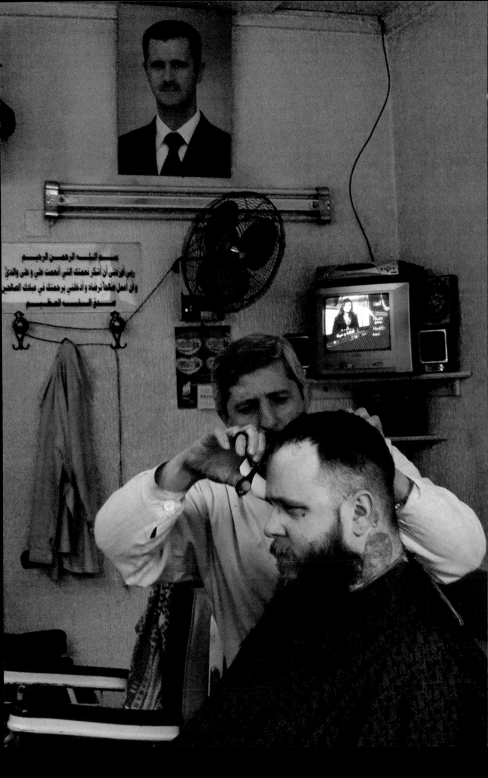

CHAD KOEPLINGER

Chad Koeplinger was born
on 3 August 1976 and began
tattooing on 16 August 1997,
in Saginaw, Michigan, USA. He
has made tattoos in cities all
over the world, including "Los
Angeles, Youngstown, Pittsburgh,
Montgomery, Jasper, Cleveland,
New Orleans, Sacramento, San
Francisco, Oakland, Seattle,
Olympia, Lincoln, Washington
D.C., Wheaton, Baltimore, Salt Lake
City, Orlando, Miami, Chicago,
New York, Philadelphia, Savannah,
Atlanta, Jersey City, Manchester,
Lansing, Reno, Barcelona, Madrid,
Gijón, London, Stockholm,
Lidköping, Malmö, Helsinki,
Trieste, Rome, Milan, Berlin,
Dorsten, Stirling, Amsterdam,
Athens, Buenos Aires, Melbourne,
Sydney, Cairo, St Petersburg, and
some others I forgot".

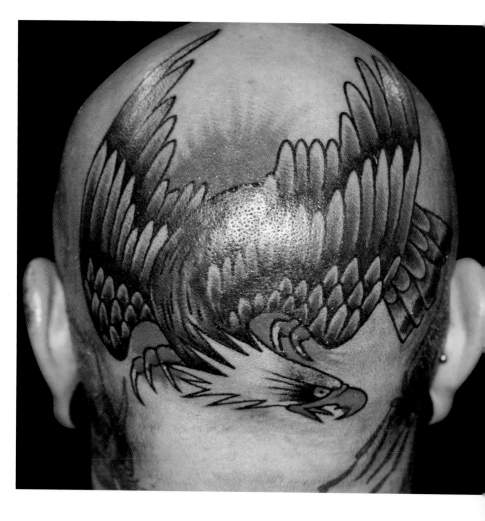

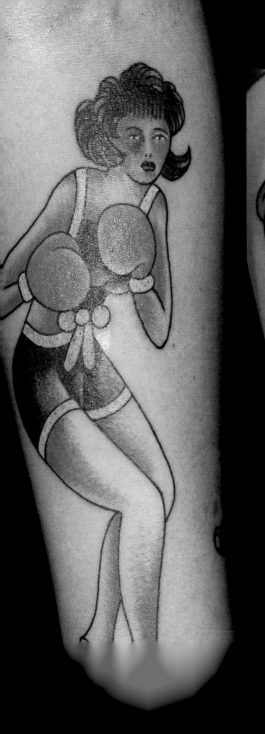
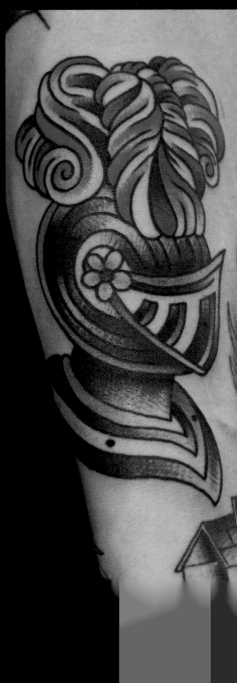

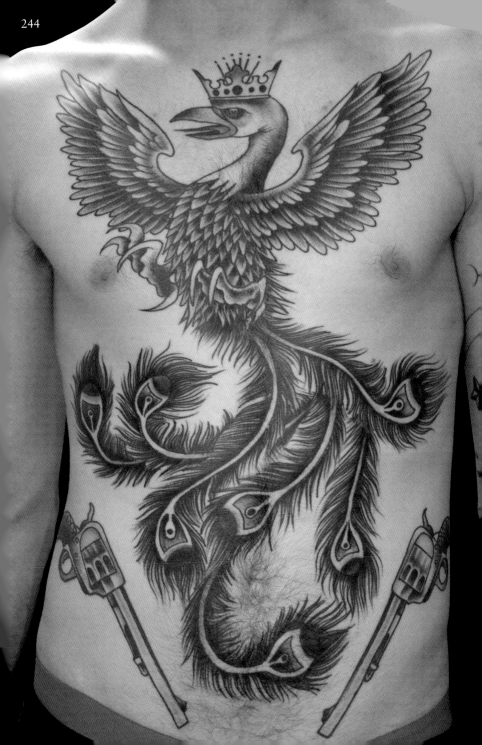

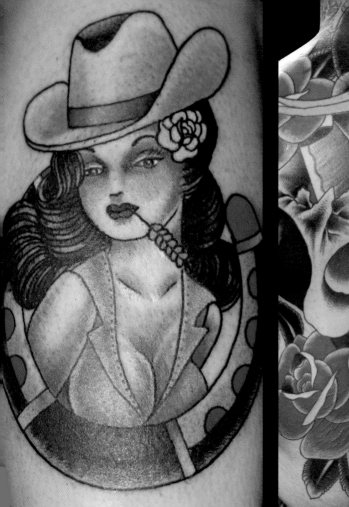
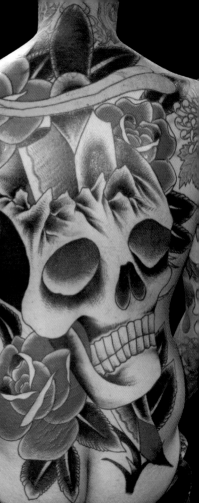

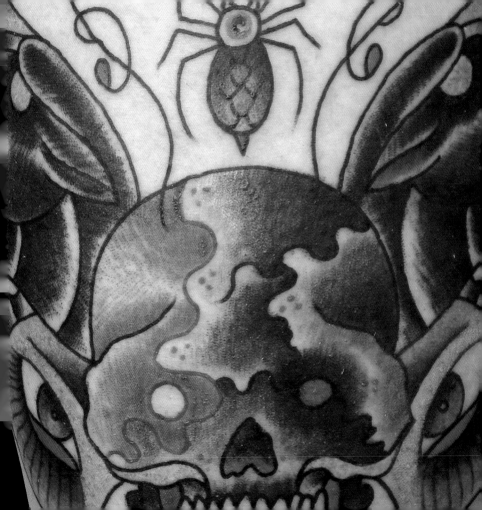

PHIL KYLE

Phil Kyle started off as an apprentice in the 1990s in Baltimore, Maryland, on the east coast of the United States. After working there for several years, he travelled around the States, working in various places, before ending up at Permanent Productions in Cincinnati, Ohio. Subsequently he moved to France where he worked in a couple of studios, as well as doing guest spots and attending conventions throughout Europe. He was approached by Discovery for the London Ink show, which he describes as a great experience and a tremendous opportunity. London Ink enabled him to open a studio in Brighton, England, which had been in the pipeline for many years and is now his main place of work. As well as tattooing, he also paints, plays music, and enjoys spending time with his daughter, Willow.

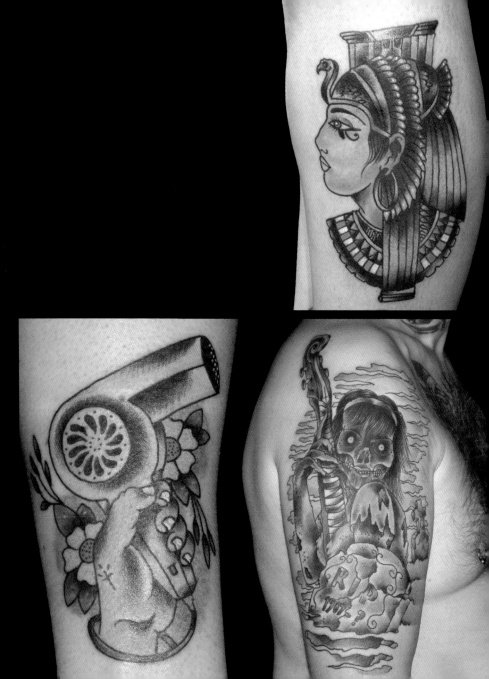

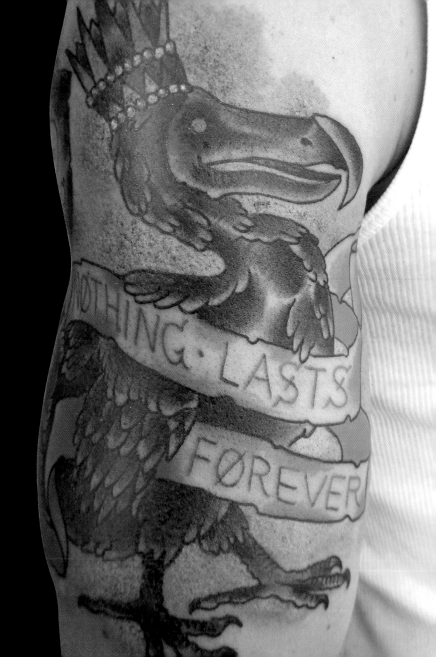

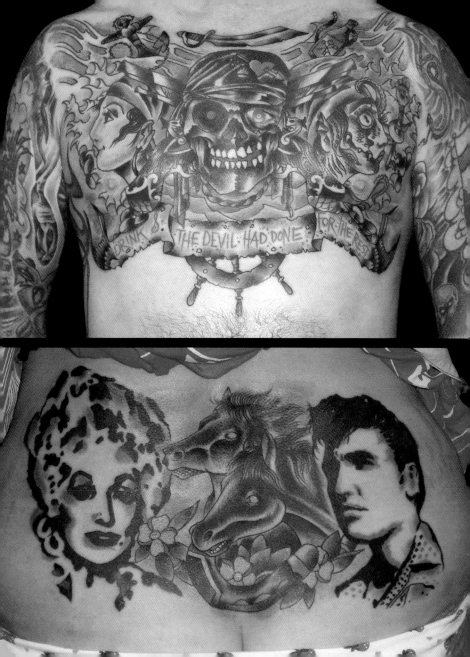

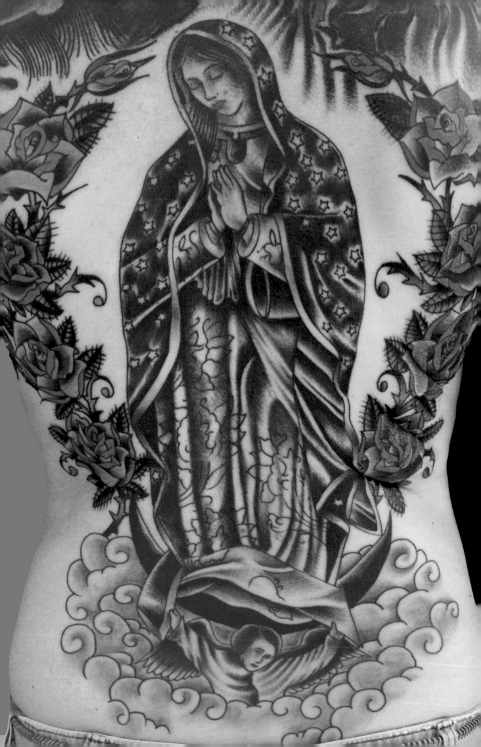

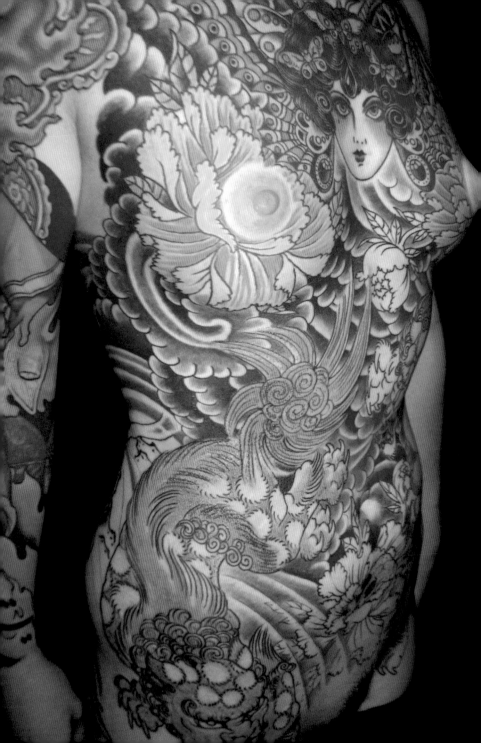

TIM LEHI

"Tattooing over 18 years now, I tattoo in many styles and also paint and make music . . . uh, what else? Still stoked on tattooing tho' it's gone through many drastic, not-so-good changes and become a bit mainstream – with the right reasons it will survive. The rest? Who cares?"

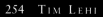

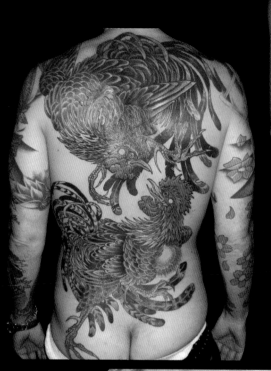

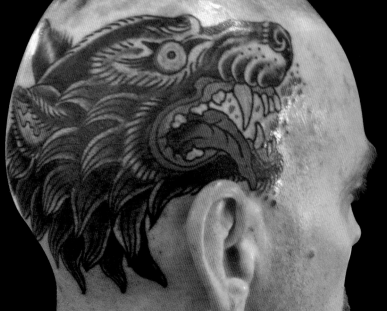

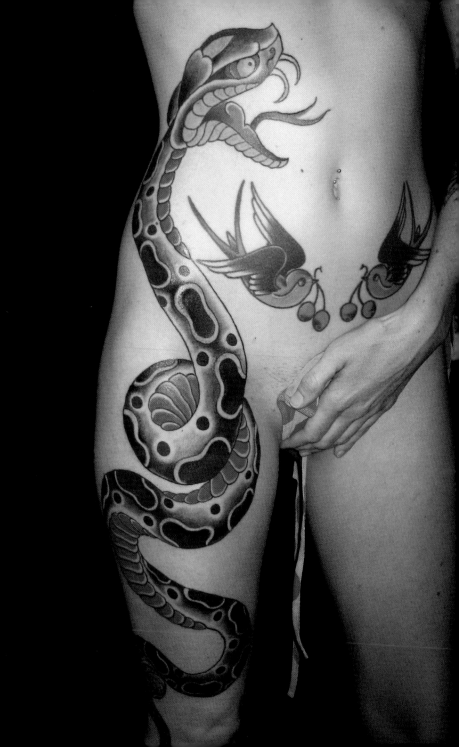

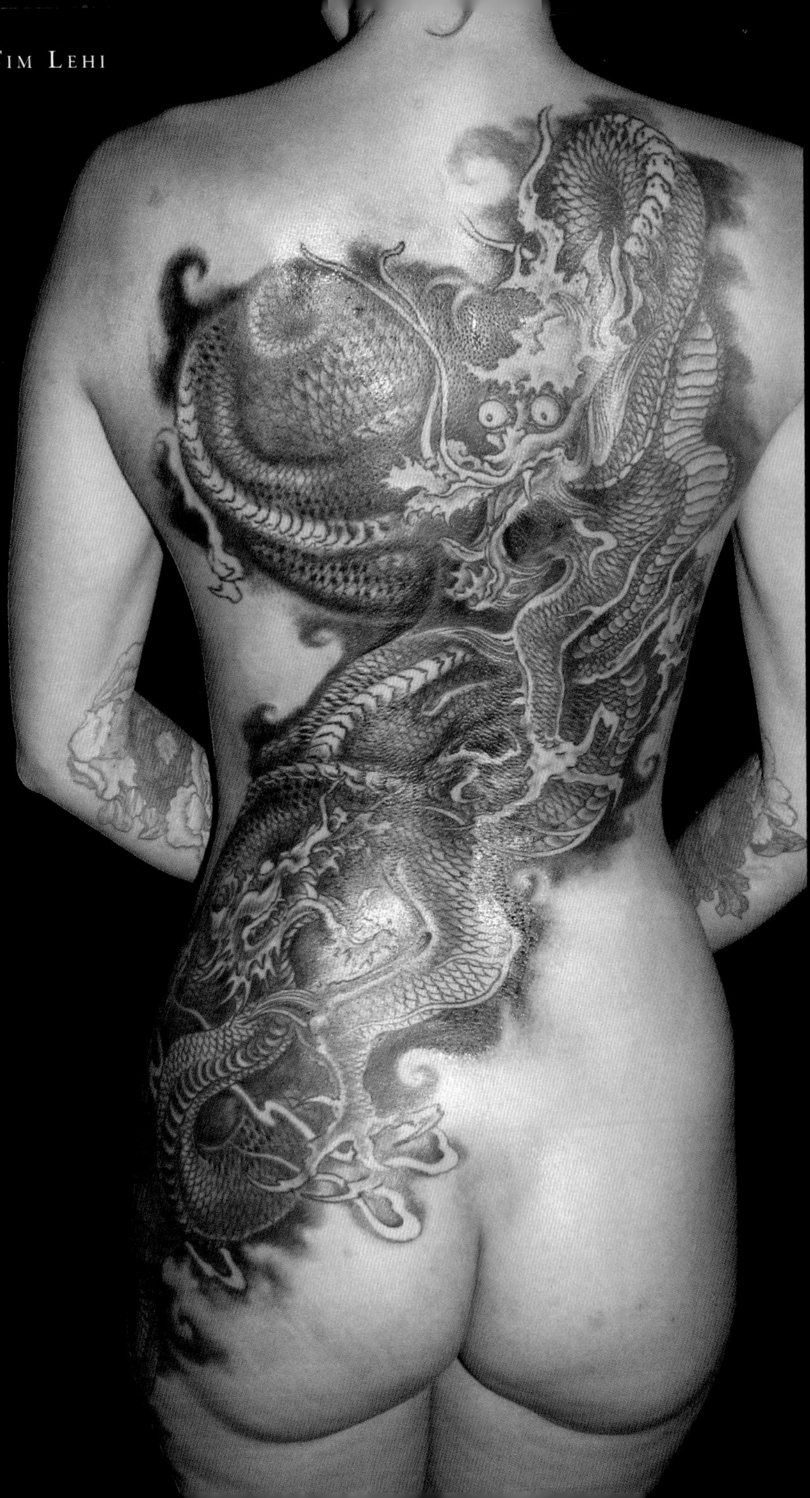

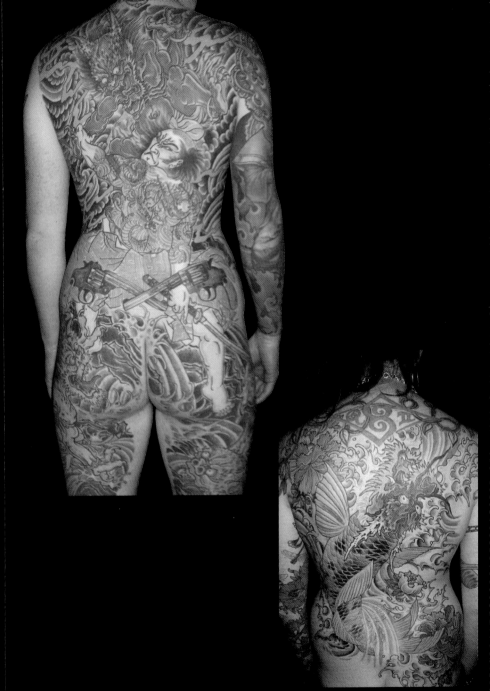

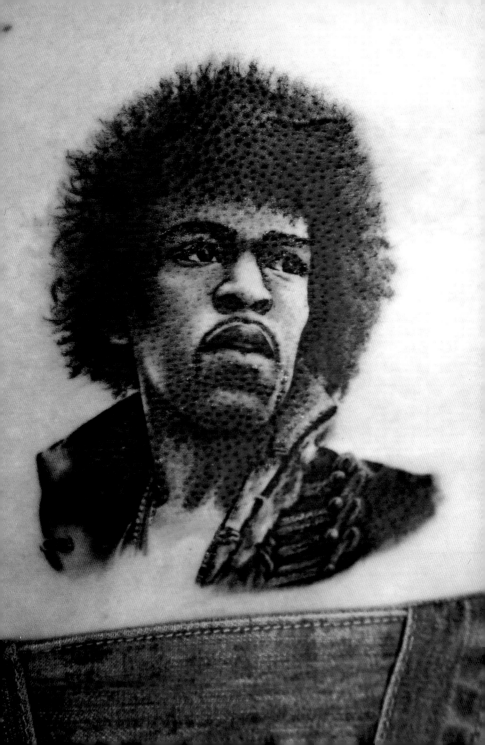

Low

Allan Low owns and runs Northside Tattooz in the north-east of England. "As a young punk in the 70s I got into tattooing and persevered in life to get to where I am now. I am self-taught and a real self-made bloke. Northside is a street shop, working in any style and doing custom work to the customers' requirements. Like all true relationships I have a love/hate relationship with tattooing – it is in me blood, it's my life 24/7."

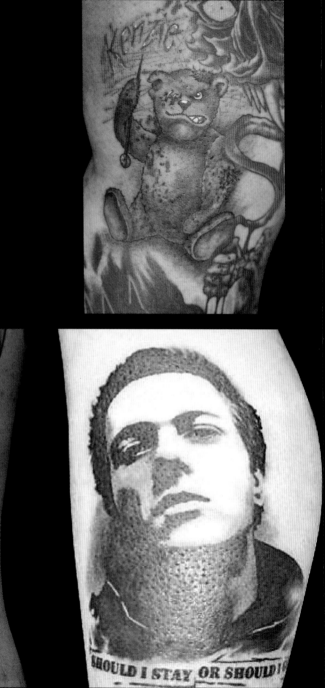
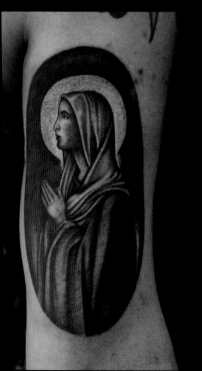

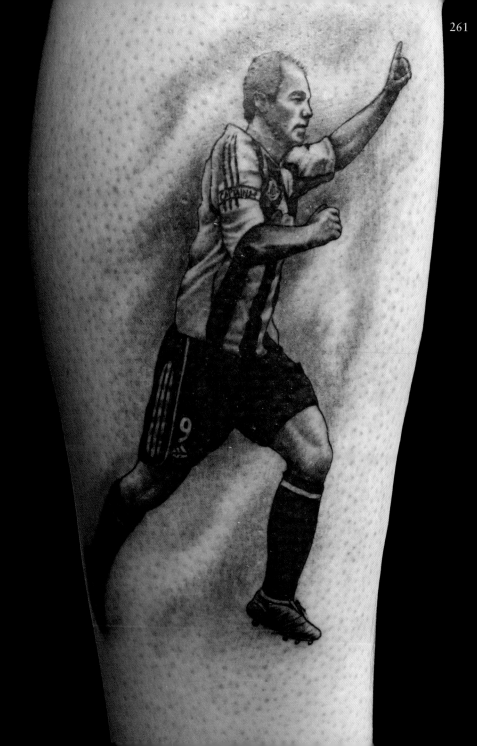

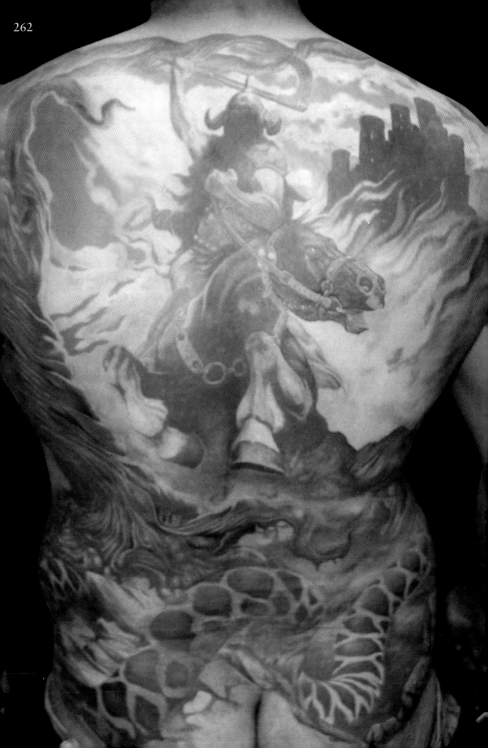

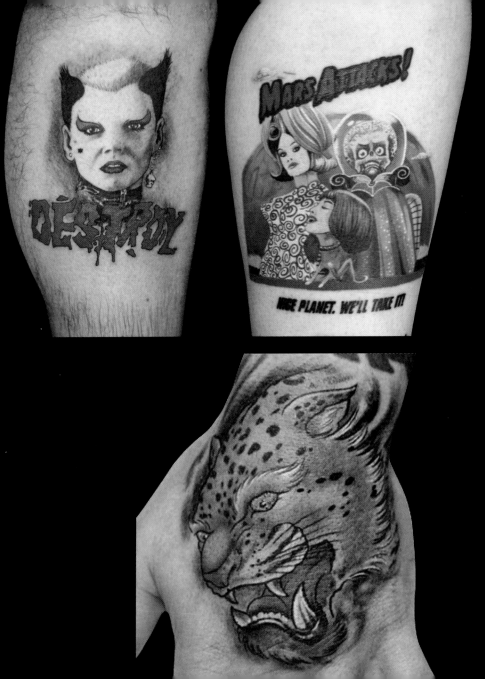

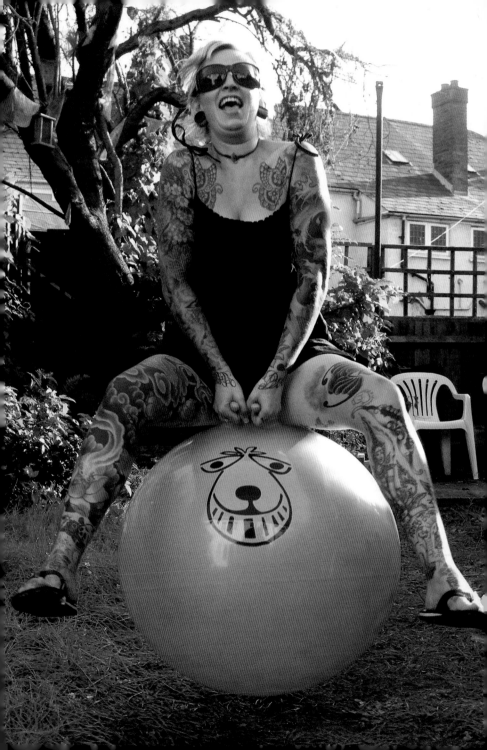

NIKOLE LOWE

"I never thought I'd be where I
am today when I was growing up.
I never knew where I'd be, but
I was open-minded to anything
that came my way. I found
myself drawing a lot which led to
tattooing. I focused on things I was
good at until one day everything
seemed to fall into place. Tattooing
found me in 1991, I'm still doing
it, always learning, and loving it."

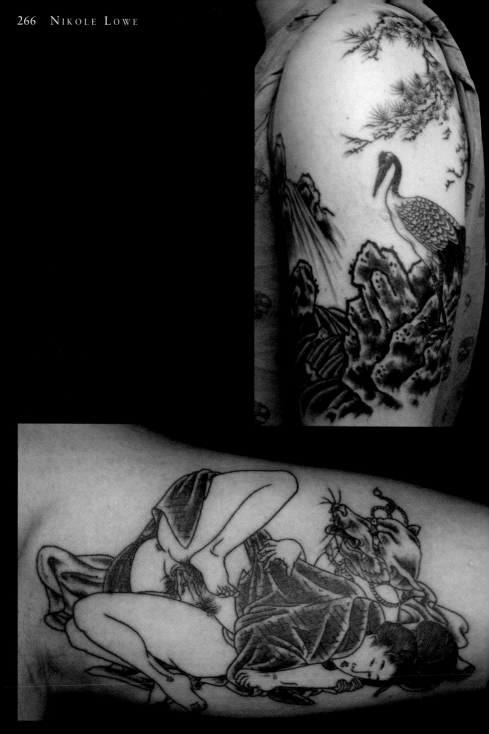

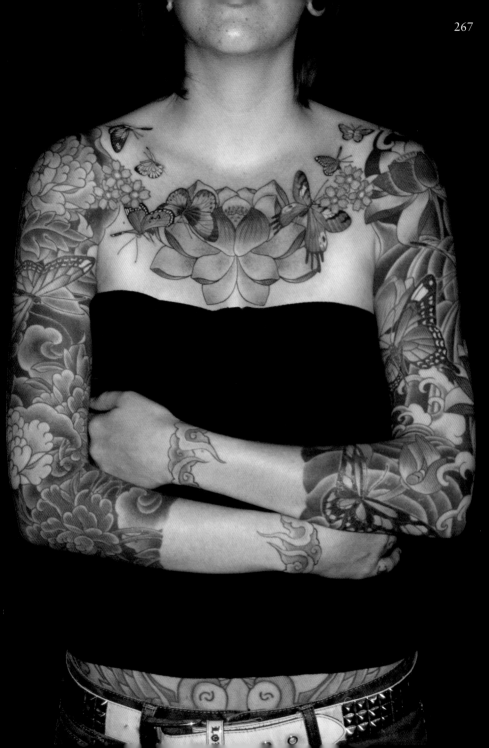

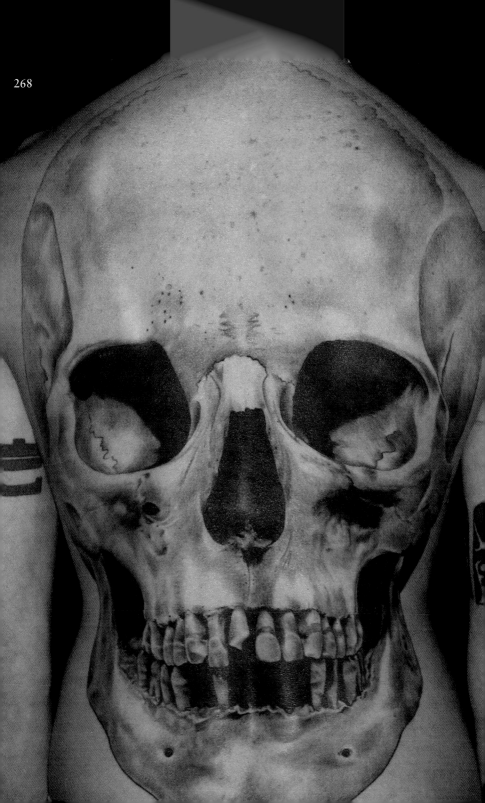

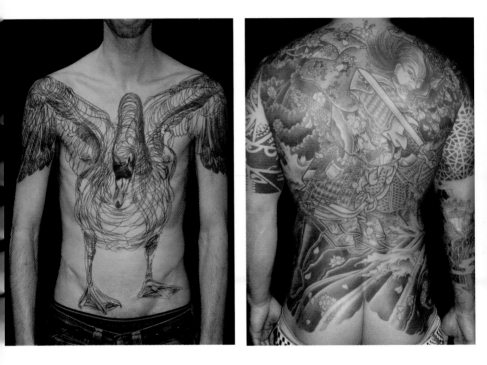

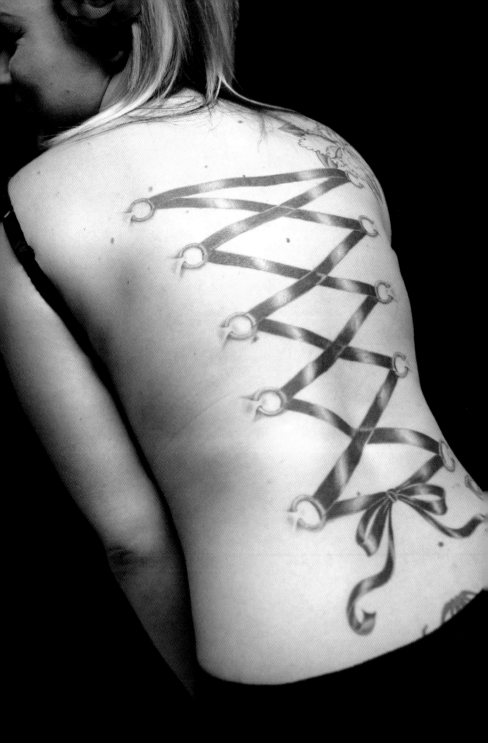

COREY MILLER

"The circus hasn't changed,
but the tent is really fuckin' big
right now . . ."

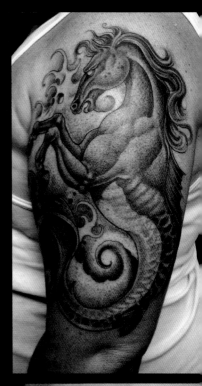

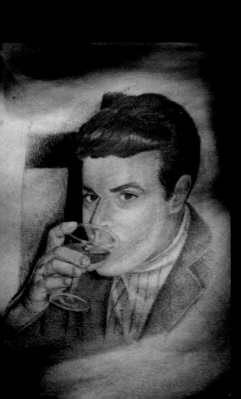

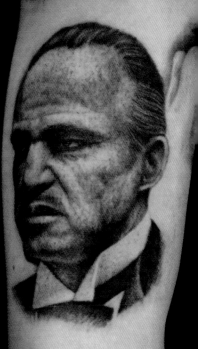

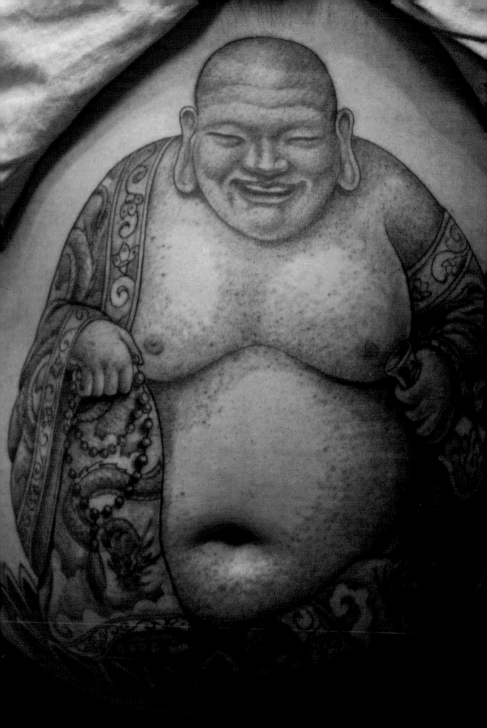

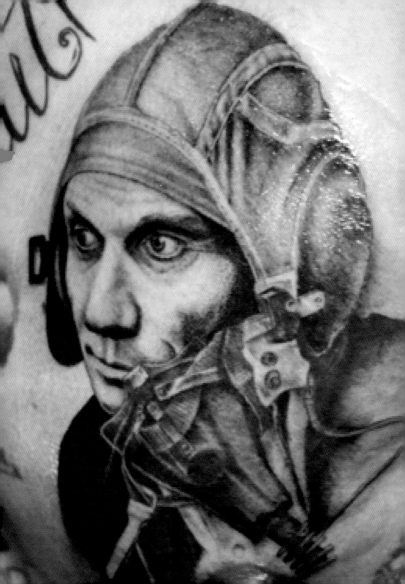

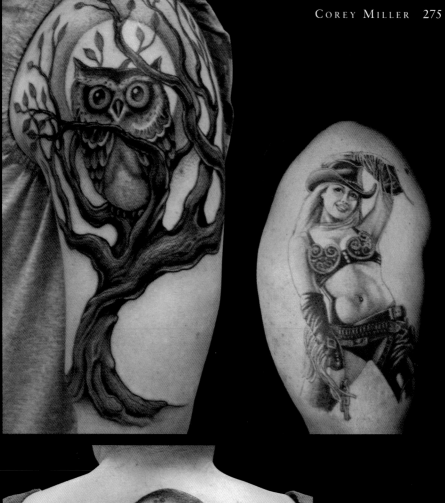

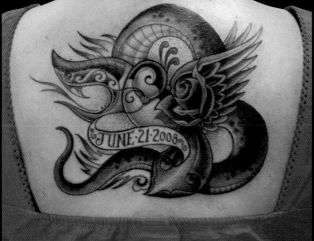

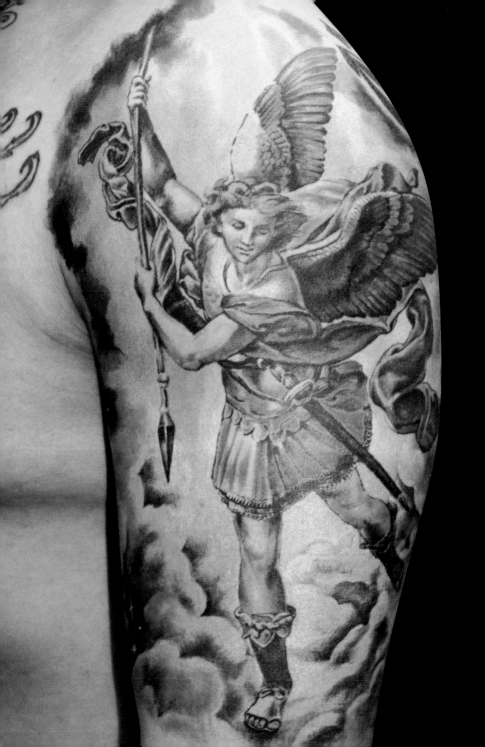

MIREK

Mirek, whose nickname is Stotker (a German version of his Polish nickname Szczota), is originally from Poland, where he started tattooing in 1992. In 1993 he opened one of the first tattoo studios in Poland, Joker Tattoo, in Kraków. After working for seven years in his studio he left Poland to travel around Europe and the rest of the world, gaining valuable tattooing experience. He now has his own tattoo and body piercing studio, Stotker Tattoo, in Angel, London. He has won awards from tattoo conventions in Berlin, Vienna, and Tahiti. He likes to do realistic-style tattoos and specializes in portraits, of both humans and animals.

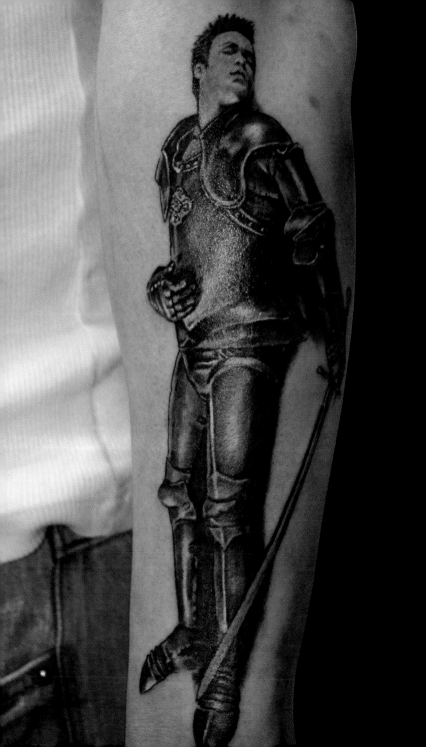

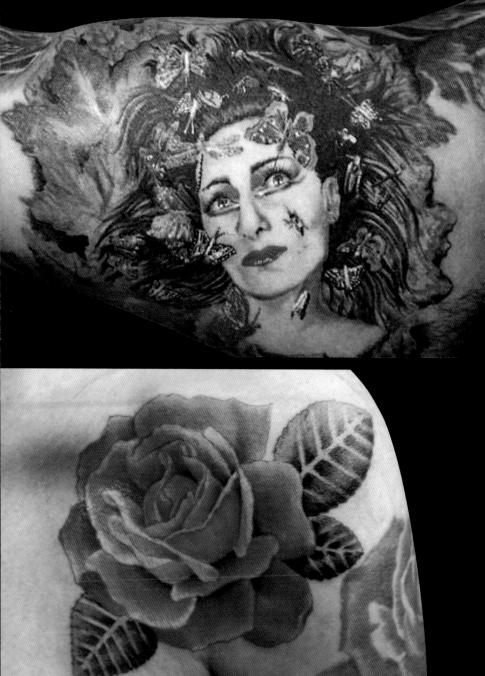

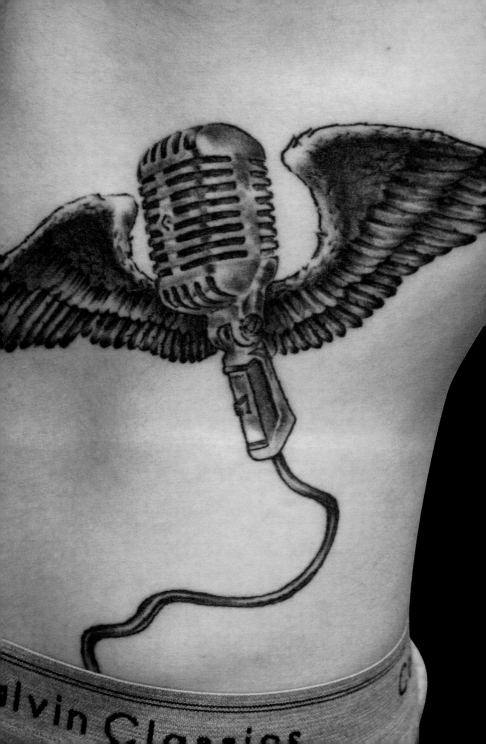

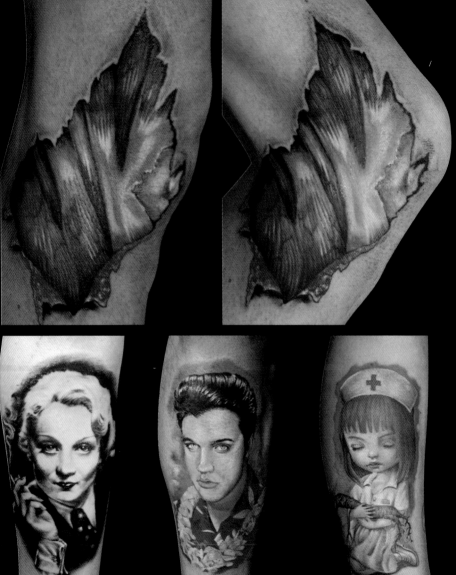

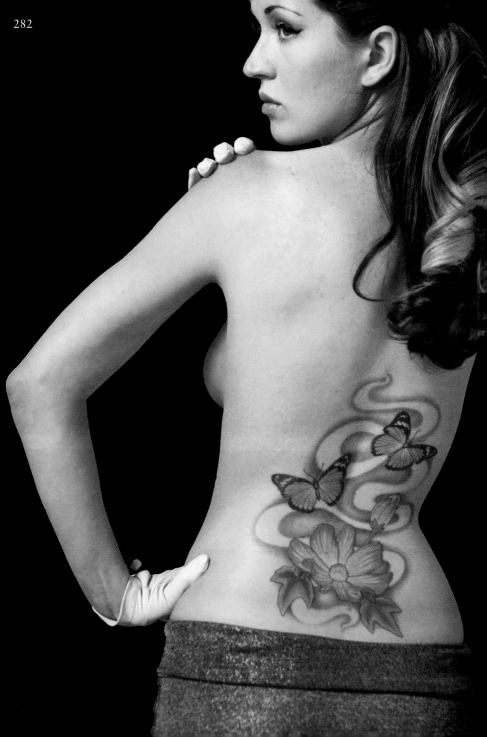

Louis Molloy

Louis Molloy opened the Middleton Tattoo Studio in 1981 at the age of 18. He's still in the same studio and expects to remain there until the day he dies. Rather than choosing to become a tattoo artist, he feels it chose him and has become "hardwired at [his] very core" where he carries it "like a life sentence". He describes himself as being "always at its disposal". Occasionally he looks up to see the devastation this sentence causes to himself and to the people around him, yet still he feels compelled to carry on "this love affair". He feels that it is impossible to glean individuality from the pages of Flash books and magazines – either you have it, or you don't, and if you don't have it, you never will.

Comic-book sleeve photograph © Matt Wright.

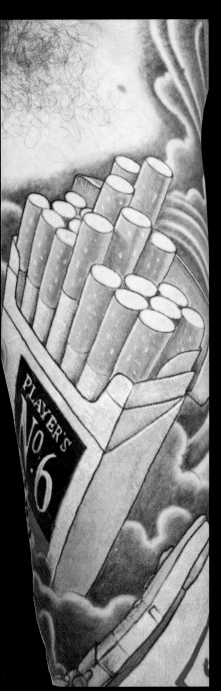

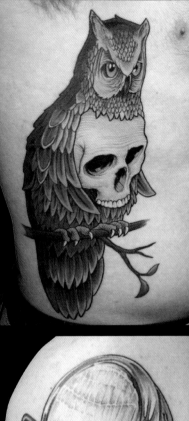

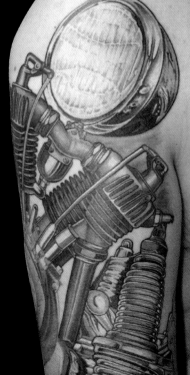

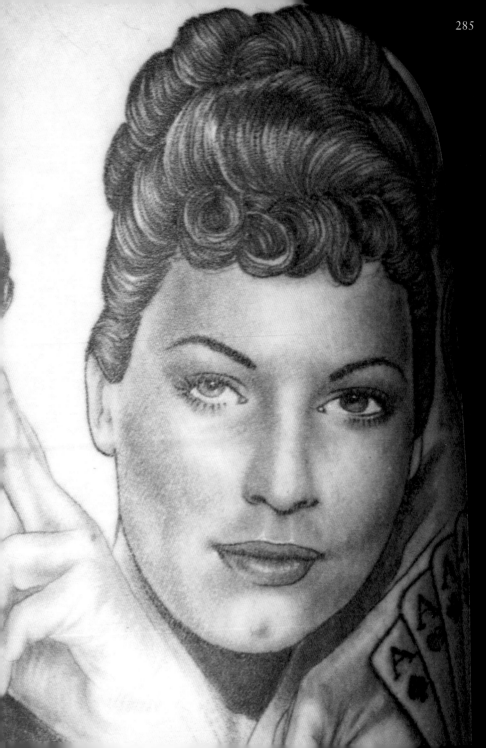

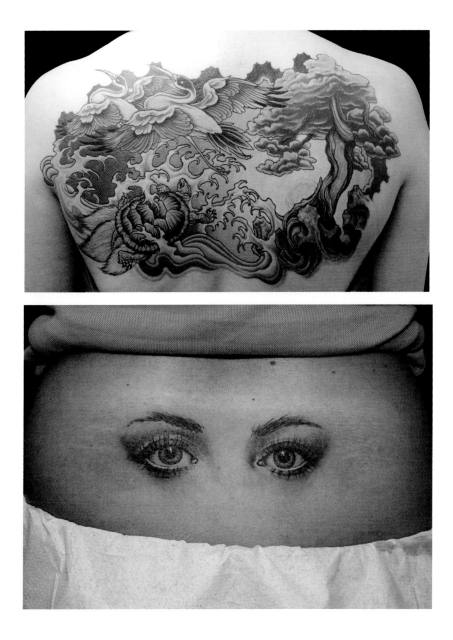

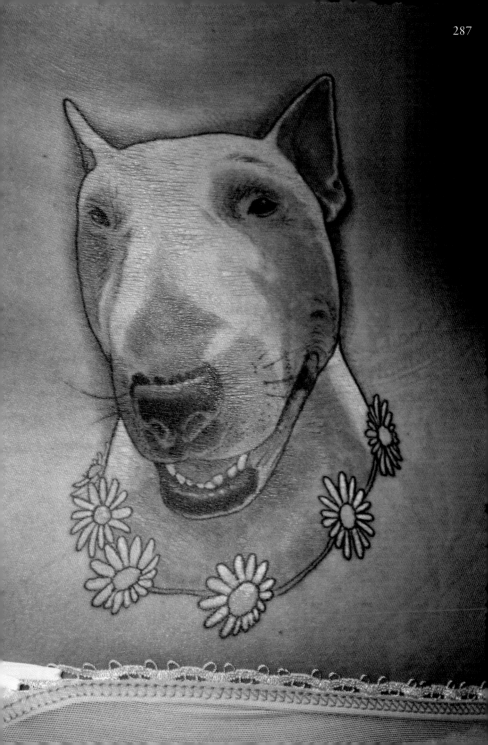

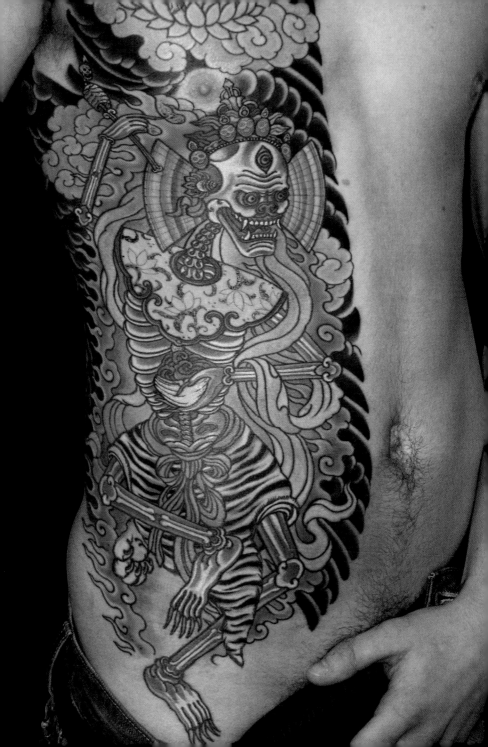

CHRIS O'DONNELL

Chris O'Donnell started
tattooing in 1993 and
moved to New York City
in 2000. He works at New
York Adorned where he
specializes in large-scale,
Japanese-inspired tattooing,
though he enjoys most
styles that are open to
interpretation.

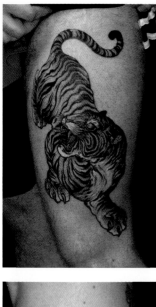

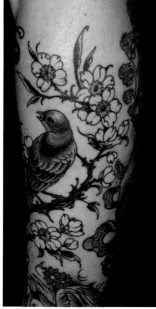

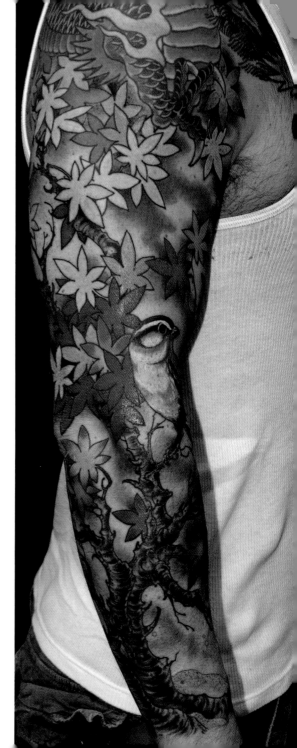

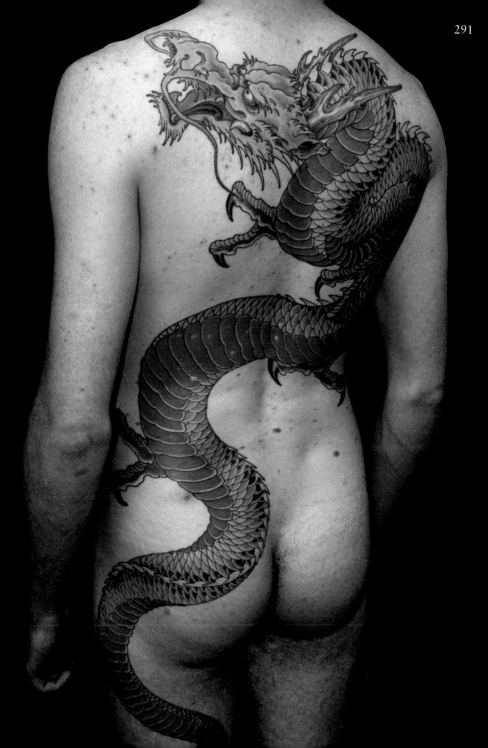

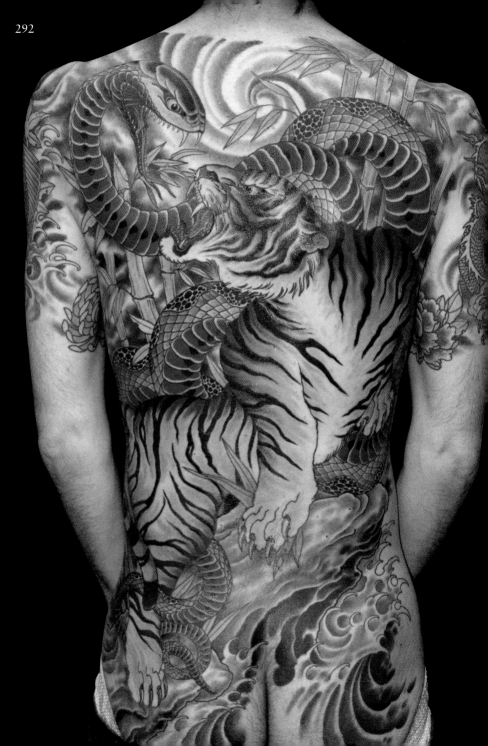

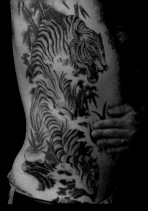
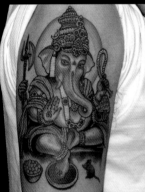
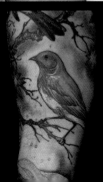
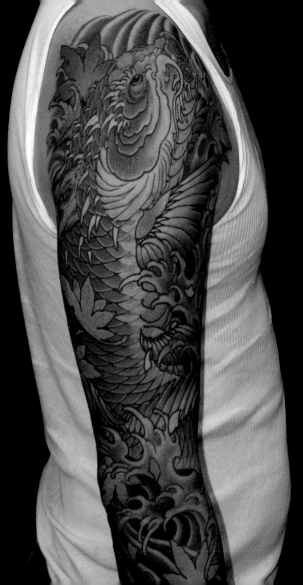

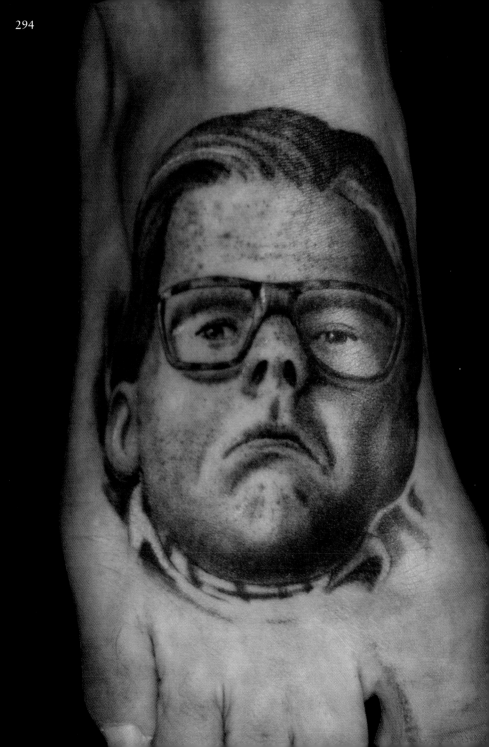

LEIGH OLDCORN

Leigh Oldcorn's studio, Cosmic
Tattoo, is in Colchester, Essex,
England. He was born in 1969
and raised in a children's home.
He left in 1985 and hung around
at Scorpio Tattoo Studio in
Middlesbrough, Cleveland,
collecting tattoos, and acting as
front desk and general dogsbody.
This was the start of his tattooing
career. He is primarily self-taught,
having gained experience at
various studios on the south coast
of England until opening his own
studio in 1998. He says, "I love
this profession dearly, particularly
black and grey work and
portraits, but I'll do pretty much
anything! My main influences
are Bob Tyrell, Tom Ptolemy,
Louis Molloy, and Paul Booth."
His main interests are cards, *Top
Gear*, weight training, and his
two Staffordshire bull terriers.

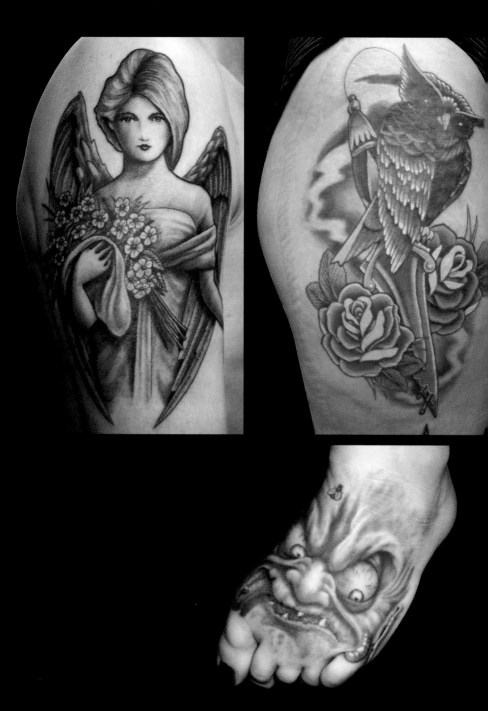

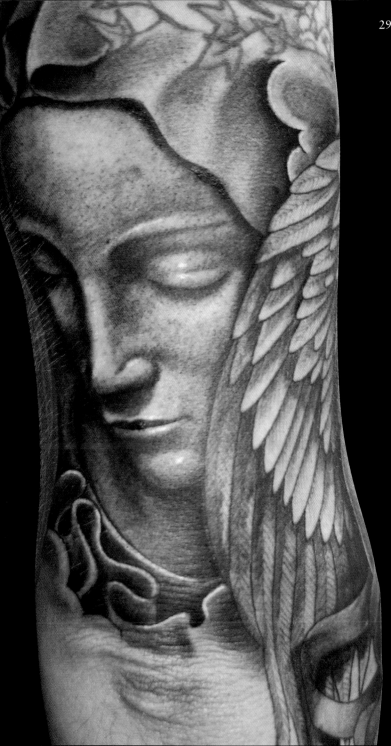

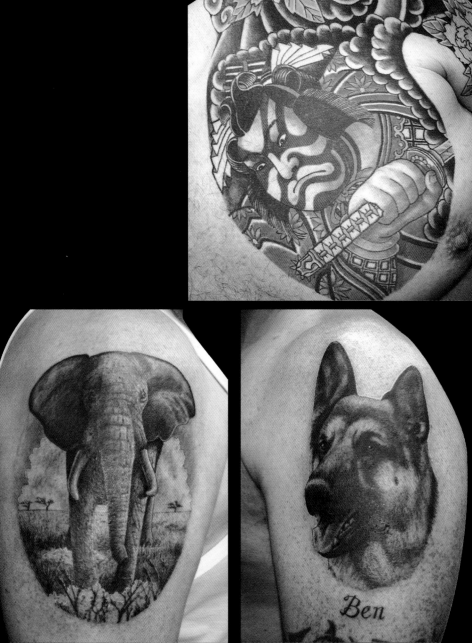

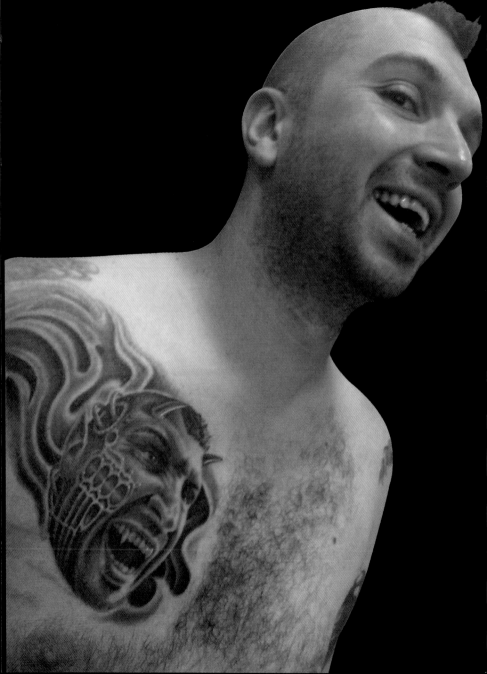

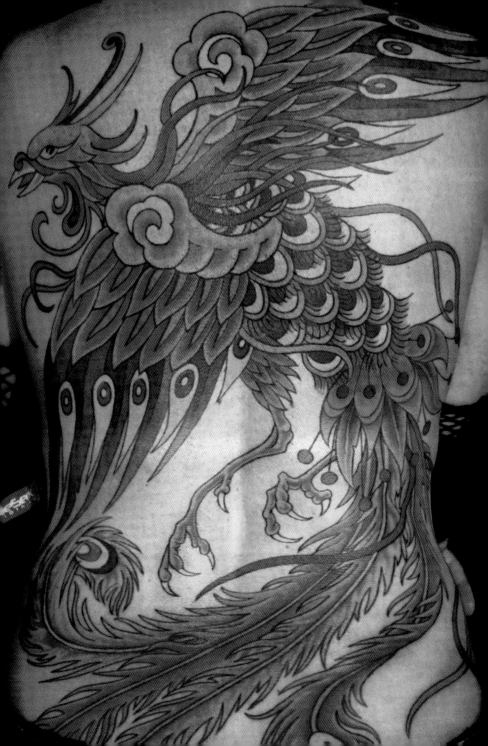

MEGAN OLIVER

Megan Oliver has been tattooing professionally since 1996. Originally from Aotearoa, New Zealand, in the early 1990s she travelled to London to begin her tattoo journey with Mark Lee of Realistic Dermagraphics on the Portobello Road. Returning to the Antipodes she spent two years tattooing under the guidance of eX de Medici at Deus Ex Machina in Canberra, Australia. Since 2001 she has been working at Cliffe Clayton's Inner Vision Tattoo in Sydney, Australia. Her favourite style of tattooing is anything graphic, unique, meaningful, and personal.

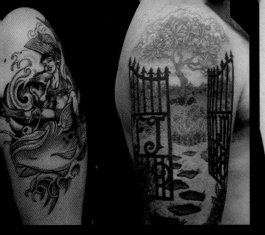

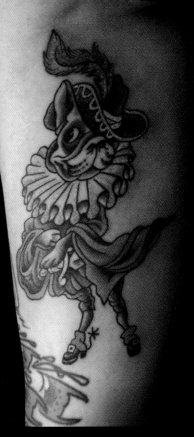

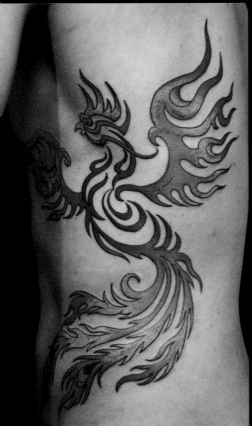

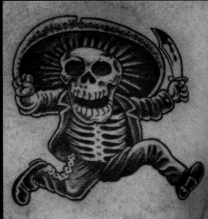

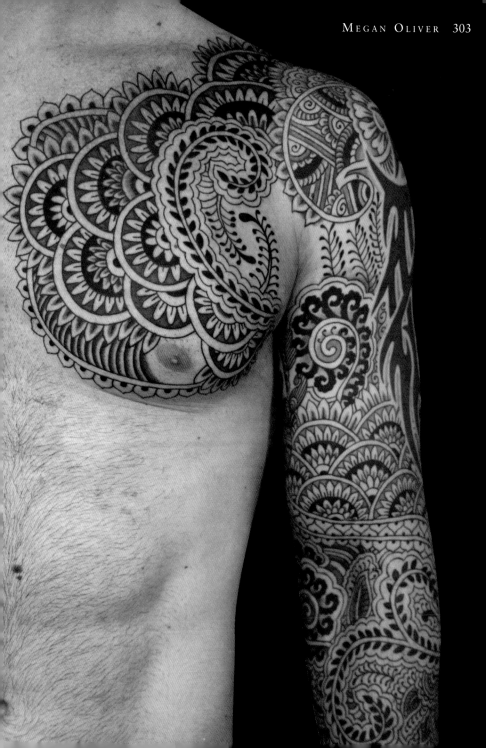

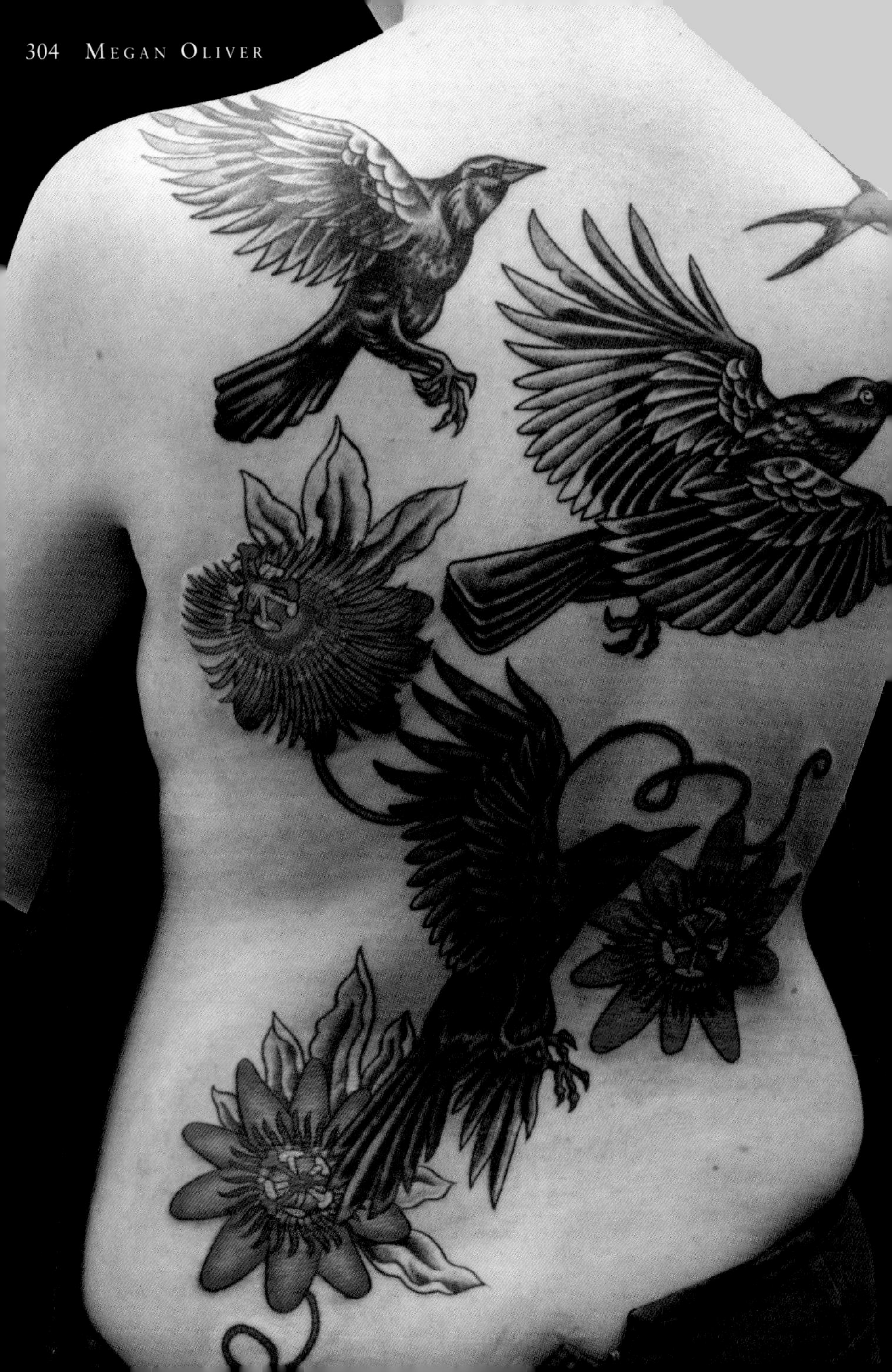

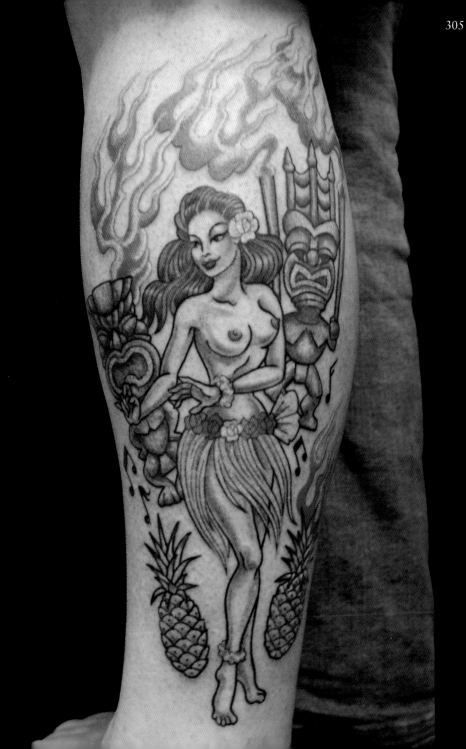

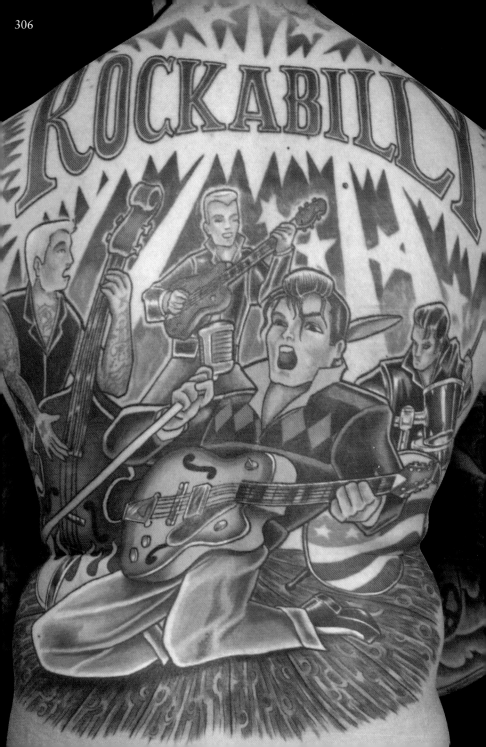

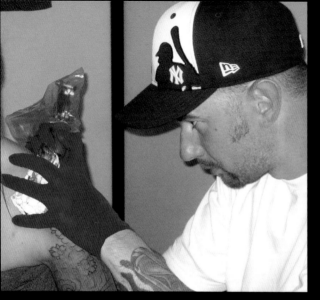

Jeff Ortega

Currently at Evil from the Needle, Jeff Ortega cut his teeth at Rising Dragon Tattoo in New York. He learned the old school way which took him from scrubbing the floors/cleaning the toilet/making needles etc. right up to the present day when he owns his own studio, Evil from the Needle, in London's thriving Camden Town/Market area. His artistic influences range from Michelangelo to the graffiti scene. He has been tattooing for over 15 years.

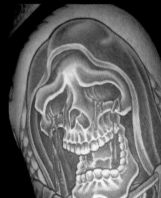

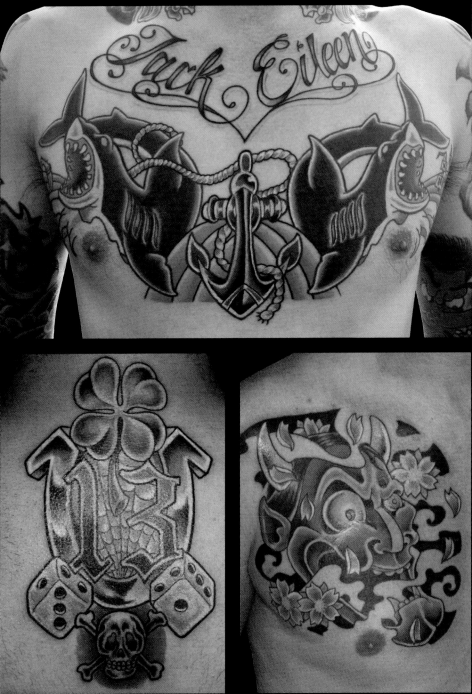

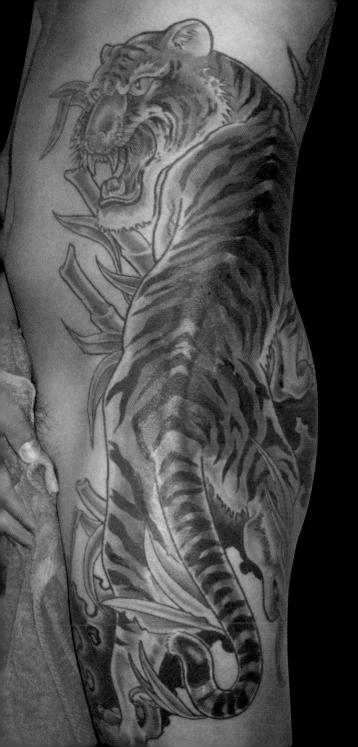

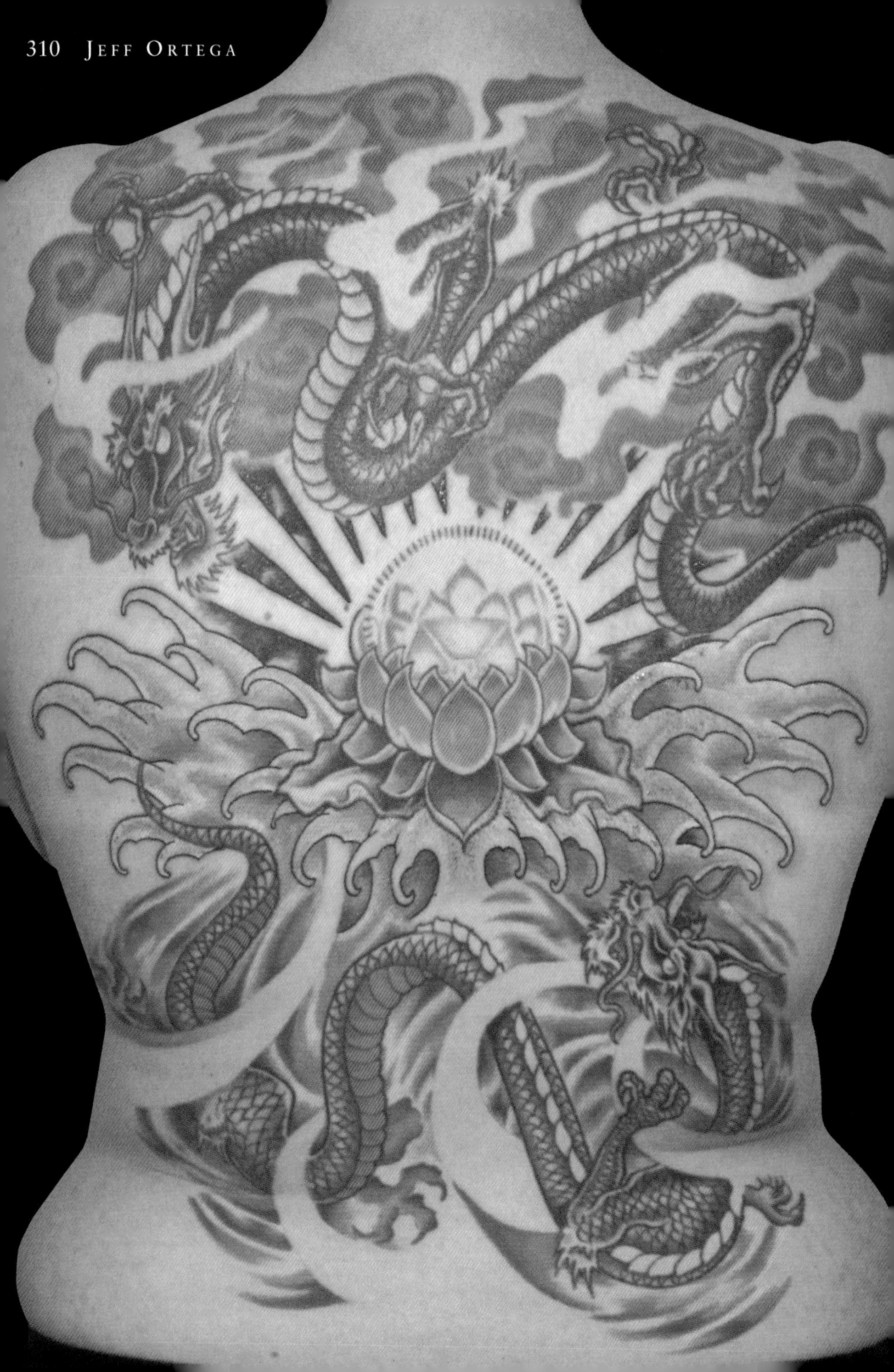

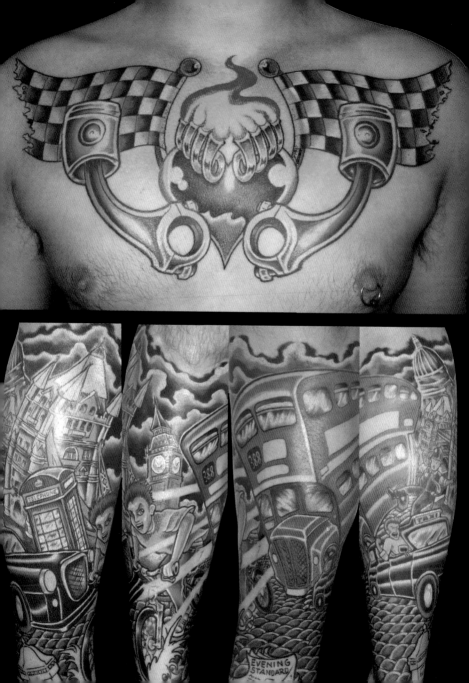

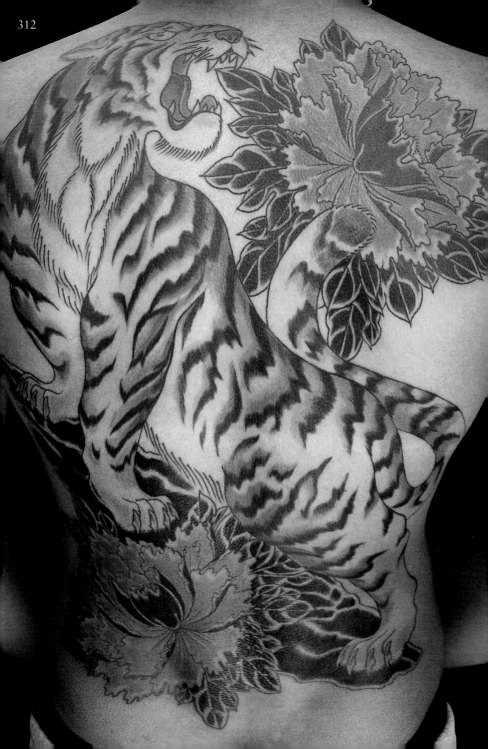

LUCA ORTIS

Luca Ortis was born in
Luxembourg so he soon decided
to try his luck elsewhere. While
travelling through Chile he was
given a tattoo machine by a
mysterious stranger who told him
it would be a great way to live.
After scratching his way around
for a while he realized someone
would eventually break his hands
if he carried on carving havoc
on unsuspecting skins. He then
set about lying and cajoling so
as to get his foot in the door of a
proper tattoo shop and was lucky
enough to come across kind souls
who took pity on his potential
customers and decided to teach
him what they knew.

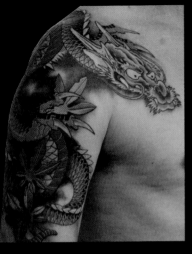

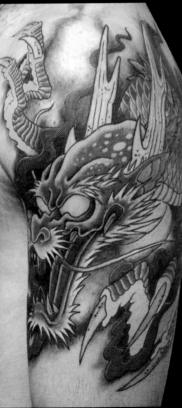

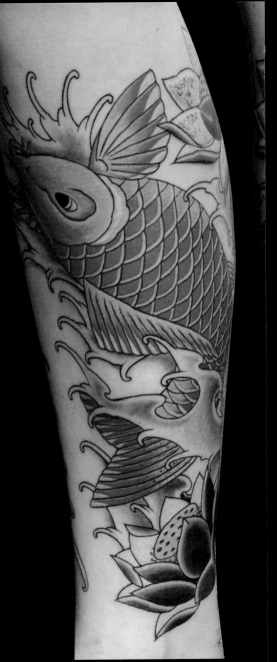

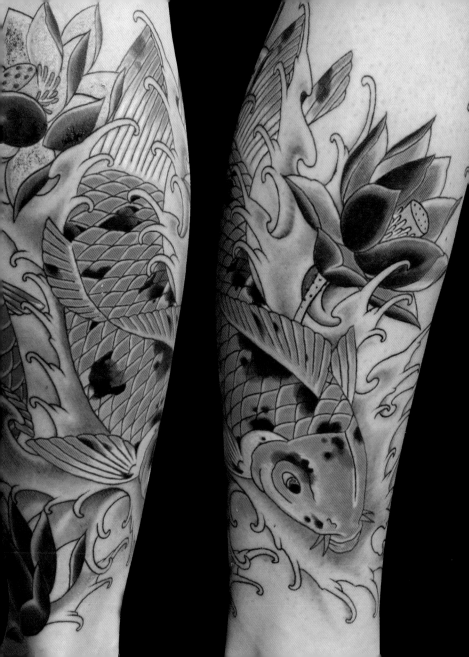

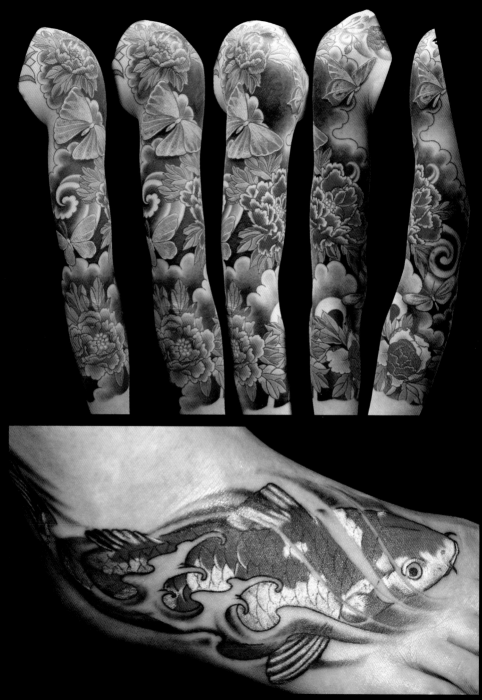

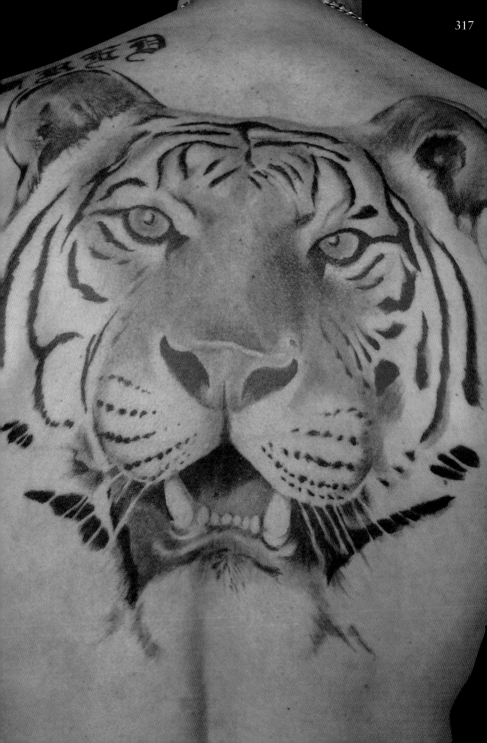

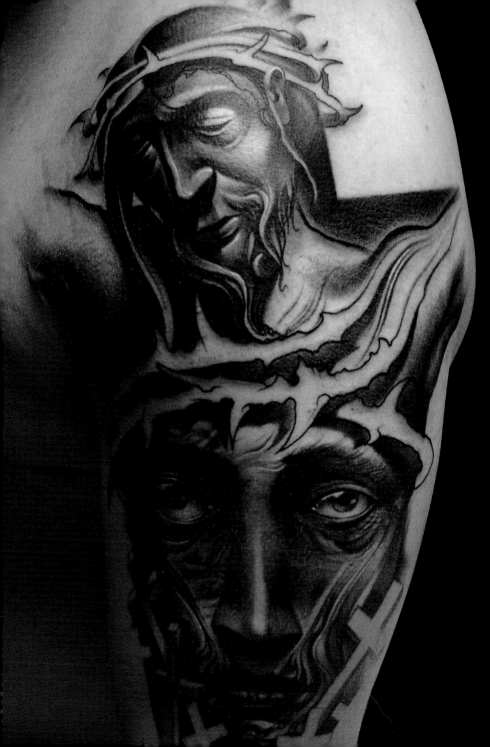

PIOTREK

Piotrek was born and raised in Poland, in a small mountain village named Rabaka. He studied chemistry at school before moving on to do medical research. After travelling to the United Kingdom in 2000 he found himself pursuing a career as a tattoo artist in London. He is open to all styles of tattooing.

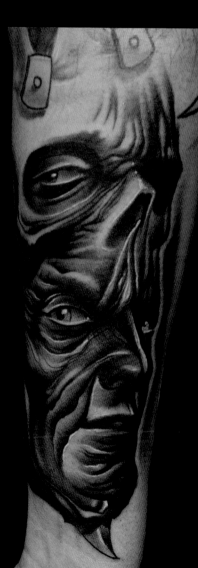

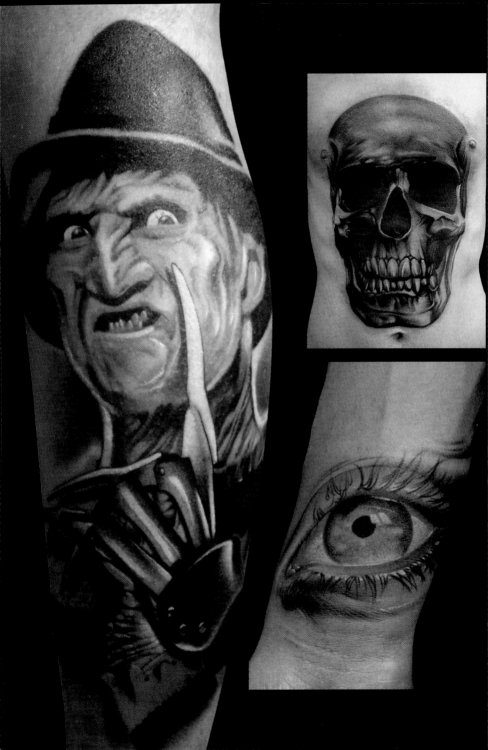

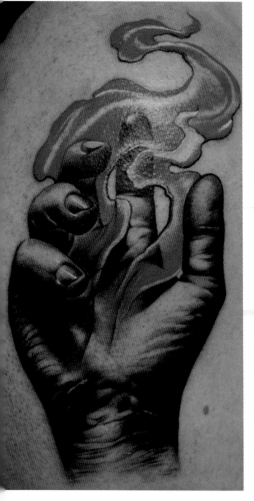

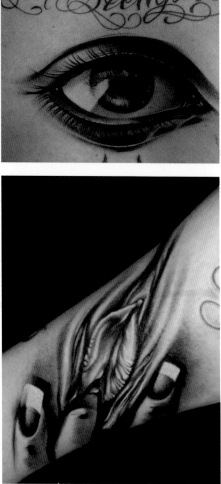

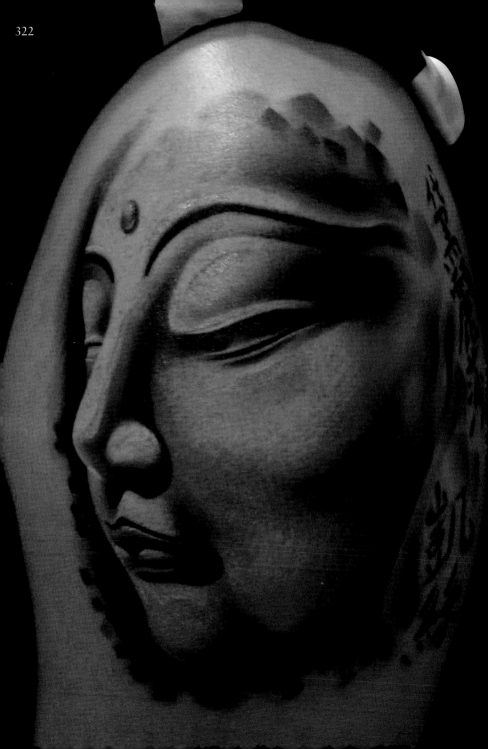

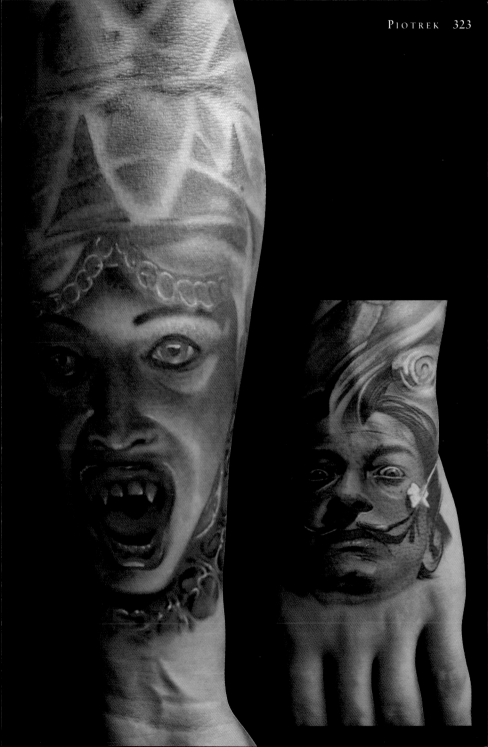

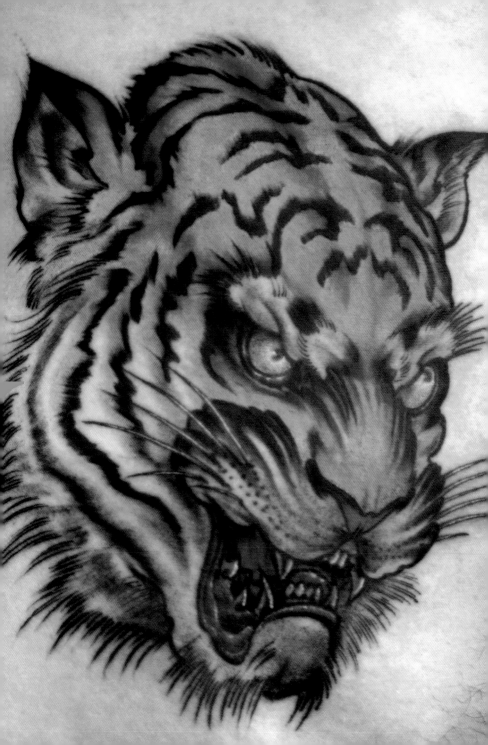

RODNEY RAINES

While studying visual arts at Lander
University in South Carolina, Rodney
Raines spent a semester in 1992 studying
at Polytechnic South West (now the
University of Plymouth), in England. It
was then that he received his first tattoo,
from Tattoo Paul. He graduated in 1995
and, with the help of Shay Cannon
and Phil Colvin, he began to tattoo
professionally in 1997, at Point Blank in
Hendersonville, North Carolina. Later
that year he moved to work with Randy
Herring at Skin Art in Gastonia, NC. After
two years of "street shop" tattooing, he
moved to Ace Custom Tattoo in Charlotte,
NC, to work for Nick Hughes, where,
with Colin LaRocque, he focused on
tattoo conventions. Finally, in 2003, he
bought Ace Custom Tattoo. Now, when
not tattooing or painting, he travels all
over the world, tattooing at conventions
and doing guest spots. He also owns,
together with Lise Barnet, Twenty-Two, an
art gallery in Charlotte.

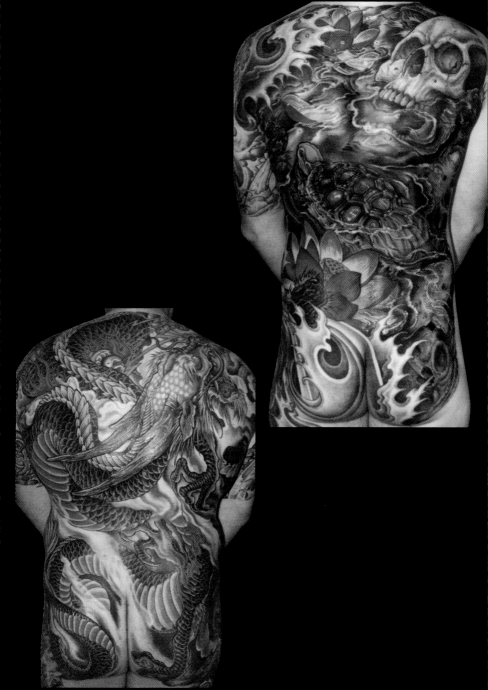

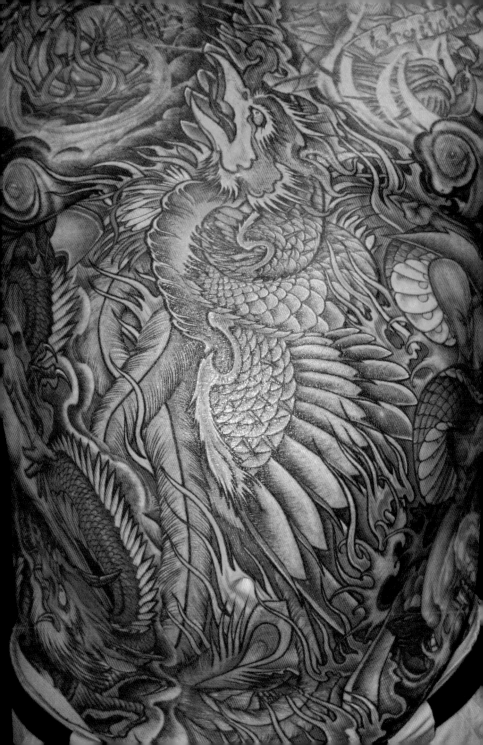

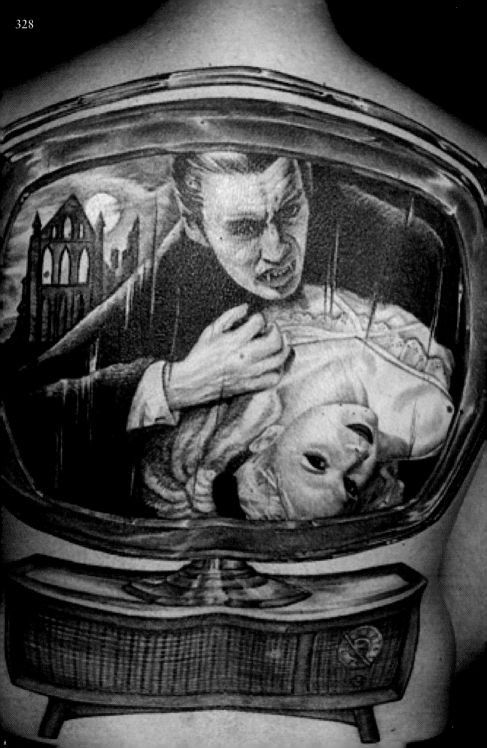

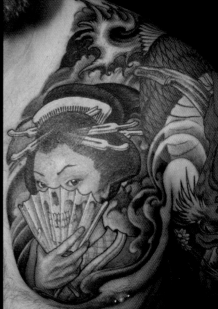

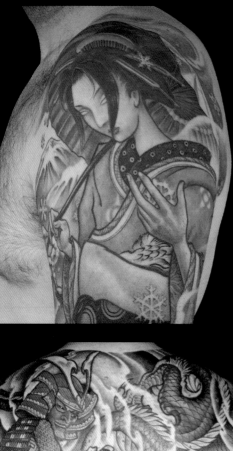

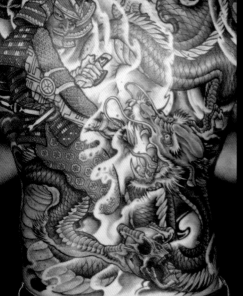

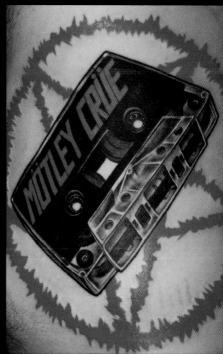

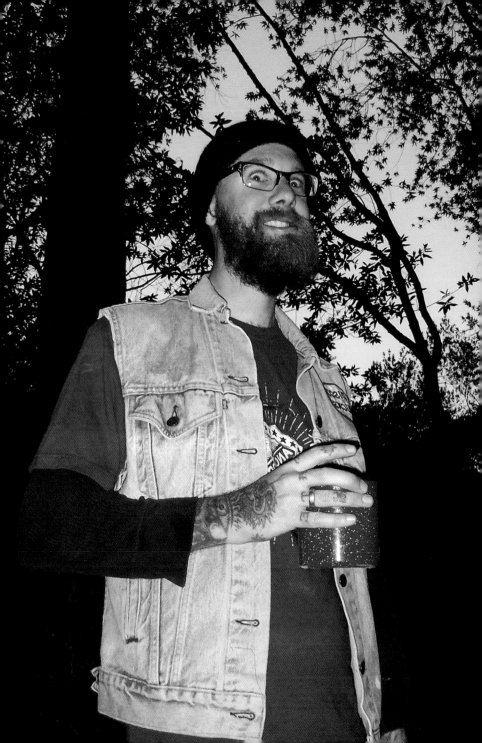

JEFF RASSIER

"I started tattooing in Santa Barbara, but soon moved to San Francisco. At the time the energy in the city was incredible, especially for a young tattooer – man, it was the best! In that seven-mile little city you had Ed Hardy, Eddy Deutsche, Freddy Corbin, Dan Higgs, Marcus Pacheco, Aaron Cain, Henry Goldfield, Bill Salmon, Timothy Hoyer, Elio, E.F. Whithead, Scott Sylvia, Tim Lehi, Grime . . . all within the first few years I lived there, plus a plethora of guest artists coming through all the time. You couldn't help being motivated in San Francisco – everybody in SF had great tattoos back then. Now when I see a shitty tattoo on someone walking down the street I want to hit them with a hammer and ask them, 'What the fuck! How do you get a bad tattoo here?' It's hard to do, but they probably wouldn't answer because I hit them with a hammer rendering them unconscious – oh well, serves them right. I am really lucky to be in a shop where it feels like it did when I first moved here, all the time. I love tattooing, always will, no matter how much Hollywood tries to suck the specialness out of it. Tattooing will always be first on my mind and body."

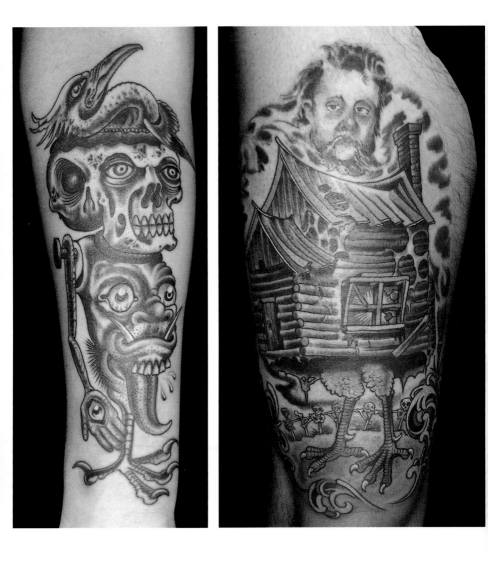

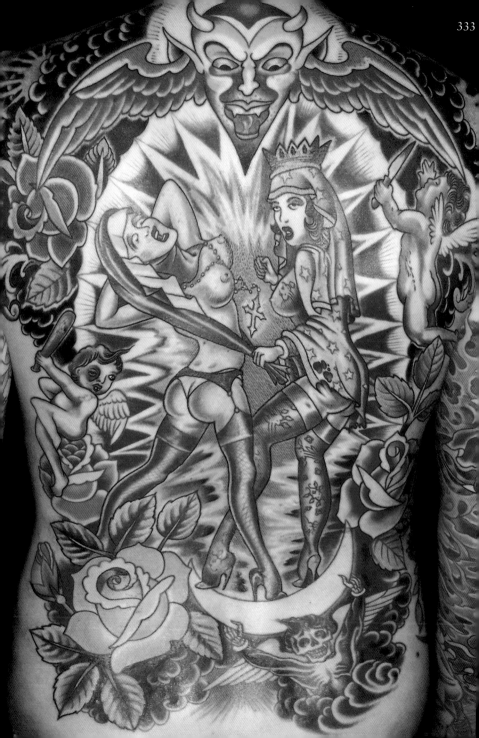

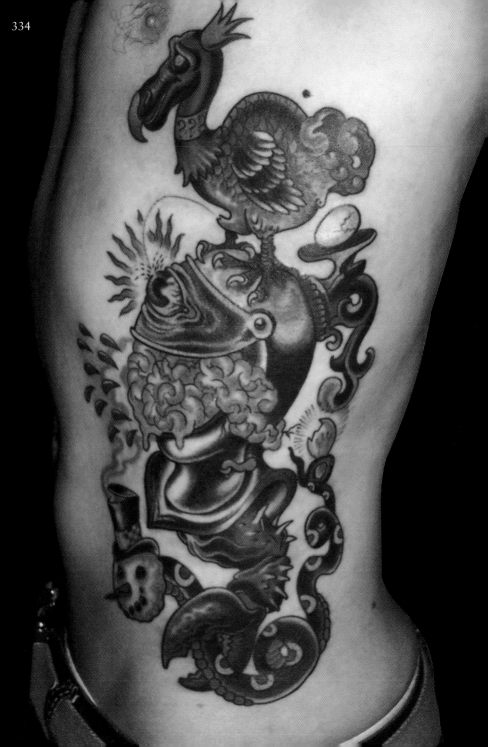

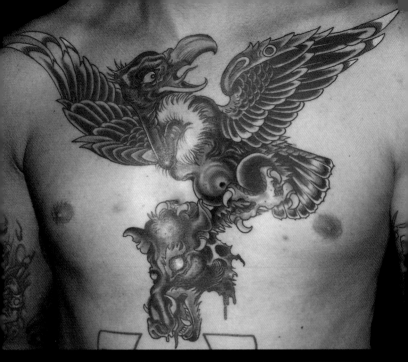

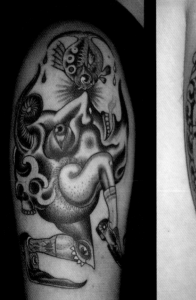

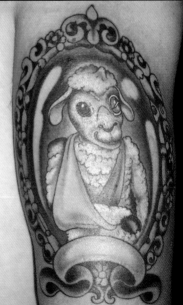

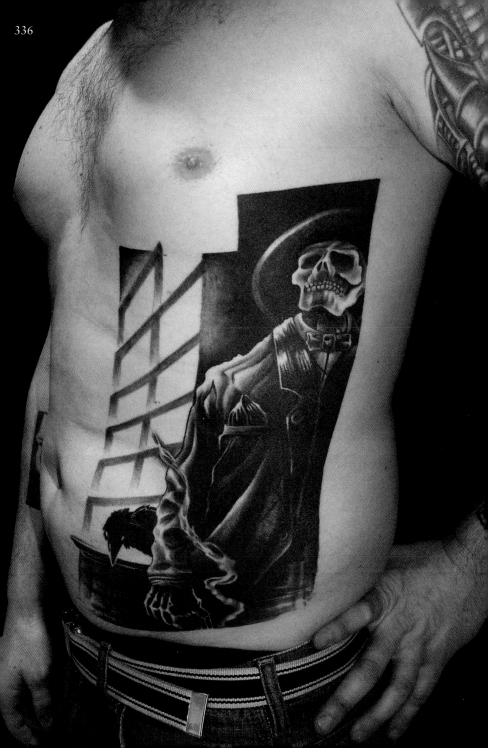

STEFF REIDER

Steff Reider describes his first experience of seeing someone getting a tattoo as being like magic. Although he was only 13 at the time, he still remembers the experience as if it had happened yesterday. He knew then that it was exactly what he wanted to do for the rest of his life. He never wanted to be an artist; he just wanted to be a tattooist, "like a tool for those who wanted to wear tattoos." He began his apprenticeship at Varry's Tattoo and Art Shop in Sissach, Switzerland, moving after four years, in 2000, to Lucerne where he now works with Frank at Hot Flash Tattoo. Travelling is an important part of his work and he has been grateful to be able to work in other countries with great tattooists like Sean Wood, Naresh, and Steve Peace, to name just a few.

Cotidie damnatur qui semper timet
Pars maior lacrimas ridet et intus habet
factum est illud fieri infectum non potest

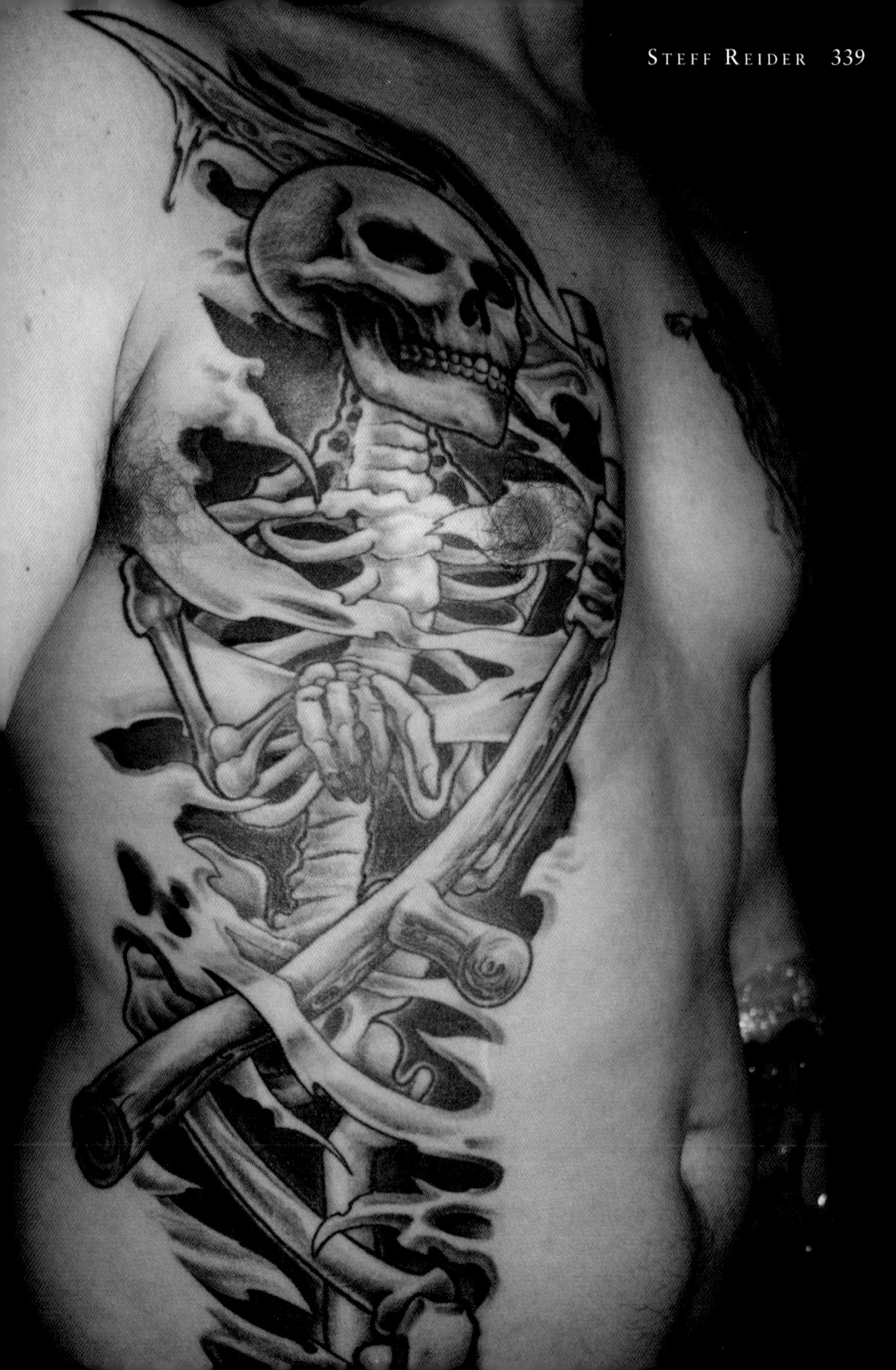

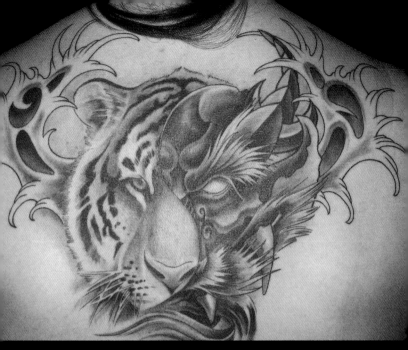

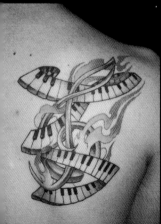

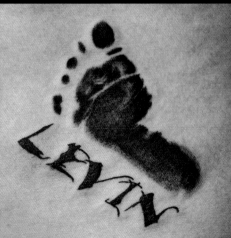

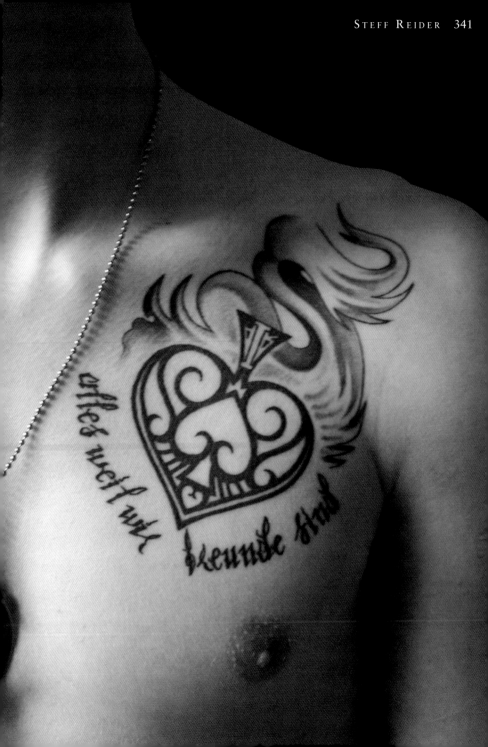

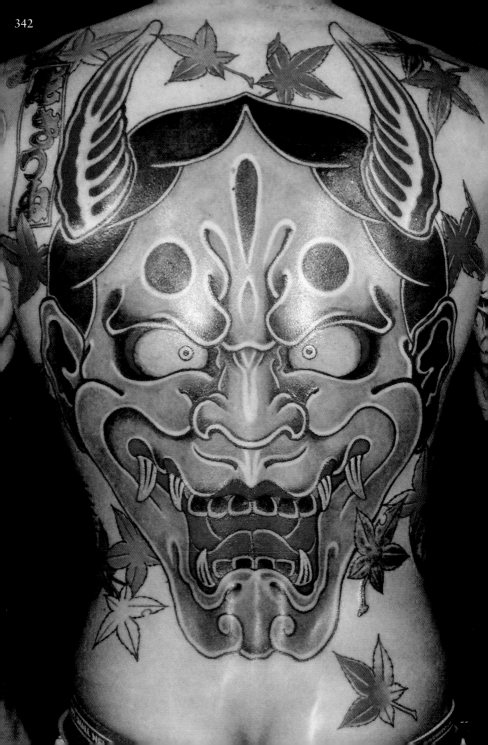

ALEX REINKE

Alex Reinke, a.k.a. Horikitsune, of Horiyoshi III's Holy Fox Tattoos, started tattooing 13 years ago. He is a student of Horiyoshi III from Yokohama, Japan. Although he is 34 years old, in Japanese terms he is nothing but a beginner in this trade. He says, "There is nothing more to know about me, really. Never forget to ask yourself: What in me is it that reads these lines, that sees, hears, tastes, feels, smells, and thinks! Look inward closely! God bless."

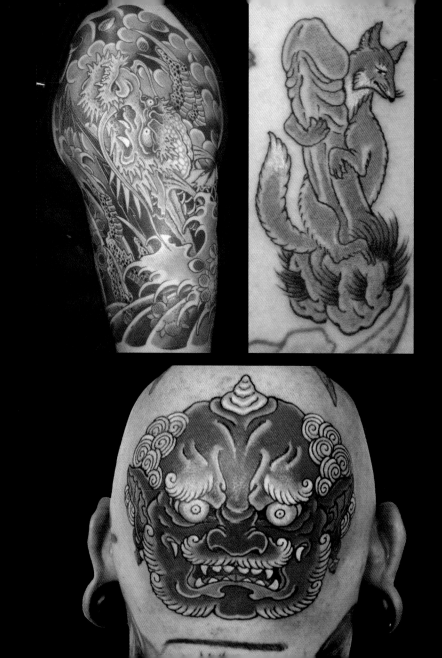

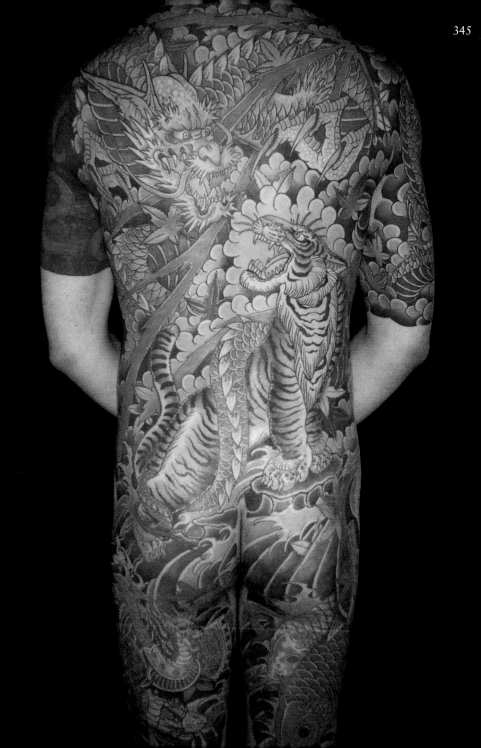

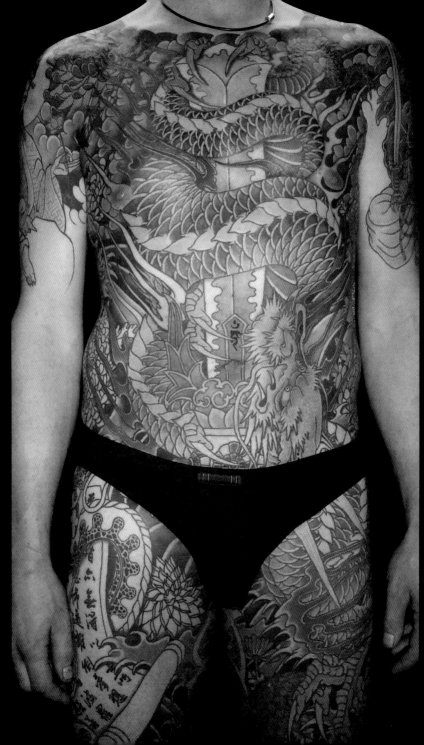

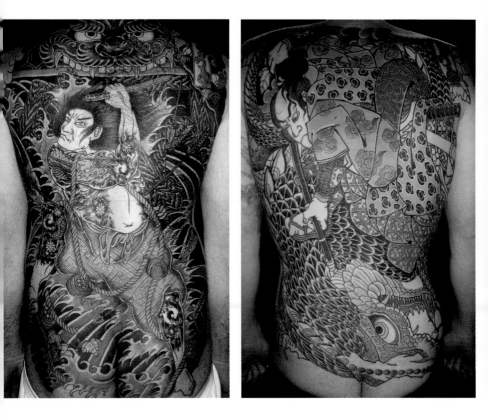

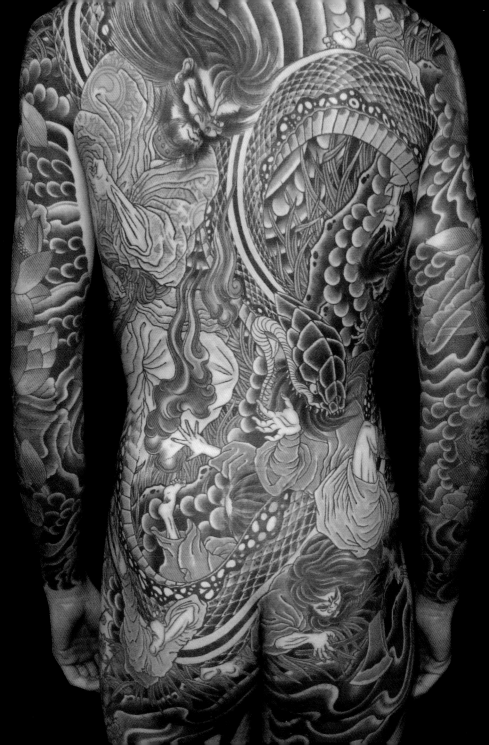

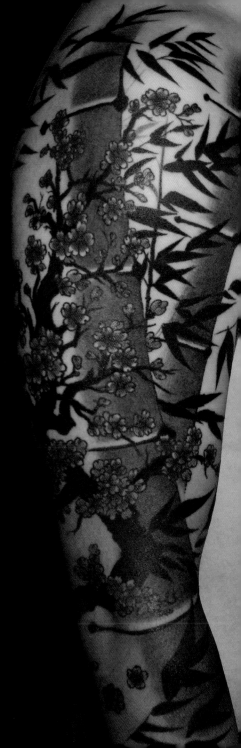

KAHLIL RINTYE

"Kahlil Rintye works in San Francisco at Ed Hardy's Tattoo City. He's been called 'too fucking polite' and 'a huge fucking grouch' by people that know him. Having worked in street shops his whole career prior to landing the fortunate slot he currently occupies, Kahlil can do anything requested but truly loves doing Japanese; classic, Western-style one-point; and spooky, epic things . . . particularly those inspired by the atmospheric writings of Mr H.P. Lovecraft. He reads too many comic books, yet finds it quite difficult to write about himself, particularly in the third person ..."
He says, "Say what you mean; do what you say."

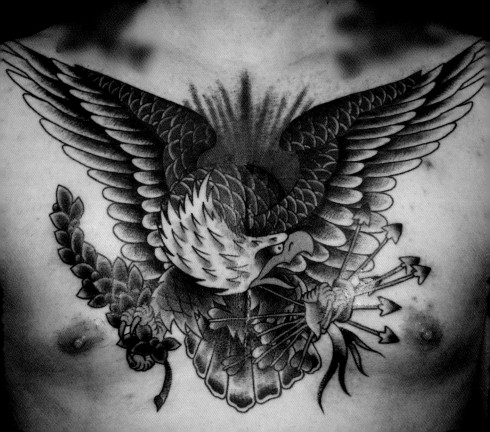

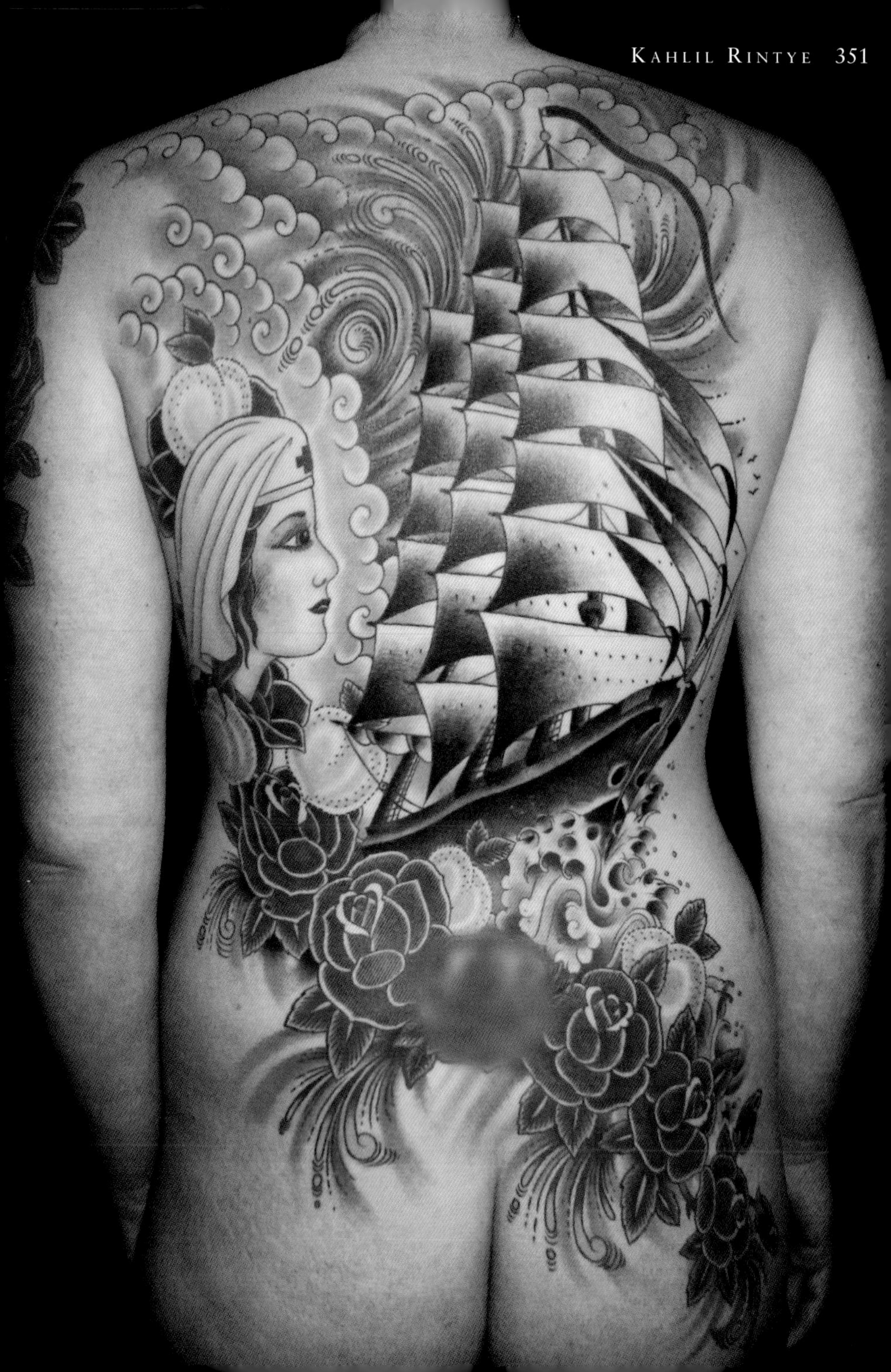

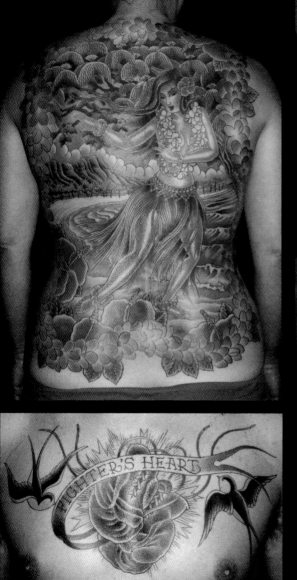
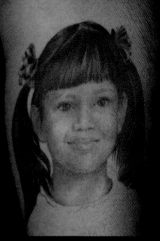
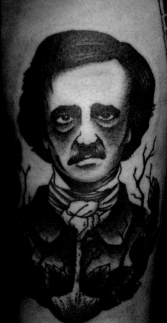

FIGHTER'S HEART

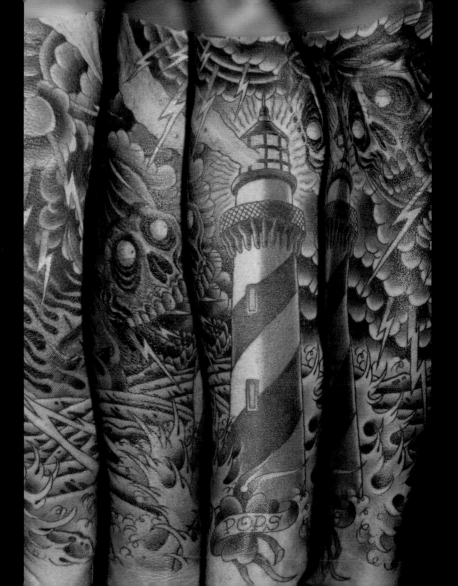

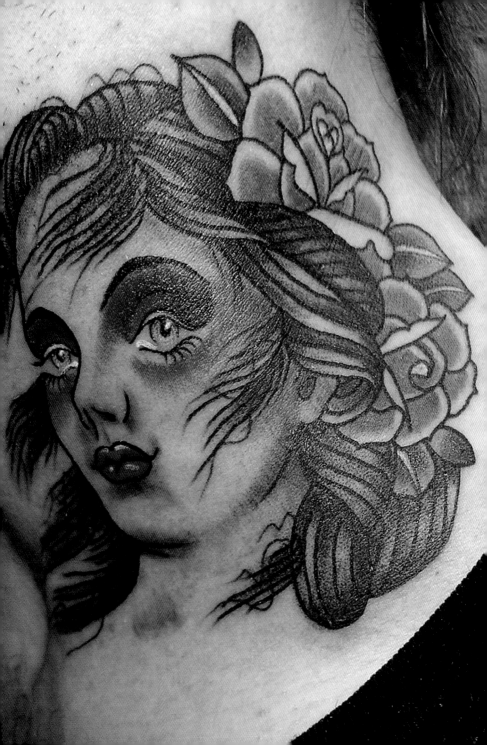

STEWART ROBSON

Stewart Robson began tattooing in early 2004, and became a full-time professional in October 2006. In July 2007 he accepted an invitation to work at Frith Street Tattoo in Soho, London. Although he is self-taught, he learned, and continues to learn, a great deal from the people he works with and the people who have tattooed him. He considers himself a tattooer, rather than an artist. He most enjoys working in several established tattoo styles: Japanese, Traditional Western and Black & Grey.

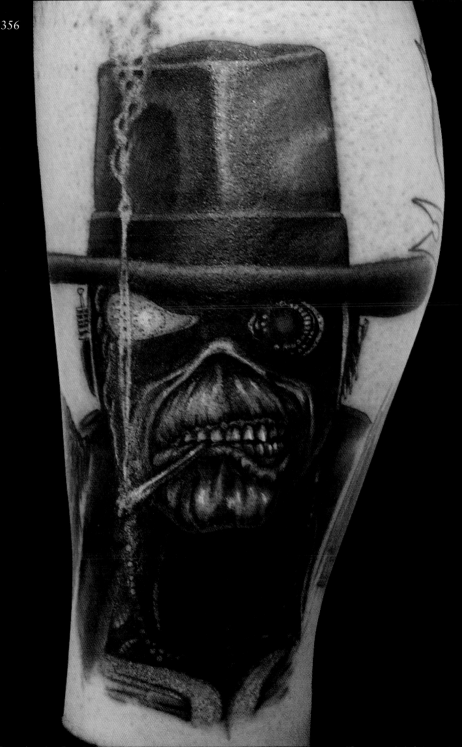

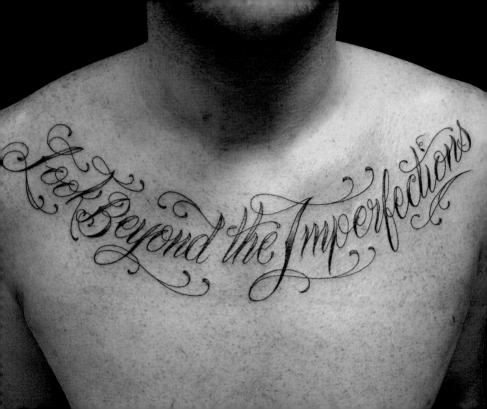

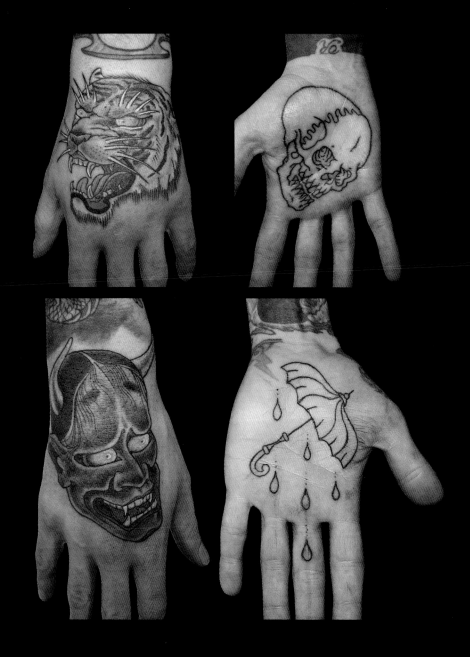

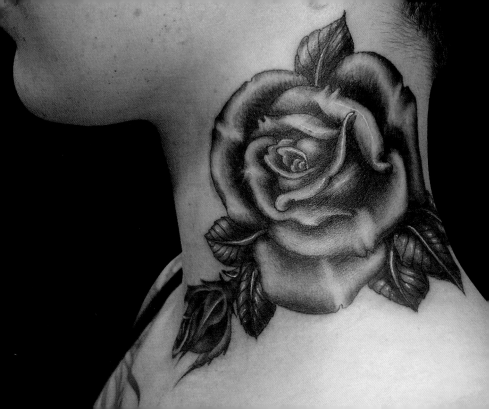

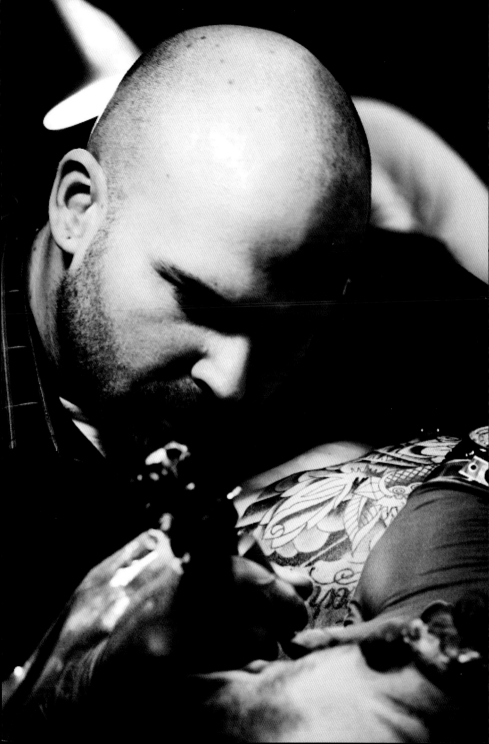

MIKE RUBENDALL

Mike Rubendall was born and raised in Long Island, New York. He began his apprenticeship in 1995 at Da Vinci Tattoo, and started work as a professional a year later. In 2003, he and Henning Jorgensen started a Flash distribution company, Tattoo Elite International. Along with his busy schedule and constant travelling, Mike opened Kings Avenue Tattoo in 2005. He currently works there full time, specializing in Chinese/Japanese designs, black and grey work, and American Traditional tattooing.

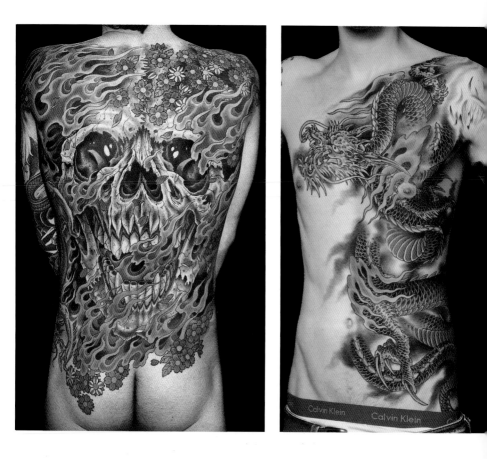

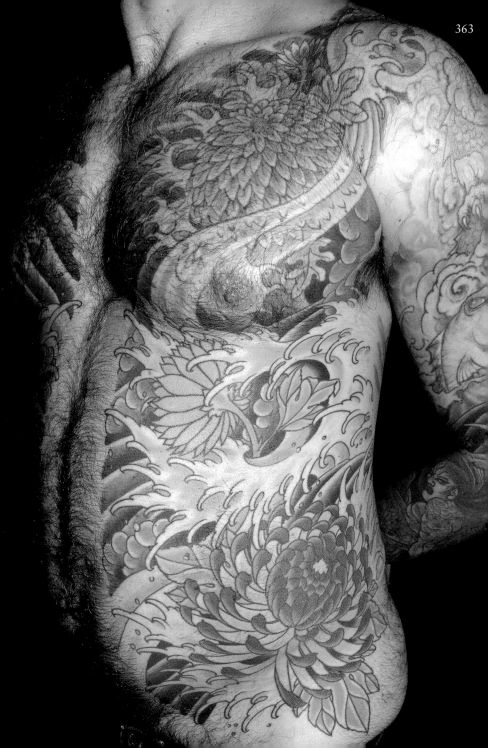

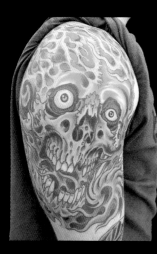

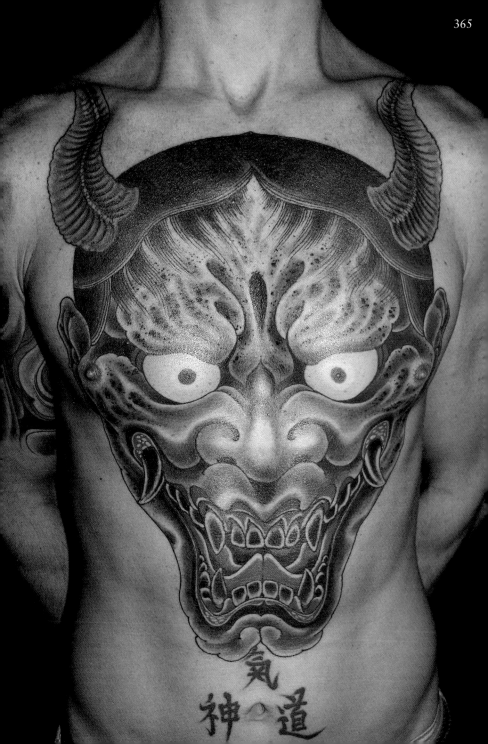

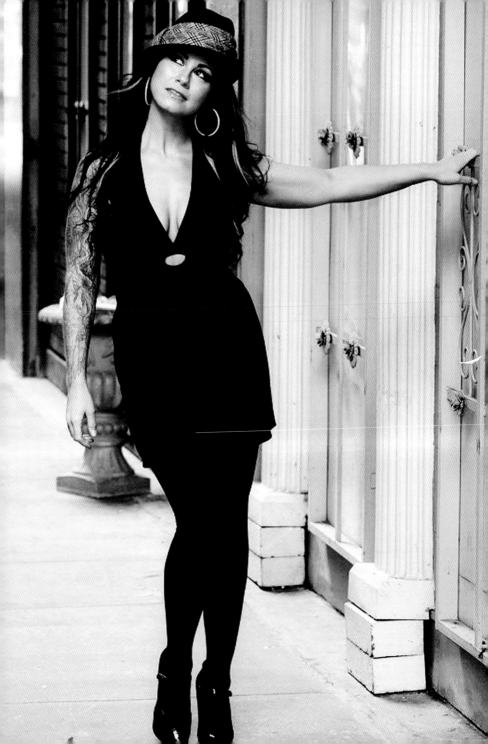

KIM SAIGH

Kim Saigh's interest in tattooing began aged 16, moments before she received her first tattoo. Apprenticed at 18 in Cleveland, Ohio, she soon relocated to Chicago to work alongside Guy Aitchison at Guilty & Innocent Productions. In 1999, she opened Cherry Bomb Tattoo in the Wicker Park neighbourhood of Chicago's North Side. She has always felt that this highly public, yet – ironically – overlooked, art form is "by far the most sacred". Her illustrative style is influenced by everything from fairy tales to iconographic religious images, from art nouveau to architecture, and from mythical imagery to nature, whose organic flow lends itself to being draped over the human body. She enjoys the freedom of having no one particular style which allows her to assimilate all her inspirations into each piece, keeping the medium new and fun. When not tattooing, she is likely to be found upside down or spending time with the love of her life, Geezer.

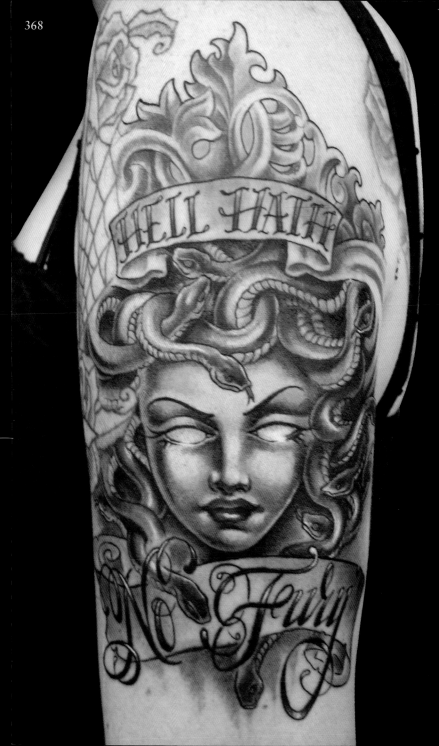

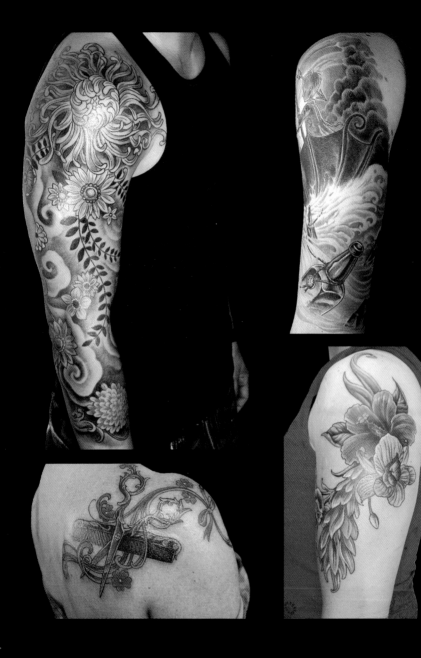

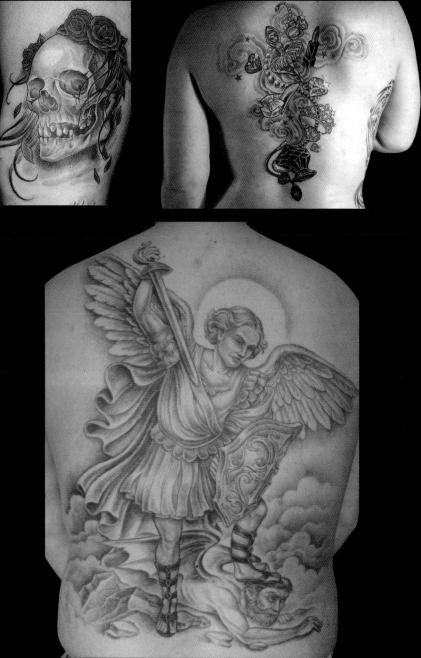

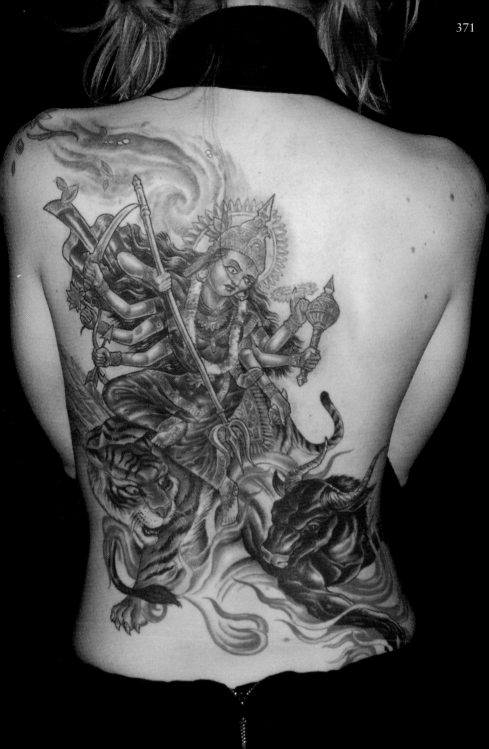

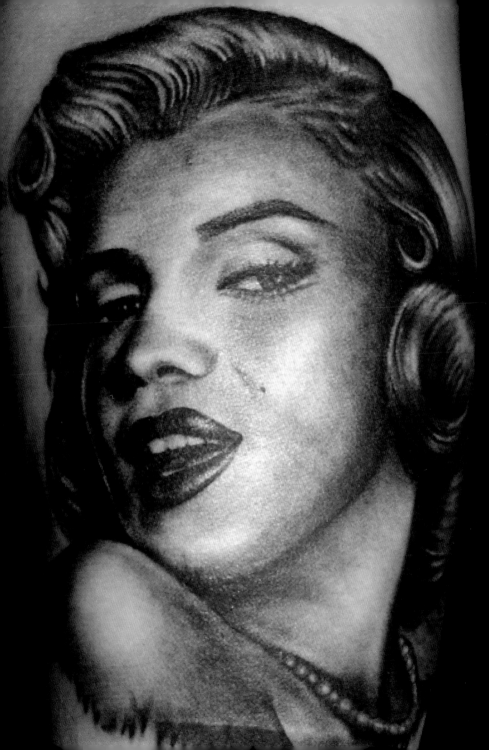

Silvia Z

Silvia Z comes from "a little town near Venice, in Italy", but she moved to London 12 years ago. She became a tattooist thanks to Alex, a French tattoo artist she met in Mexico. She did her first tattoo on him six years ago. She loves to tattoo in realistic, black-and-grey style, but also enjoys mixing that with different cultural styles, particularly Tibetan. She says, "Special thanks to Alex and those in the tattoo world who believed in me."

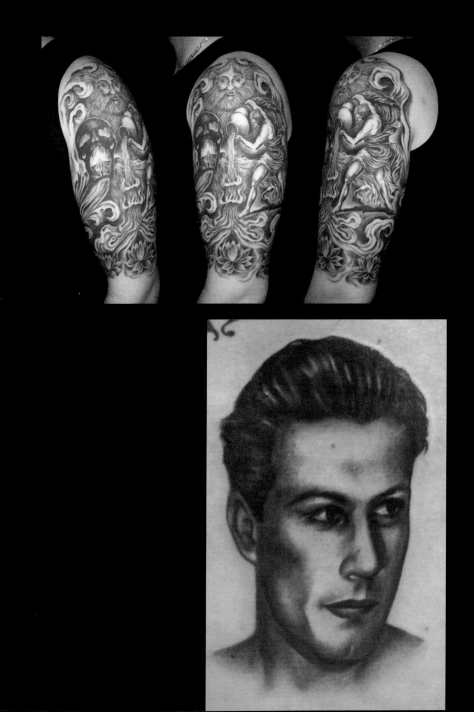

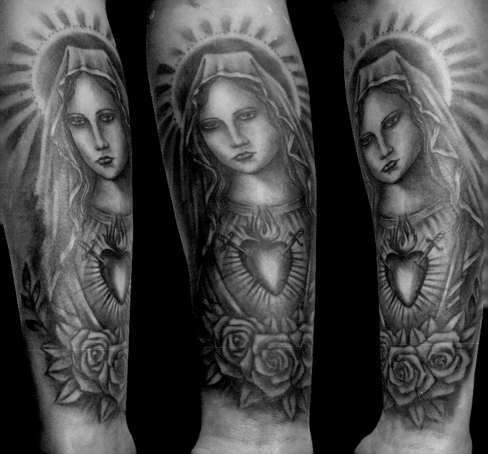

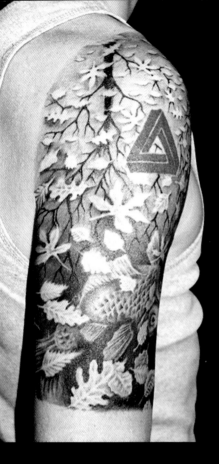
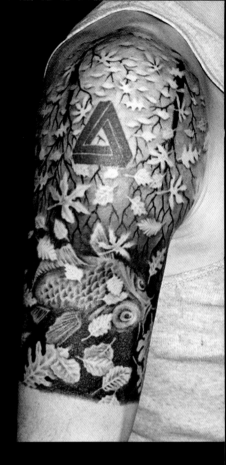
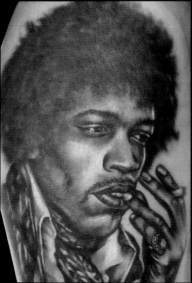

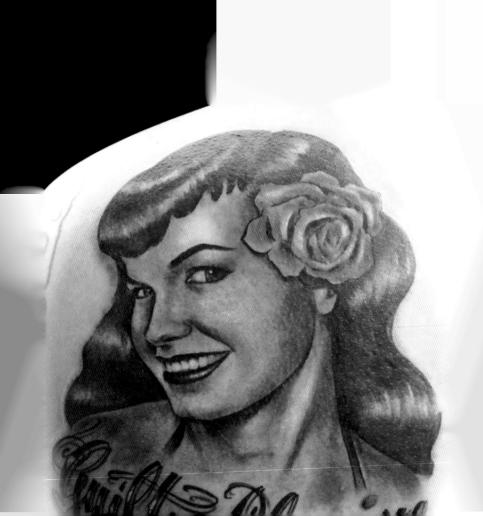

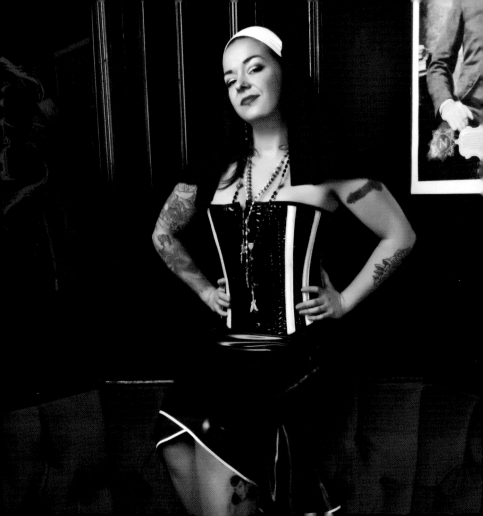

Sister Sammy

Sister Sammy has been on the tattoo scene for over ten years. She loves doing old-fashioned pin-ups and is also a big fan of the Americana comic-book style. She loves big, bold, colourful imagery, but is also quite happy to escape into a really dark, lustrous, Japanese piece. She is often amazed and inspired by some of her customers' ideas, and loves adding her own little twist to their concepts. As she says, "Making someone fall in love with their own arm or leg is hilarious, I love my job!"

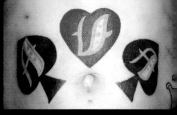

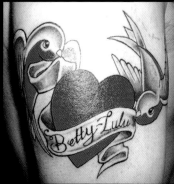

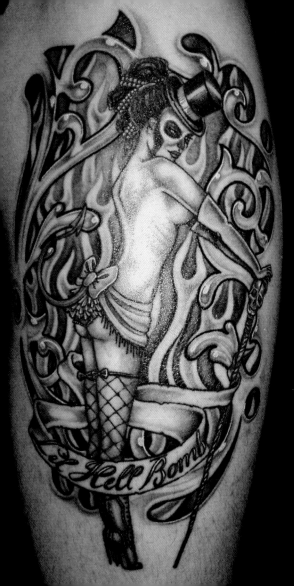

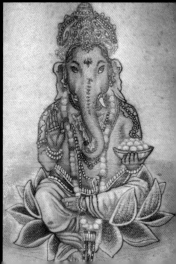

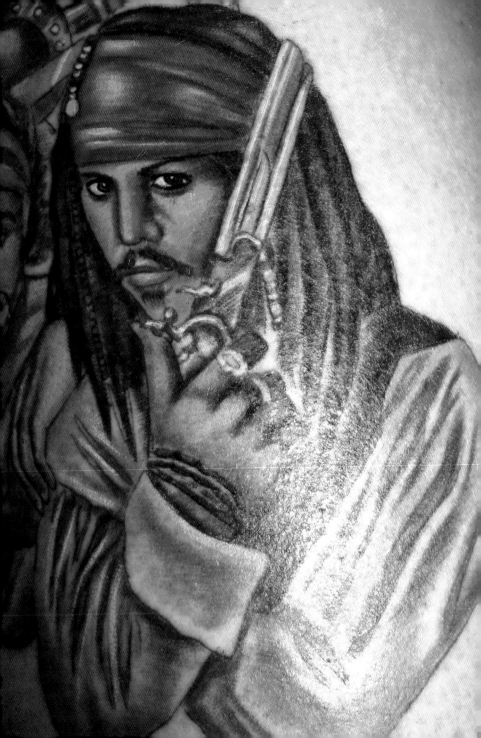

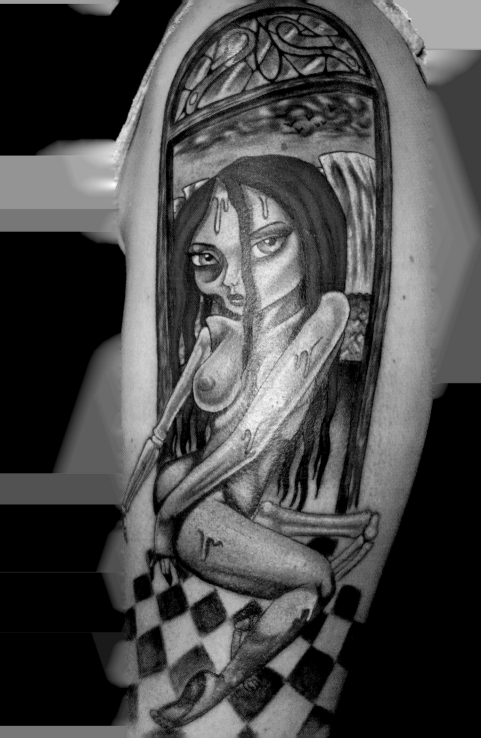

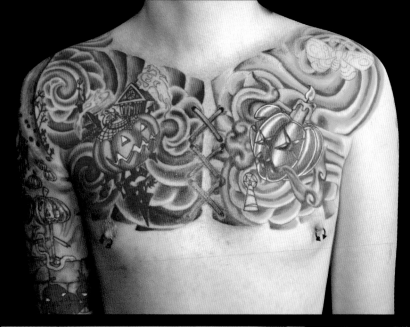
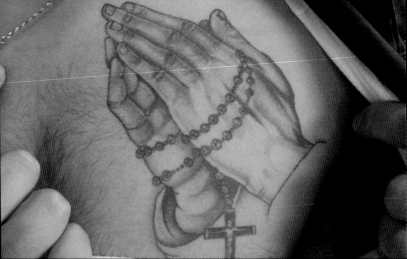

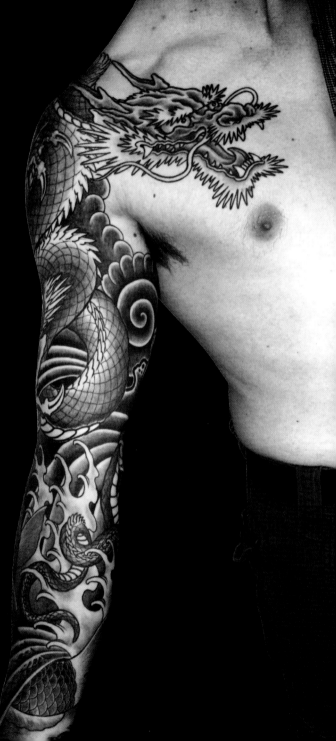

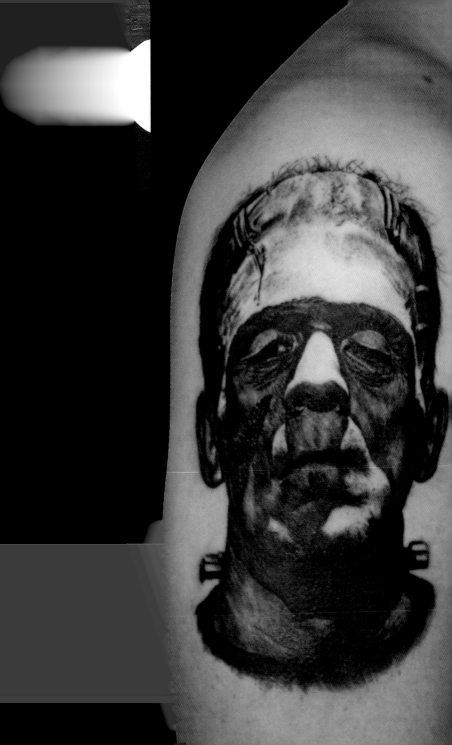

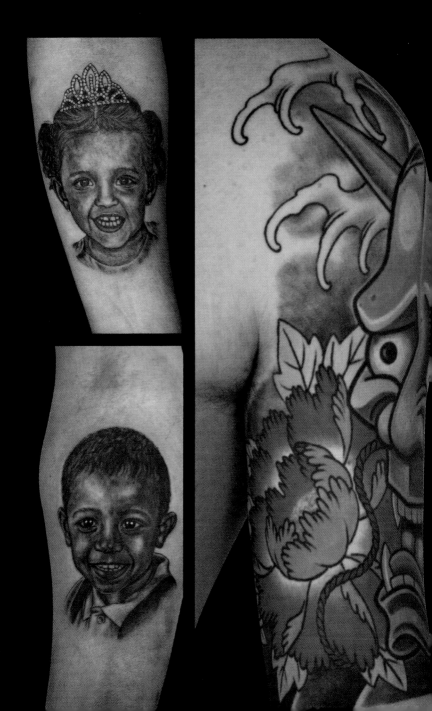

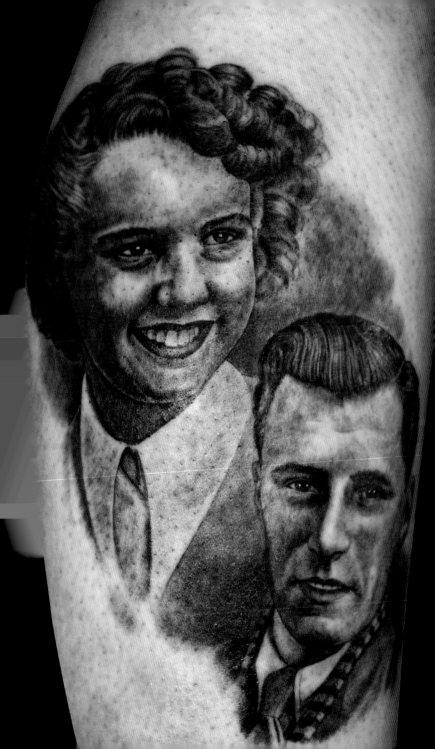

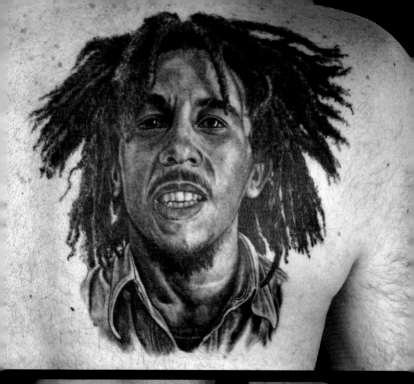

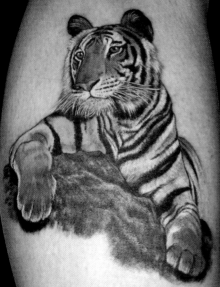

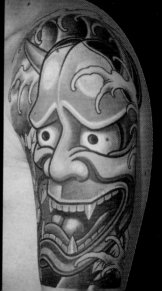

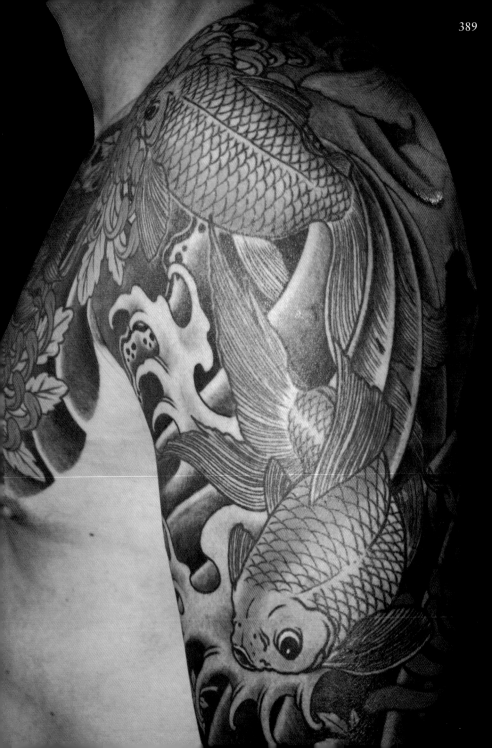

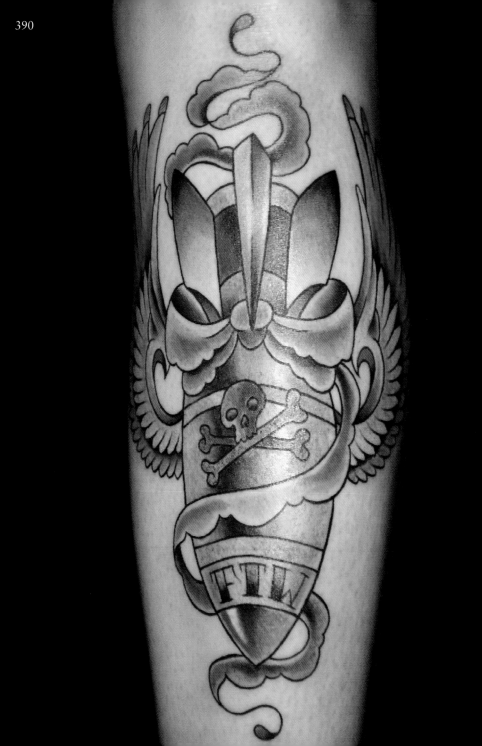

Suzi Q

Suzi Q has gone from a sleepy Welsh village to the most geographically isolated city in the world. She grew up in south Wales, in the United Kingdom, in the 70s and it was not until 2001, in the United States, that she first picked up a tattoo machine as part of her apprenticeship at Lucky Lady Studios, in North Carolina. During the following seven years she worked at studios and conventions throughout the United States, Europe, New Zealand, and Australia, which she now calls home. She works at Holdfast Tattoo, a busy, modern, custom studio just ten minutes outside Perth, tattooing her favourite neo-traditional style as well as others, such as black and grey, 50s' pin-ups, rockabilly, zombie, and Vegas-themed designs.

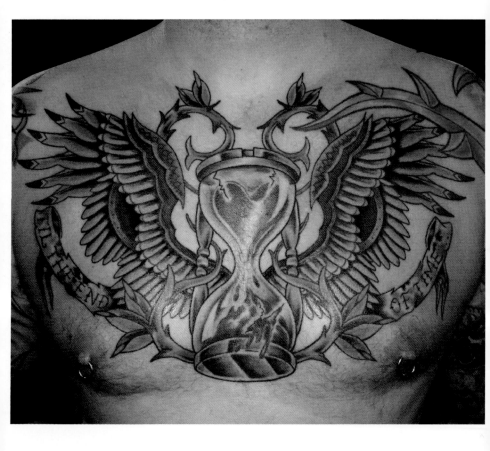

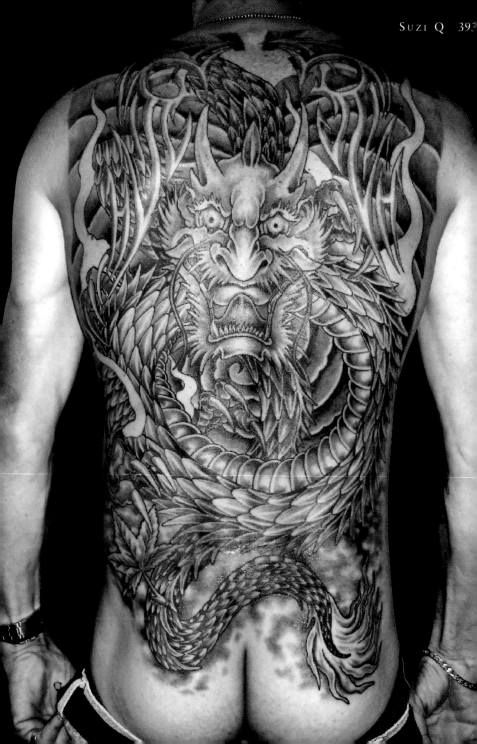

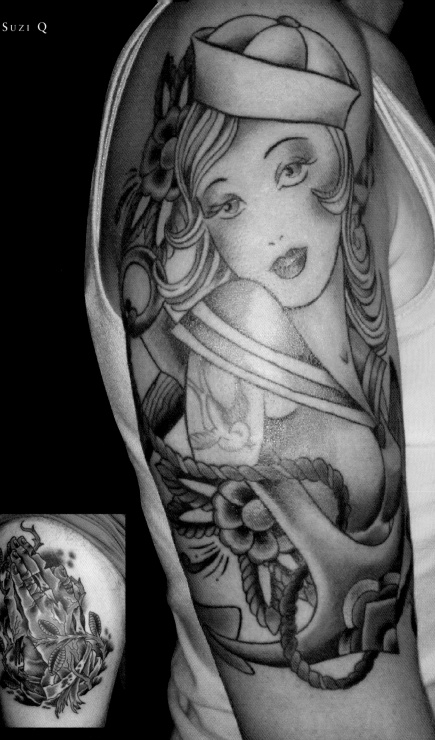

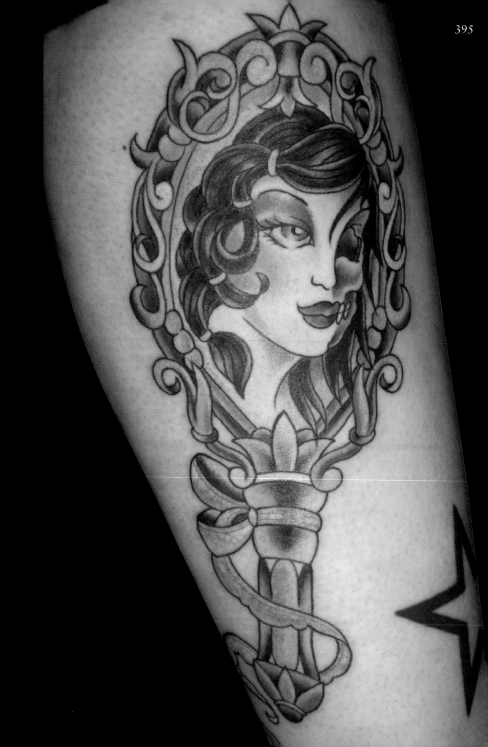

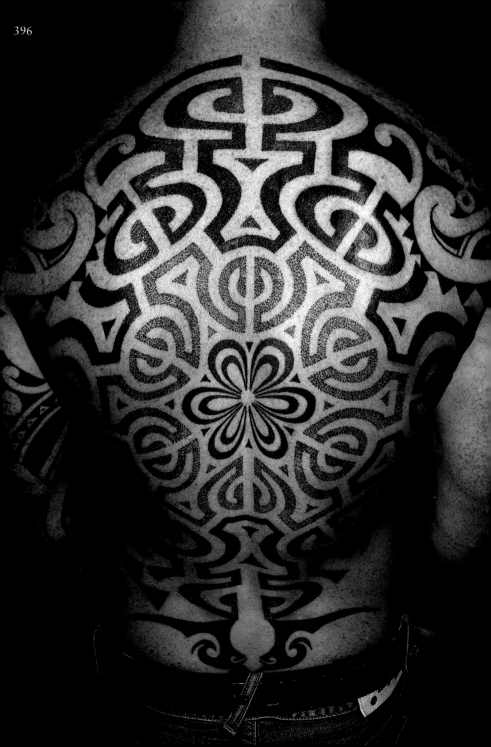

TOMAS TOMAS

Tomas Tomas has declined
interviews in the last decade,
nevertheless he issued this
statement: "In the recent years,
too much has been written
and said about tattooing and
tattooists . . . let's face it, none
of it is actually any interesting
or relevant. My only wish is that
the readers of this book enjoy the
tattoos in these photos as much as
I have enjoyed tattooing them."
Thank you.

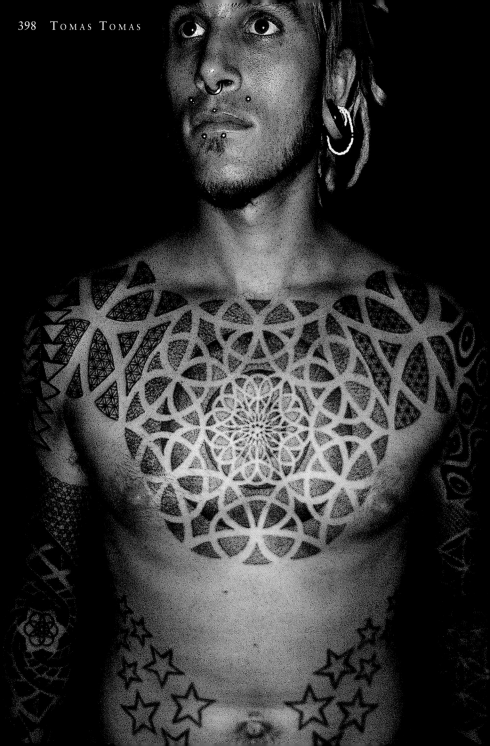

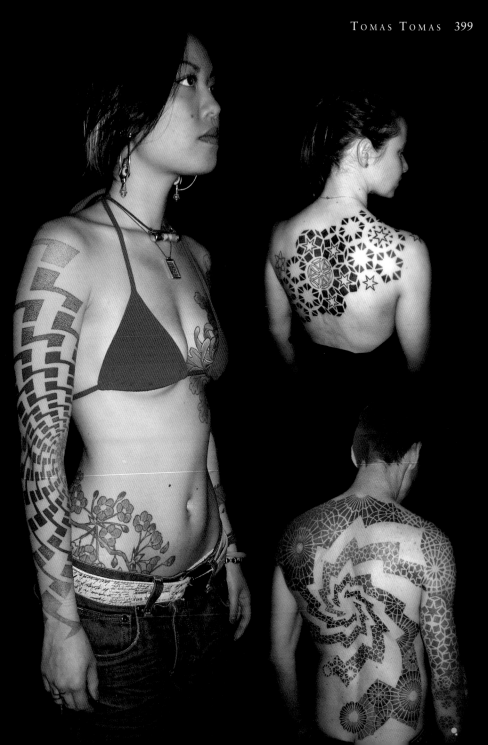

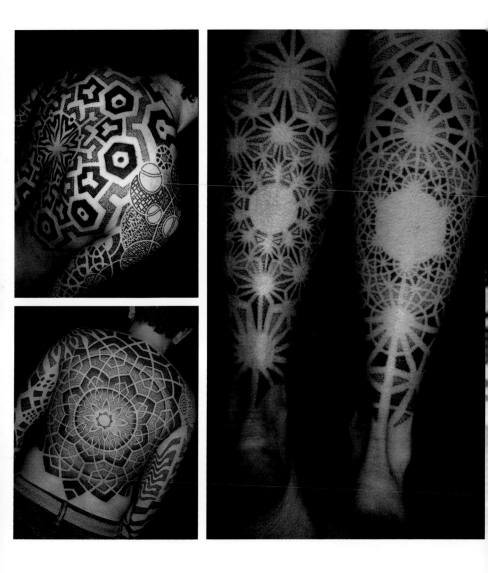

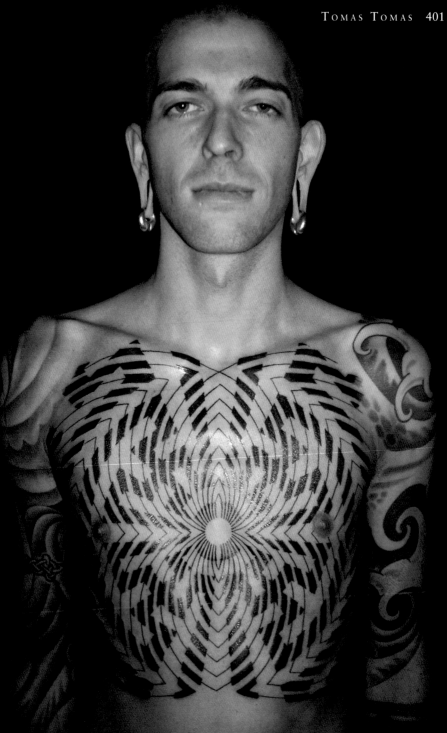

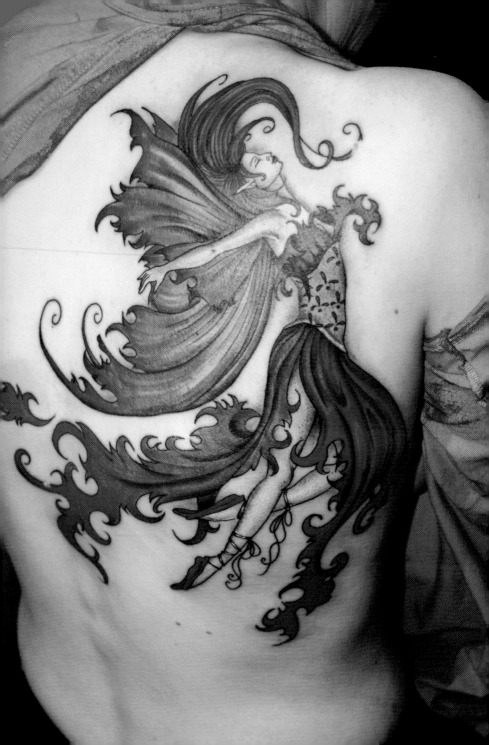

MICK TOMO

Mick Tomo first opened Ruby Arts
n York, England, at the age of 17.
He has been tattooing for around
28 years, but professionally for
only about 25. He has enjoyed
watching the industry progress
from strength to strength over
the years, and has attended many
tattoo shows around the globe
where he met many great friends,
artists, and enthusiasts. He likes
all kinds of styles and loves a
good challenge to keep him on his
toes. He says, "I definitely think
tattooing is more than a job; it is
a way of life – one which I love!
Rock on . . ."

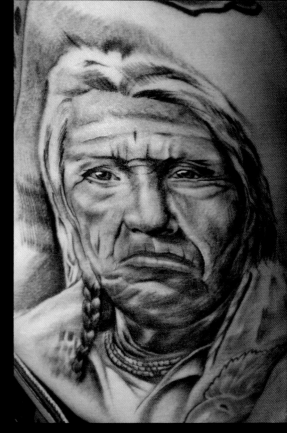

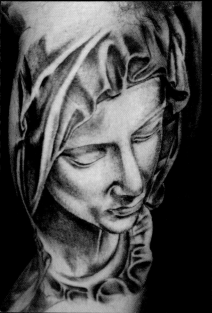

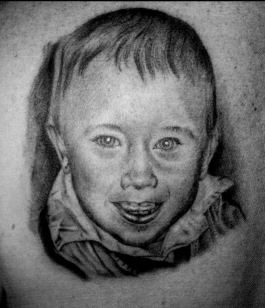

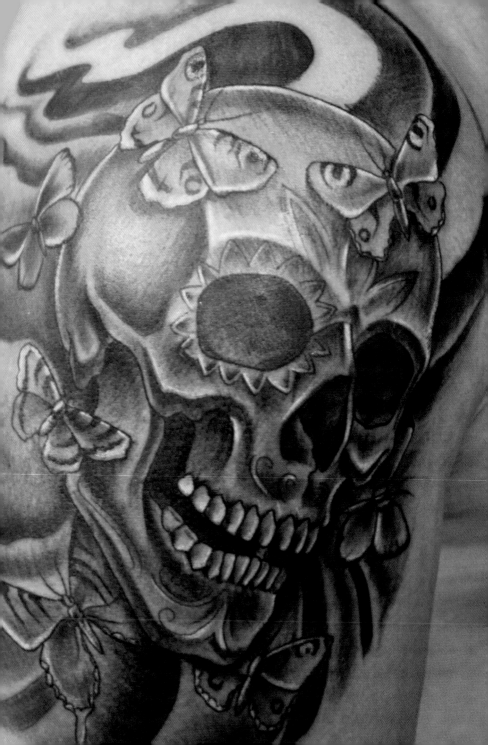

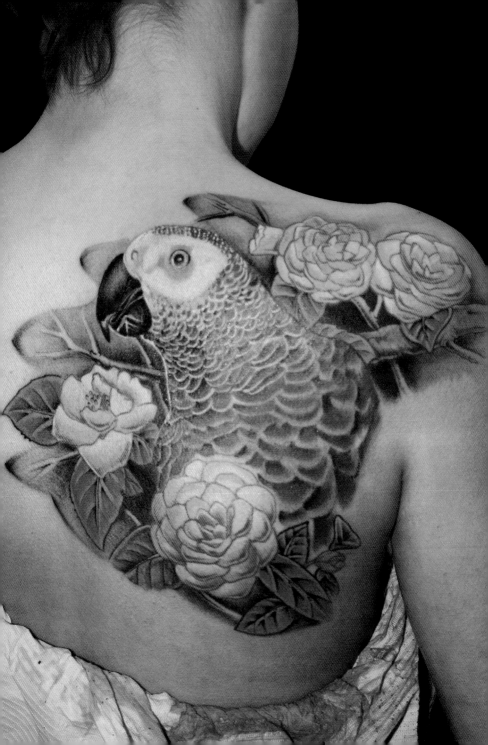

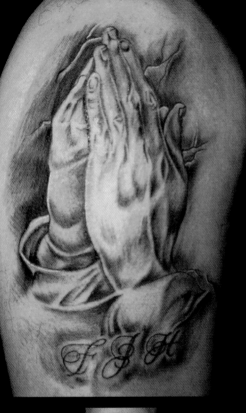

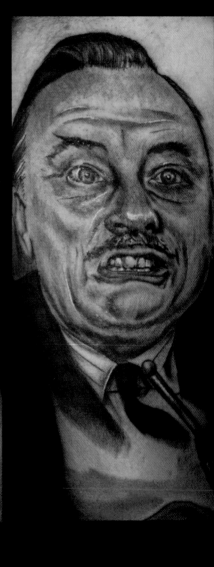

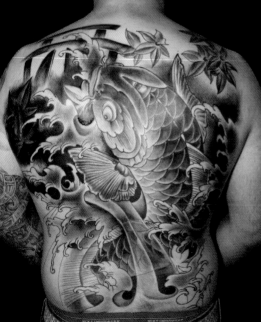

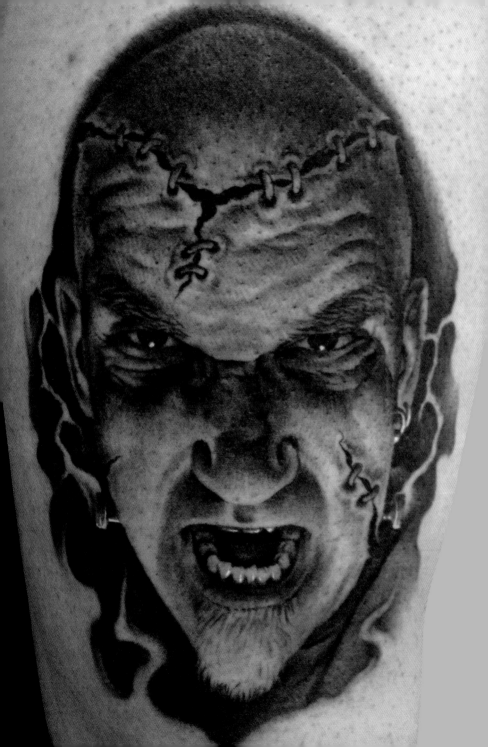

BOB TYRRELL

Having an incredible artist for a father, Bob Tyrrell grew up wanting to be an artist himself. But he started playing guitar in his teens, and spent the next 15 years playing in heavy metal bands and working a factory job. He got his first tattoo just before he turned 30 and was immediately hooked, soon getting his sleeves and a full back piece done. He got back into drawing and showed some of his work to Tramp, of Eternal Tattoos, in the Detroit area where he grew up. He was offered an apprenticeship and within three months he was tattooing full time. He is forever grateful to Tramp and to Tom Renshaw, who took him under his wing. After six years at Eternal he opened his own studio, Night Gallery, in Detroit. These days he'd like to cut back on travelling so he can learn to paint, do more fine art, and tattoo more, but he just can't stop!

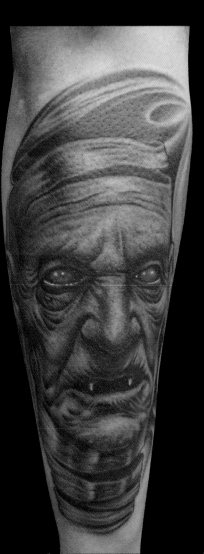

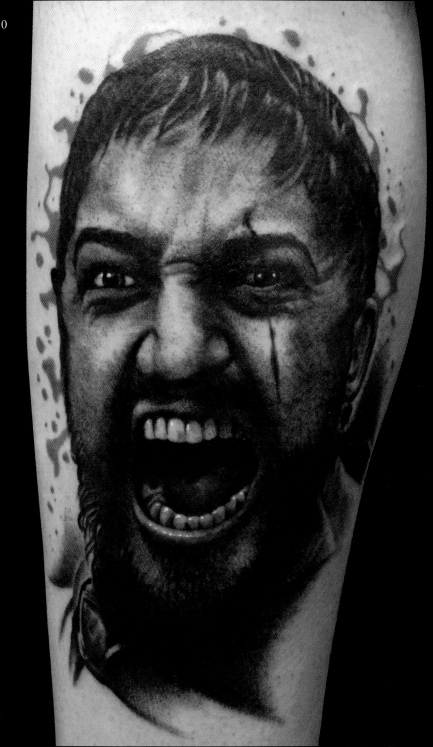

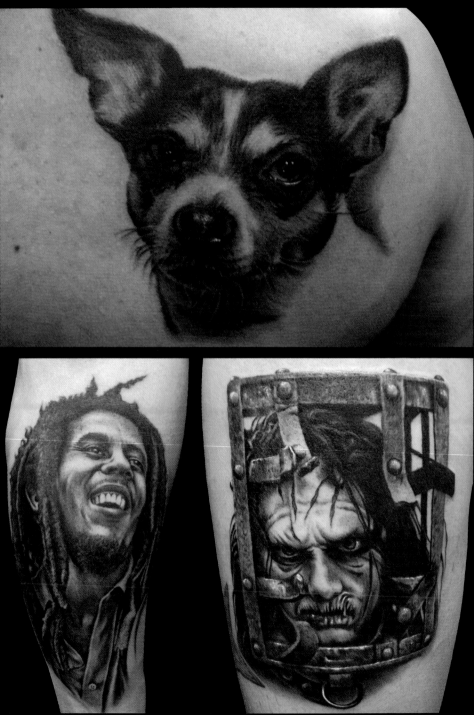

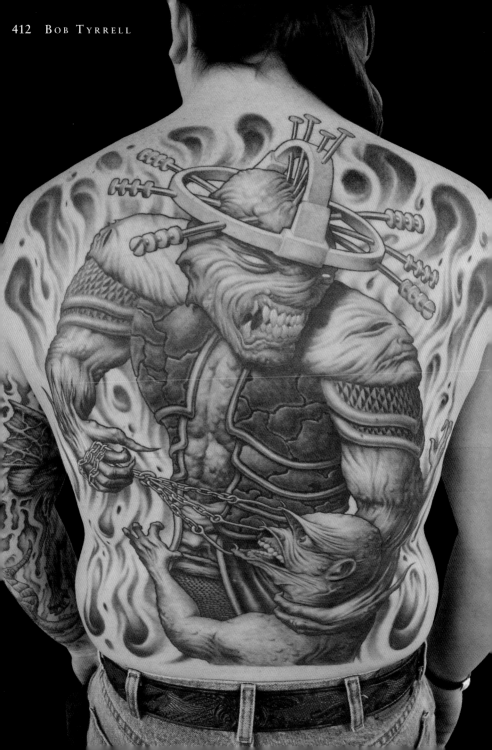

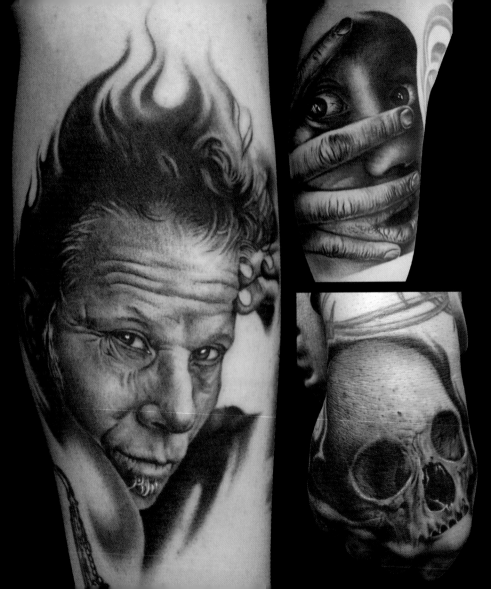

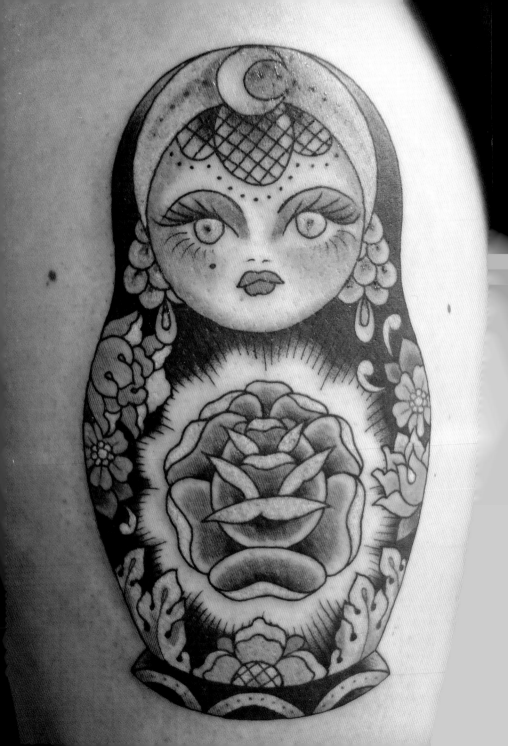

VALERIE VARGAS

Valerie Vargas started tattooing
professionally in 2007 after leaving
Scotland where she had lived since her
teenage years. Six months later she
moved to London where she began
working at Soho's longest established
studio, Frith Street Tattoo, where she
has been ever since.

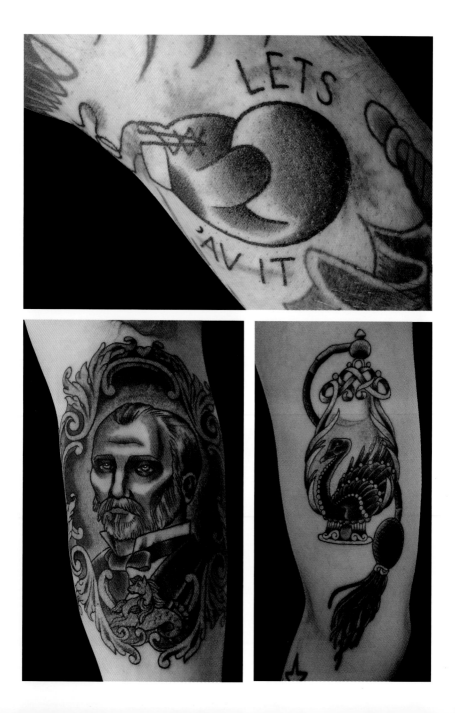

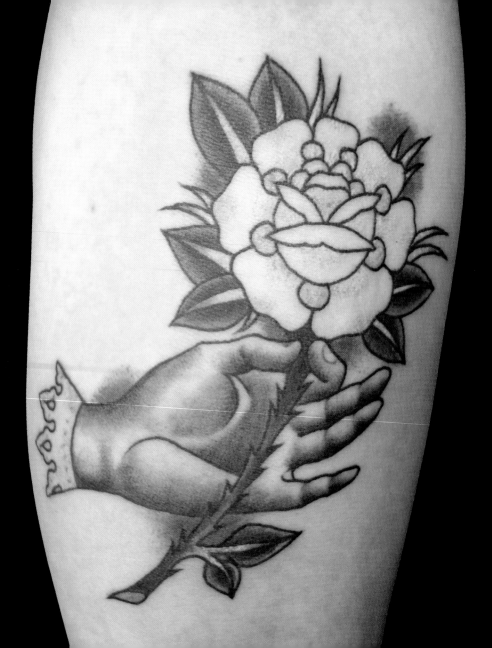

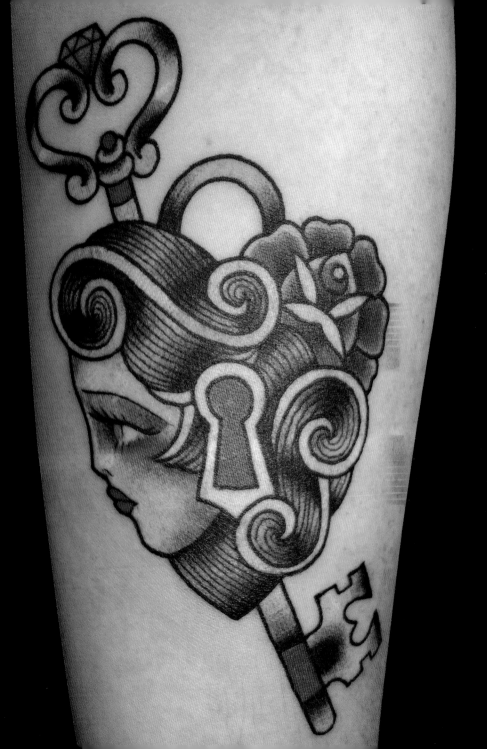

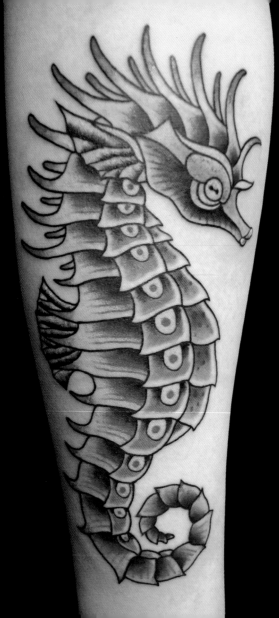
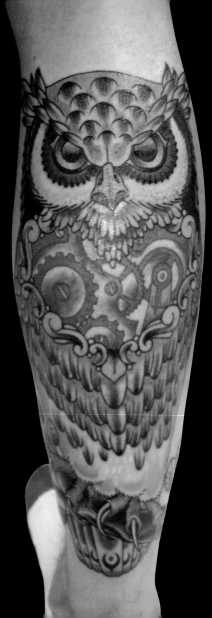

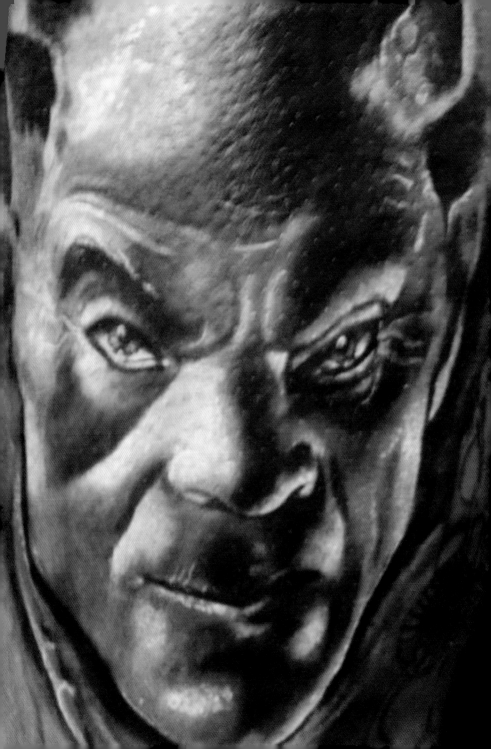

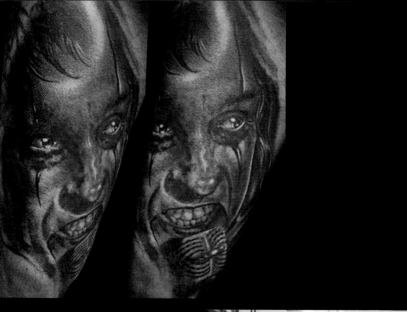

DARRIN WHITE

Darrin White started tattooing when he was 18, working as an apprentice in a tattoo shop in Atlanta, Georgia. For a few years, he had his own shop in Atlanta, but, deciding that he would rather not work in just one spot, he shut up shop and moved to Ashville, North Carolina. At the same time he began to travel, doing guest spots all over the world. Every day he gets to work with new artists that he can learn from. Teaching seminars and going to conventions have become a big part of what he does and he "wouldn't change a thing".

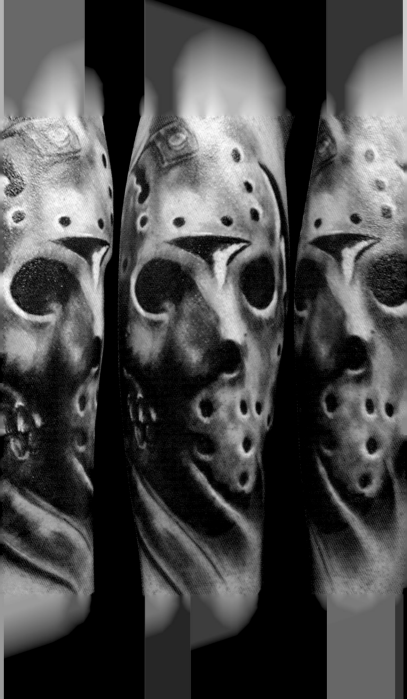

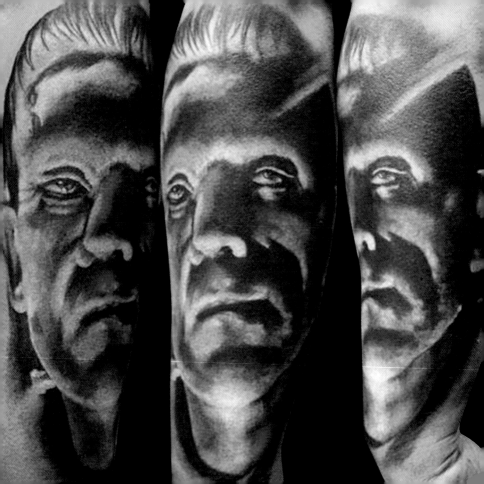

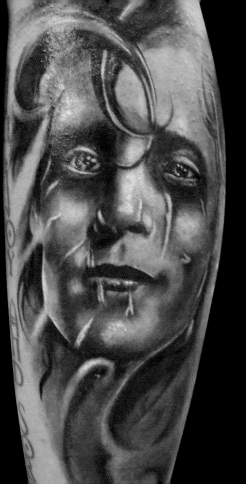
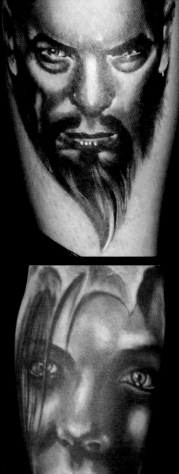

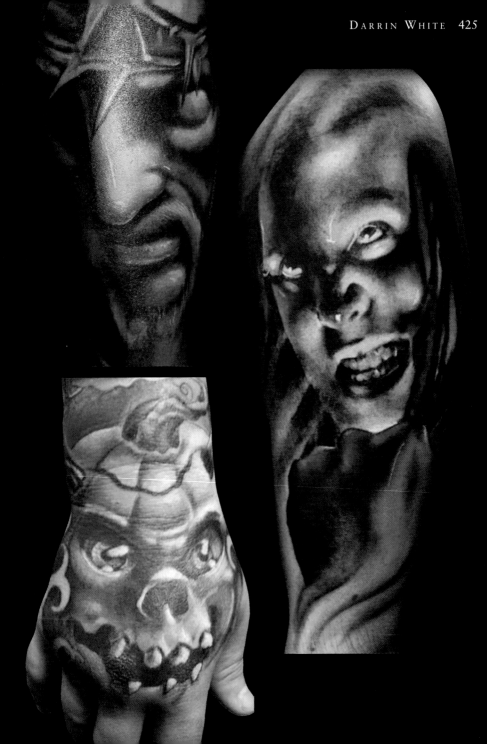

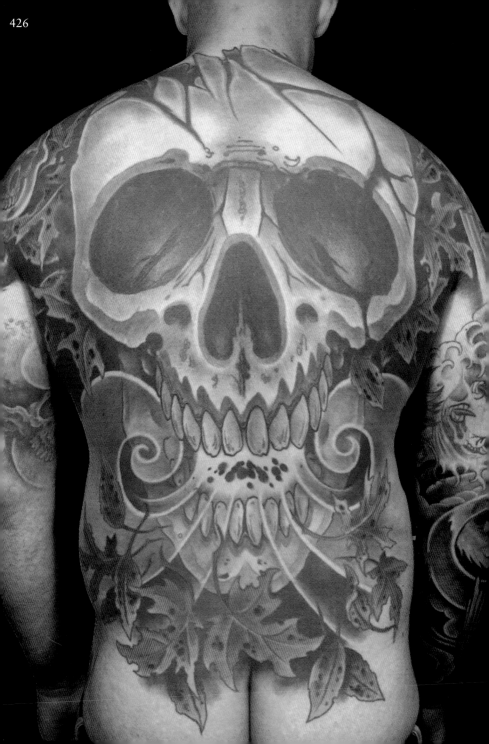

Kurt Winscombe

Kurt Winscombe works with Alex Adams at Tattoos for the Individual, established in 1996. With many years of tattooing experience, Kurt is constantly striving to push the boundaries of his art and "put it to skin" on the dedicated group of people who come from near and far to have tattoos done. Kurt also creates art using other media.

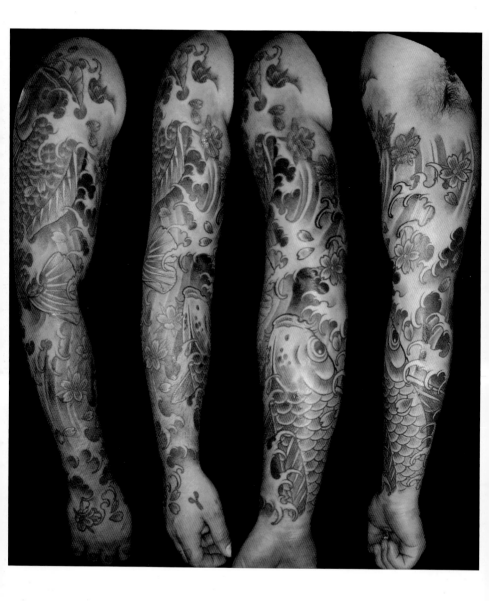

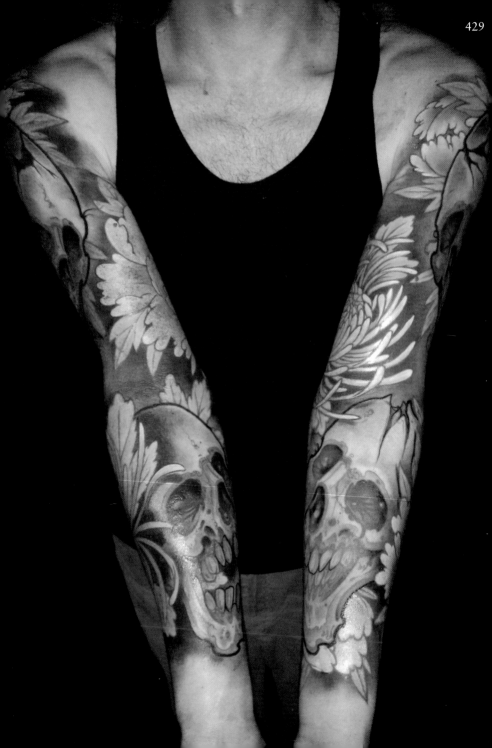

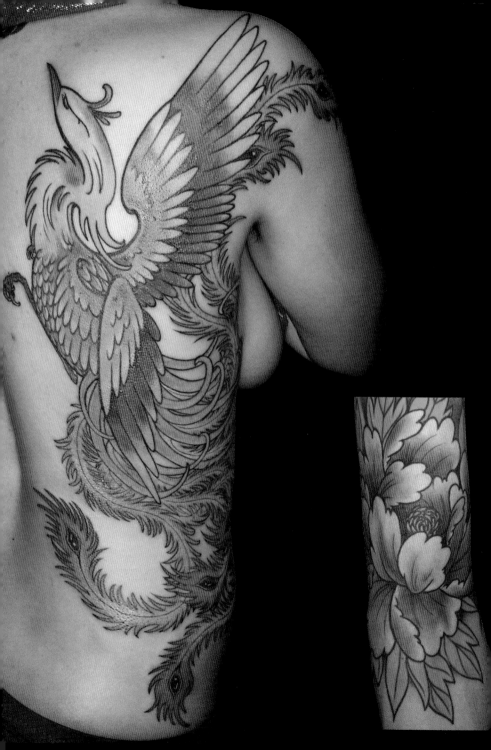

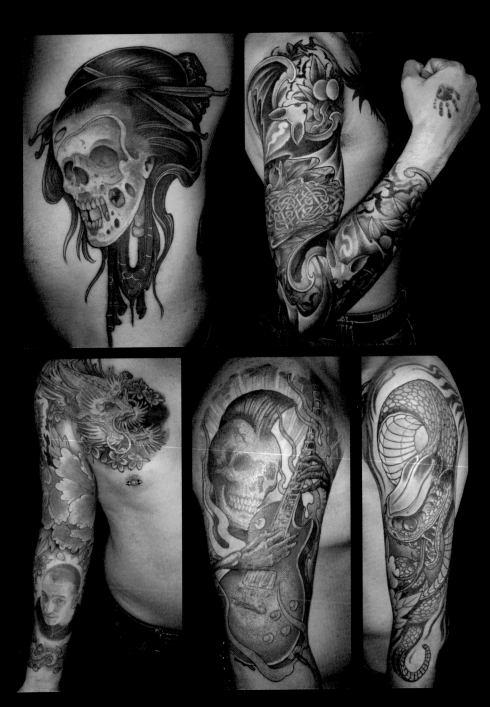

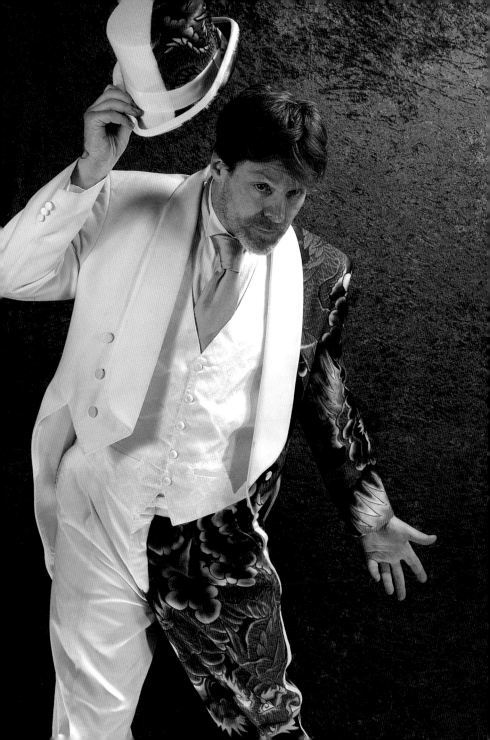

SEAN "WOODY" WOODS

Woody describes his occupation as being a "cure for wealthy Chroma-Junkies." As he puts it, "In an otherwise cardboard-coloured world where mediocrity is accepted as standard and bland is the usual there will always be a need for agents of change charged with the task of uplifting the lead-weighted souls from the drudging reality of normality." He feels a duty to a "higher task" which has never been to put images into bodies, but is "to break through the armour of the astral being to free the higher person within." He adds: "An organo-mechanical future awaits all those who choose the path of reaching out of the mundane to the very heart of the Gods" before acknowledging, "This hyperbolic and psychedelic crap was beaten out of me by brain-stupefying lack of slumber. The typewriters made me do it."

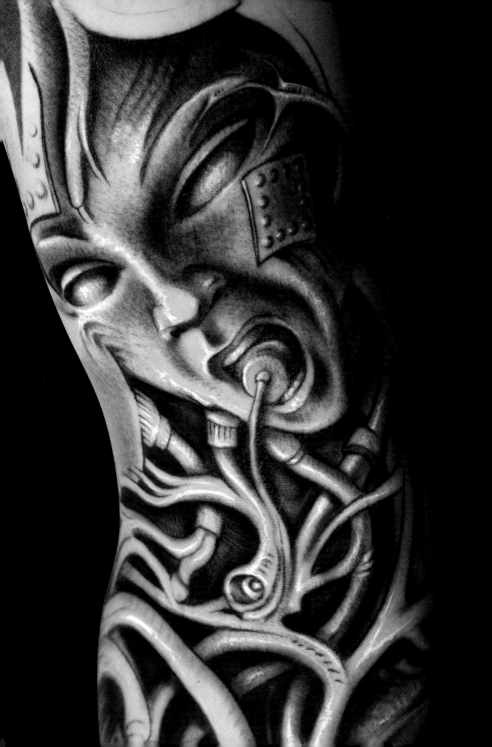

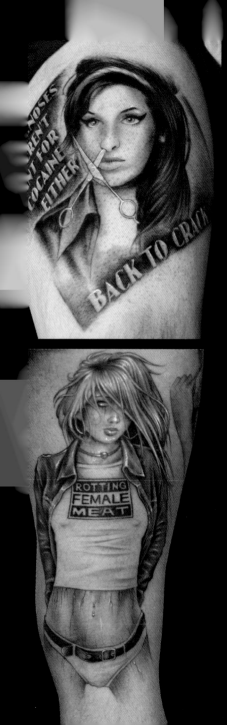
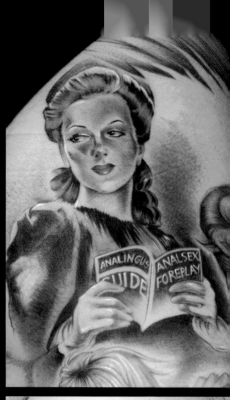
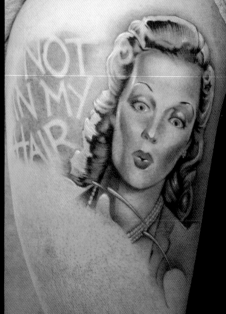

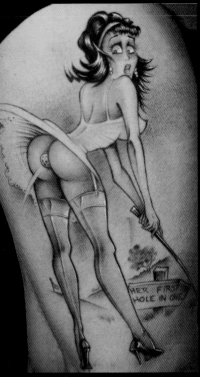

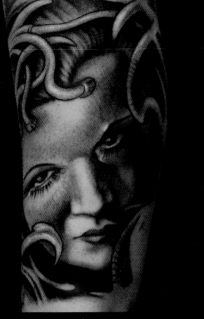

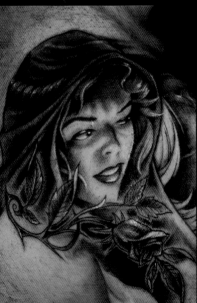

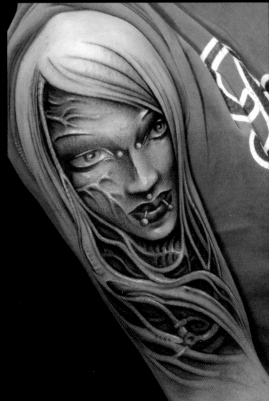

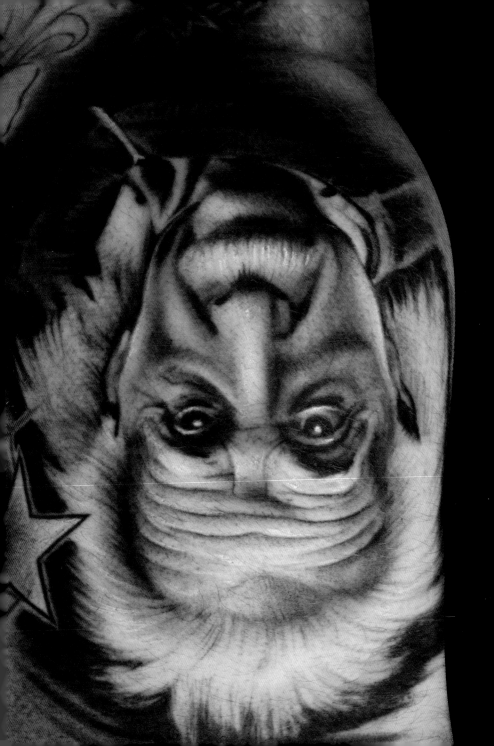

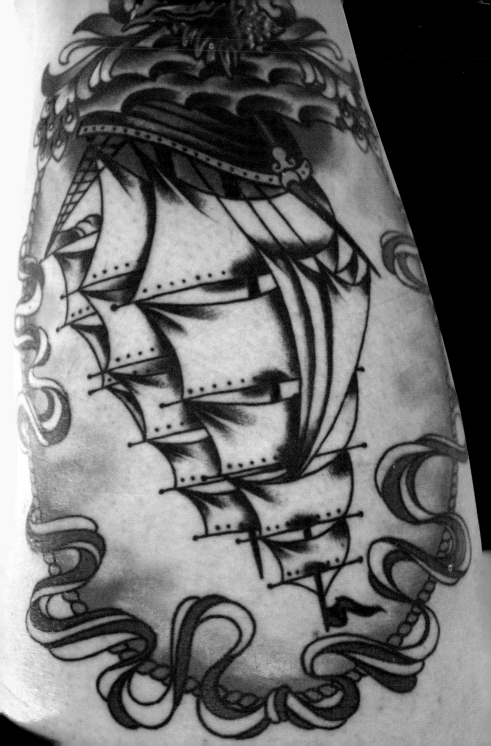

Xam

Xam was born in Spain in 1975
and has been tattooing since 1997.
He is currently working in London.
He says, "Everything has been
said, everything has been done."

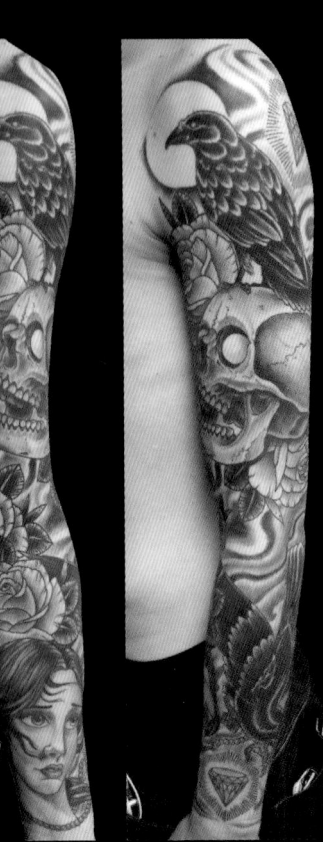

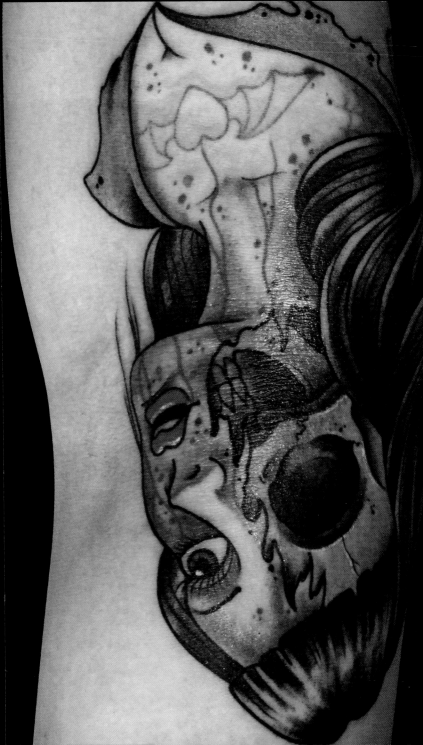

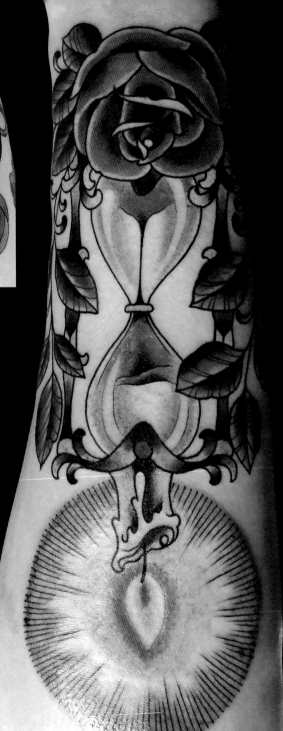
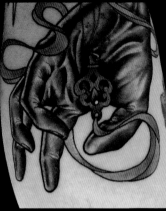

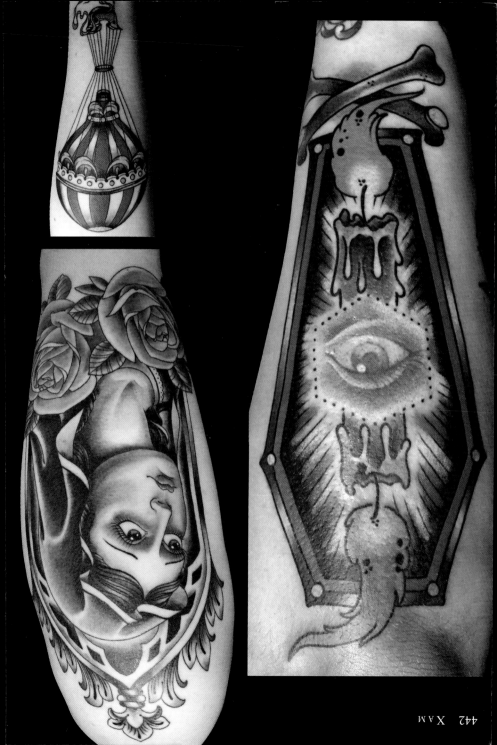

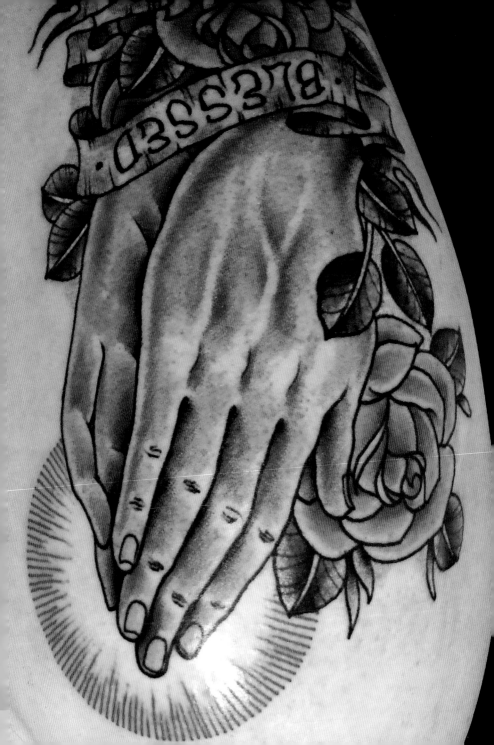

Also available

The Mammoth Book of
TATTOOS